סידור קורן לליל שבת

The Koren Shabbat Evening Siddur

קוֹרֵן ירושלים

סידור קורן ללילל שבת

THE KOREN SHABBAT EVENING SIDDUR

טוב
להדות
לה׳
ולזמר
לשמך
עליון

WITH TRANSLATION AND COMMENTARIES BY

Rabbi Lord Jonathan Sacks

EDITED BY

Rabbi Yehuda Sarna

CO-EDITED BY

Rabbi Binyamin Lehrfield

•

KOREN PUBLISHERS JERUSALEM

The Koren Shabbat Evening Siddur
Third Edition, 2018

Koren Publishers Jerusalem Ltd.
POB 4044, Jerusalem 91040, ISRAEL
POB 8531, New Milford, CT 06776, USA

www.korenpub.com

The English translation and commentary of Minḥa, Kabbalat Shabbat, and Ma'ariv in this edition are based on the English translation and commentary first published in Great Britain in 2006 in the Authorised Daily Prayer Book of the United Hebrew Congregations of the Commonwealth: New Translation and Commentary by Chief Rabbi Jonathan Sacks, (Fourth Edition, Compilation © United Synagogue) by Collins, a division of HarperCollins Publishers, London.

The creation of this Siddur was made possible through
the generous support of Torah Education in Israel.

Printed in the PRC

Personal Size, Hardcover, ISBN 978 965 301 277 6
CS Edition, Hardcover, ISBN 978 965 301 278 3

FN03

CONTENTS

FOREWORD

Prayer moves us simultaneously in three directions. We offer a word to God, a word to each other, and a word to ourselves.

For the vast majority of young Jews today, the prayer style of yesterday does not move anything at all. The erosion of meaning in the highly formal style of worship, detailed by suburban synagogues with sprawling pews and lengthy cantorial performances has given way to more intimate gatherings of young Jews in informal settings which inspire authenticity, sincerity and creativity. The spirituality present in prayer contexts such as trips to Israel, weekend retreats, summer camps, or independent *minyanim* speak to our generation with a profound sense of community and self-revealing purpose. The contexts exist, the people are coming, but until now we did not have all the accessories.

> It has been taught in accordance with Rabbi Yose bar Ḥanina: Abraham established the morning prayer, as it says, 'And Abraham rose up early in the morning to the place where he had stood' (Genesis 19:27), and there is no 'standing' but for prayer, as it says, 'Then stood up Pinehas and prayed' (Psalms 106:30).
>
> Isaac established the afternoon prayer, as it says, 'And Isaac went out to meditate in the fields at dusk' (Genesis 24:63), and there is no 'meditation' but for prayer, as it says, 'A prayer of the poor when he wraps himself and before God he pours out his meditation' (Psalms 102:1).
>
> Jacob established the evening prayer, as it says, 'And he encountered the place' (Genesis 28:2), and there is no 'encounter' but for prayer, as it says, 'Therefore do not pray for this people; do not lift up prayer nor cry for them; do not encounter me [on their behalf]' (Jeremiah 7:16).
>
> *Berakhot* 26a

The Talmud offers us instruction in how prayer ought to move a person. For Abraham, prayer directs an individual upwards, towards God: "to the place where he had stood." A person rises to pray in concert with the morning sun – an upward orientation. Prayer must inspire a degree of transcendence, truth and divine experience. Separation from God happens through the presence of intermediaries. The desired mode of prayer, in contrast, brings each worshiper in direct contact with the divine by pulling away the barriers of formality and enabling the expression of individuality. Rabbi Nachman of Breslov teaches that the truest form of prayer comes in one's own words, in the middle of the night, on a path where no one else travels. Upward.

For Isaac, prayer directs an individual closer to others. "And Isaac went out to meditate in the fields at dusk" (Genesis 24:63). According to Ḥizkuni, a 13th century French commentator, Isaac goes out "to speak to whomever would need to speak with him" (ad loc.) – an outward oritentaion. A prayer gathering should be neither a tense social event nor a coincidental meeting, but an expression of a community's fundamental values. Unless the community's core principles and purpose become expressed in the nature and tone of a prayer event, it is not *siḥa,* meditation. Going to a synagogue "just because" is to go for no reason. Part of a person's presence in prayer is the demonstration of care for the other and an acceptance of their care. Territoriality, entitlement, and snobbery denude our words of their meaning. Outward.

For Jacob, prayer directs inward. "He encountered the place" – the Hebrew word for prayer, *vayifga,* means to wound or to penetrate – an inward motion. Self-consciousness induces anxiety, shallowness, and competitiveness; consciousness can bring about awareness, inner peace, and clarity. When a person feels safe, the conditions for openness are enabled and there is little fear to peer inside. A human being is often a bundle of contradictions, and attempts at creating coherent self-narratives can be stunted by many defense mechanisms. For a person looking to be his or her own creator, one needs to feel invited to pursue the journey. Inward.

These three vectors do not come at the expense of each other; they reinforce each other. Experience of God's Presence provides the weight to communal values. Community creates the necessary safety for individual exploration. Individuality, in turn enables the creativity and honesty which is required to meet God. The *Esh Kodesh,* Rabbi Kalonymos Kalman Shapiro, asks why one refers to God in the second person in the Amida; why do we say "Blessed are You," not "Blessed is He"? He explains that when we say "You," we invite God to bring His full Presence before us. The Divine Presence, however, does not come unless we ourselves are present. Only if the "I" is here will the "You" come.

The object you hold is not a Reader or a Prayerbook: it is a propeller of movements upward, outward, and inward. It is designed to be utilized by those navigating for the community to maximize the prayer experience by bringing each participant into full dialogue with the liturgy, consistent for the most part, across ethnic and denominational lines. To that end, we have accentuated the different dimensions of the prayer experience: Study, Imagination, and Rhythm.

Study. Much of the liturgy was originally instituted for the purpose of study, not recitation. Paradigmatic examples include the texts hosted under "Limmud Shabbat" (*Shabbat Study*). The chapter of Mishna, *Bameh Madlikin*, should engage us in thinking about how to prepare for Shabbat. For that reason, we formatted the pages as a classic page of Talmud, with a literal English translation on one side and spiritual application, adapted from the thought of Rav Kook, on the other. We also included texts, such as the Ten Commandments and selections from the Talmud, which serve as the literary source of *Lekha Dodi*, though there is no particular custom to study them as Shabbat enters.

Imagination. The lost art of prayer in our age is the freelance articulation, visualization, or application of routine phrases. To recover it, we provided a visual commentary to the sections of the liturgy, notably *Lekha Dodi* and *Shir HaShirim*, Song of Songs. These furnish rich, compelling images designed to clarify and to challenge, to focus and to distract, to enliven and to discipline – all essential habits of the imagination. Most importantly, prayer ought be a playful exercise; and the myriad associations, hopefully fresh with every prayer experience, will invite each participant into a playground for hearts and minds.

Rhythm. By varying the visual presentations of the different sections of the Shabbat evening service, we hope to enable users to appreciate its texture and rhythm . The commentary details the sources and customs of each segment, virtually inescapable given the change in appearance. In this way, we also tried to echo the popular Carlebach musical interpretation of the service – a standard weekday beat for Minḥa, a creative energy for Kabbalat Shabbat, and a respectful tone for Ma'ariv.

Our aim is to produce an accessory to prayer which is open and friendly to novices, yet inspiring and familiar to veterans. The result, we hope, is a succesful and welcome compromise. *The Koren Shabbat Evening Siddur* can serve as a reliable companion to an educator looking to bring out themes in the Friday night prayer service. It can be a mentor to a student organizing and leading a service for the first time. It can be a guide to parents who want to pray with their children at home.

The grand narrative of Jewish prayer begins with our ancestors seeing the possibilities of prayer to connect us to God, to each other, to ourselves. This siddur hopes not to be the story's end, but an assurance of its future.

Rabbi Yehuda Sarna
New York 5771/2011

ערב שבת

EREV SHABBAT

Minḥa for Erev Shabbat

אַשְׁרֵי Happy are those who dwell in Your House; *Ps. 84*
they shall continue to praise You, Selah!
Happy are the people for whom this is so; *Ps. 144*
happy are the people whose God is the Lord.

A song of praise by David. *Ps. 145*

I will exalt You, my God, the King, and bless Your name for ever and all time. Every day I will bless You, and praise Your name for ever and all time. Great is the Lord and greatly to be praised; His greatness is unfathomable. One generation will praise Your works to the next, and tell of Your mighty deeds. On the glorious splendor of Your majesty I will meditate, and on the acts of Your wonders. They shall talk of the power of Your awesome deeds, and I will tell of Your greatness. They shall recite the record of Your great goodness, and sing with joy of Your righteousness. The Lord is gracious and compassionate, slow to anger and great in loving-kindness. The Lord is good to all, and His compassion extends to all His works. All Your works shall thank You, Lord, and Your devoted ones shall bless You. They shall talk of the glory of Your kingship, and speak of Your might. To make known to mankind His mighty deeds and the glorious majesty of His kingship. Your kingdom is an everlasting kingdom, and Your reign is for all generations. The Lord

---

The service begins with *Ashrei,* the third of three daily recitals, as a prelude to prayer. As opposed to Shaḥarit, the morning service and Ma'ariv, the evening service, the Amida is directly preceded by Ashrei, not Shema. The reason for this is based on the convergence of two issues. The first is that the biblical commandment mandates the recitation of the Shema when one goes to sleep and when one rises in the morning, hence the Shema is an integral part of Ma'ariv and Shaḥarit. The second issue relates a difference of opinion

מנחה לערב שבת

תהלים פד אַשְׁרֵי יוֹשְׁבֵי בֵיתֶךָ, עוֹד יְהַלְלְוּךָ סֶּלָה:
תהלים קמד אַשְׁרֵי הָעָם שֶׁכָּכָה לּוֹ, אַשְׁרֵי הָעָם שֶׁיהוה אֱלֹהָיו:
תהלים קמה תְּהִלָּה לְדָוִד

אֲרוֹמִמְךָ אֱלוֹהַי הַמֶּלֶךְ, וַאֲבָרְכָה שִׁמְךָ לְעוֹלָם וָעֶד:
בְּכָל־יוֹם אֲבָרְכֶךָּ, וַאֲהַלְלָה שִׁמְךָ לְעוֹלָם וָעֶד:
גָּדוֹל יהוה וּמְהֻלָּל מְאֹד, וְלִגְדֻלָּתוֹ אֵין חֵקֶר:
דּוֹר לְדוֹר יְשַׁבַּח מַעֲשֶׂיךָ, וּגְבוּרֹתֶיךָ יַגִּידוּ:
הֲדַר כְּבוֹד הוֹדֶךָ, וְדִבְרֵי נִפְלְאֹתֶיךָ אָשִׂיחָה:
וֶעֱזוּז נוֹרְאֹתֶיךָ יֹאמֵרוּ, וּגְדוּלָּתְךָ אֲסַפְּרֶנָּה:
זֵכֶר רַב־טוּבְךָ יַבִּיעוּ, וְצִדְקָתְךָ יְרַנֵּנוּ:
חַנּוּן וְרַחוּם יהוה, אֶרֶךְ אַפַּיִם וּגְדָל־חָסֶד:
טוֹב־יהוה לַכֹּל, וְרַחֲמָיו עַל־כָּל־מַעֲשָׂיו:
יוֹדְוּךָ יהוה כָּל־מַעֲשֶׂיךָ, וַחֲסִידֶיךָ יְבָרְכוּכָה:
כְּבוֹד מַלְכוּתְךָ יֹאמֵרוּ, וּגְבוּרָתְךָ יְדַבֵּרוּ:
לְהוֹדִיעַ לִבְנֵי הָאָדָם גְּבוּרֹתָיו, וּכְבוֹד הֲדַר מַלְכוּתוֹ:
מַלְכוּתְךָ מַלְכוּת כָּל־עֹלָמִים, וּמֶמְשַׁלְתְּךָ בְּכָל־דּוֹר וָדֹר:

AFTERNOON SERVICE

The afternoon service corresponds to the daily afternoon sacrifice (Num. 28:4). *Minḥa*, the "meal-offering," was not unique to the afternoon. The prayer may have acquired this name because of the verse in Psalms (141:2): "May my prayer be like incense before You, the lifting up of my hands like the afternoon offering (*minḥat arev*)." The Sages attached special significance to this prayer, noting that Elijah's prayer was answered at this time (1 Kings 18:36).

supports all who fall, and raises all who are bowed down. All raise their eyes to You in hope, and You give them their food in due season. You open Your hand, and satisfy every living thing with favor. The LORD is righteous in all His ways, and kind in all He does. The LORD is close to all who call on Him, to all who call on Him in truth. He fulfills the will of those who revere Him; He hears their cry and saves them. The LORD guards all who love Him, but all the wicked He will destroy. ▸ My mouth shall speak the praise of the LORD, and all creatures shall bless His holy name for ever and all time.

We will bless the LORD now and for ever. Halleluya! *Ps. 115*

HALF KADDISH

Leader: יִתְגַּדַּל Magnified and sanctified may His great name be,
in the world He created by His will.
May He establish His kingdom
in your lifetime and in your days,
and in the lifetime of all the house of Israel,
swiftly and soon – and say: Amen.

All: May His great name be blessed for ever and all time.

Leader: Blessed and praised, glorified and exalted,
raised and honored, uplifted and lauded
be the name of the Holy One, blessed be He,
beyond any blessing,
song, praise and consolation
uttered in the world – and say: Amen.

---

states that we do so after immersing in poetry and song. Ḥazal decided to mandate both opinions; thus we recite the Shema directly before the Amida in the evening and morning but Ashrei, a psalm, before the afternoon Amida. (JS/YR)

סוֹמֵךְ יהוה לְכָל־הַנֹּפְלִים, וְזוֹקֵף לְכָל־הַכְּפוּפִים:
עֵינֵי־כֹל אֵלֶיךָ יְשַׂבֵּרוּ, וְאַתָּה נוֹתֵן־לָהֶם אֶת־אָכְלָם בְּעִתּוֹ:
פּוֹתֵחַ אֶת־יָדֶךָ, וּמַשְׂבִּיעַ לְכָל־חַי רָצוֹן:
צַדִּיק יהוה בְּכָל־דְּרָכָיו, וְחָסִיד בְּכָל־מַעֲשָׂיו:
קָרוֹב יהוה לְכָל־קֹרְאָיו, לְכֹל אֲשֶׁר יִקְרָאֻהוּ בֶאֱמֶת:
רְצוֹן־יְרֵאָיו יַעֲשֶׂה, וְאֶת־שַׁוְעָתָם יִשְׁמַע, וְיוֹשִׁיעֵם:
שׁוֹמֵר יהוה אֶת־כָּל־אֹהֲבָיו, וְאֵת כָּל־הָרְשָׁעִים יַשְׁמִיד:
◂ תְּהִלַּת יהוה יְדַבֶּר פִּי, וִיבָרֵךְ כָּל־בָּשָׂר שֵׁם קָדְשׁוֹ לְעוֹלָם וָעֶד:
וַאֲנַחְנוּ נְבָרֵךְ יָהּ מֵעַתָּה וְעַד־עוֹלָם, הַלְלוּיָהּ: תהלים קטו

חצי קדיש

ש״ץ: יִתְגַּדַּל וְיִתְקַדַּשׁ שְׁמֵהּ רַבָּא (קהל: אָמֵן)
בְּעָלְמָא דִּי בְרָא כִרְעוּתֵהּ
וְיַמְלִיךְ מַלְכוּתֵהּ
בְּחַיֵּיכוֹן וּבְיוֹמֵיכוֹן וּבְחַיֵּי דְכָל בֵּית יִשְׂרָאֵל
בַּעֲגָלָא וּבִזְמַן קָרִיב, וְאִמְרוּ אָמֵן. (קהל: אָמֵן)

קהל וש״ץ: יְהֵא שְׁמֵהּ רַבָּא מְבָרַךְ לְעָלַם וּלְעָלְמֵי עָלְמַיָּא.

ש״ץ: יִתְבָּרַךְ וְיִשְׁתַּבַּח וְיִתְפָּאַר וְיִתְרוֹמַם וְיִתְנַשֵּׂא
וְיִתְהַדָּר וְיִתְעַלֶּה וְיִתְהַלָּל
שְׁמֵהּ דְּקֻדְשָׁא בְּרִיךְ הוּא (קהל: בְּרִיךְ הוּא)
לְעֵלָּא מִן כָּל בִּרְכָתָא
/ בעשרת ימי תשובה: לְעֵלָּא לְעֵלָּא מִכָּל בִּרְכָתָא/
וְשִׁירָתָא, תֻּשְׁבְּחָתָא וְנֶחֱמָתָא
דַּאֲמִירָן בְּעָלְמָא, וְאִמְרוּ אָמֵן. (קהל: אָמֵן)

---

as to how we approach the Creator before the Amida. One opinion states that we do so directly following an immersion in Torah study; the second opinion

THE AMIDA

The following prayer, until "in former years" on page 24, is said silently, standing with feet together. If there is a minyan, the Amida is repeated aloud by the Leader. Take three steps forward and at the points indicated by ▾, bend the knees at the first word, bow at the second, and stand straight before saying God's name.

When I proclaim the LORD's name, give glory to our God. *Deut. 32*
O LORD, open my lips, so that my mouth may declare Your praise. *Ps. 51*

PATRIARCHS

▾בָּרוּךְ▾ Blessed are You, LORD our God and God of our fathers,
God of Abraham, God of Isaac and God of Jacob;
the great, mighty and awesome God, God Most High,
who bestows acts of loving-kindness and creates all,
who remembers the loving-kindness of the fathers
and will bring a Redeemer to their children's children
for the sake of His name, in love.

Between Rosh HaShana & Yom Kippur: Remember us for life, O King who desires life,
and write us in the book of life –
for Your sake, O God of life.

King, Helper, Savior, Shield:
▾Blessed are You, LORD, Shield of Abraham.

DIVINE MIGHT

אַתָּה גִּבּוֹר You are eternally mighty, LORD.
You give life to the dead and have great power to save.

The phrase "He makes the wind blow and the rain fall" is added from Simḥat Torah until Pesaḥ. In Israel the phrase "He causes the dew to fall" is added from Pesaḥ until Shemini Atzeret.

In fall & winter: He makes the wind blow and the rain fall.

In Israel, in spring & summer: He causes the dew to fall.

"I am not a man of words… I am heavy of speech and tongue." Isaiah said, "I am a man of unclean lips." Jeremiah said, "I cannot speak for I am a child." So our first prayer is for Divine help in the act of prayer itself.

עמידה

The following prayer, until קַדְמֹנִיּוֹת *on page 25, is said silently, standing with feet together. If there is a* מנין*, the* עמידה *is repeated aloud by the* שליח ציבור*. Take three steps forward and at the points indicated by* ˚*, bend the knees at the first word, bow at the second, and stand straight before saying God's name.*

דברים לב כִּי שֵׁם יהוה אֶקְרָא, הָבוּ גֹדֶל לֵאלֹהֵינוּ:

תהלים נא אֲדֹנָי, שְׂפָתַי תִּפְתָּח, וּפִי יַגִּיד תְּהִלָּתֶךָ:

אבות

˚בָּרוּךְ אַתָּה יהוה, אֱלֹהֵינוּ וֵאלֹהֵי אֲבוֹתֵינוּ
אֱלֹהֵי אַבְרָהָם, אֱלֹהֵי יִצְחָק, וֵאלֹהֵי יַעֲקֹב
הָאֵל הַגָּדוֹל הַגִּבּוֹר וְהַנּוֹרָא, אֵל עֶלְיוֹן
גּוֹמֵל חֲסָדִים טוֹבִים, וְקוֹנֵה הַכֹּל
וְזוֹכֵר חַסְדֵי אָבוֹת
וּמֵבִיא גוֹאֵל לִבְנֵי בְנֵיהֶם לְמַעַן שְׁמוֹ בְּאַהֲבָה.

בעשרת ימי תשובה: זָכְרֵנוּ לְחַיִּים, מֶלֶךְ חָפֵץ בַּחַיִּים
וְכָתְבֵנוּ בְּסֵפֶר הַחַיִּים, לְמַעַנְךָ אֱלֹהִים חַיִּים.

מֶלֶךְ עוֹזֵר וּמוֹשִׁיעַ וּמָגֵן.
˚בָּרוּךְ אַתָּה יהוה, מָגֵן אַבְרָהָם.

גבורות

אַתָּה גִּבּוֹר לְעוֹלָם, אֲדֹנָי
מְחַיֵּה מֵתִים אַתָּה, רַב לְהוֹשִׁיעַ

The phrase מַשִּׁיב הָרְוּחַ *is added from* שמחת תורה *until* פסח*.*
In ארץ ישראל *the phrase* מוֹרִיד הַטָּל *is added from* פסח *until* שמיני עצרת*.*

בחורף: מַשִּׁיב הָרְוּחַ וּמוֹרִיד הַגֶּשֶׁם / בארץ ישראל בקיץ: מוֹרִיד הַטָּל

אֲדֹנָי, שְׂפָתַי תִּפְתָּח *O Lord, open my lips:* Standing in the presence of God, we feel our inadequacy. The greatest of the prophets felt tongue-tied. Moses said,

He sustains the living with loving-kindness,
and with great compassion revives the dead.
He supports the fallen, heals the sick,
sets captives free,
and keeps His faith with those who sleep in the dust.
Who is like You, Master of might,
and who can compare to You,
O King who brings death and gives life,
and makes salvation grow?

Between Rosh HaShana & Yom Kippur: Who is like You, compassionate Father,
who remembers His creatures in compassion, for life?

Faithful are You to revive the dead.
Blessed are You, LORD, who revives the dead.

When saying the Amida silently, go to "You are holy" on the next page.

KEDUSHA

During the Leader's Repetition, the following is said standing with feet together, rising on the toes at the words indicated by ▲.

Cong. then Leader: נְקַדֵּשׁ We will sanctify Your name on earth,
as they sanctify it in the highest heavens,
as is written by Your prophet,
"And they [the angels] call to one another saying: *Is. 6*

Cong. then Leader: ▲Holy, ▲holy, ▲holy is the LORD of hosts
the whole world is filled with His glory."
Those facing them say "Blessed – "

Cong. then Leader: ▲"Blessed is the LORD's glory from His place." *Ezek. 3*
And in Your holy Writings it is written thus:

Cong. then Leader: ▲"The LORD shall reign for ever. He is your God, Zion, *Ps. 146*
from generation to generation, Halleluya!"

Leader: From generation to generation we will declare Your greatness,
and we will proclaim Your holiness for evermore.
Your praise, our God, shall not leave our mouth forever,
for You, God, are a great and holy King. Blessed are You, LORD,
the holy God. / *Between Rosh HaShana & Yom Kippur:* the holy King./

The Leader continues with "You grace humanity" on the next page.

מְכַלְכֵּל חַיִּים בְּחֶסֶד, מְחַיֵּה מֵתִים בְּרַחֲמִים רַבִּים
סוֹמֵךְ נוֹפְלִים, וְרוֹפֵא חוֹלִים, וּמַתִּיר אֲסוּרִים
וּמְקַיֵּם אֱמוּנָתוֹ לִישֵׁנֵי עָפָר.
מִי כָמְוֹךָ, בַּעַל גְּבוּרוֹת
וּמִי דְּוֹמֶה לָּךְ
מֶלֶךְ, מֵמִית וּמְחַיֶּה וּמַצְמְיחַ יְשׁוּעָה.

בעשרת ימי תשובה: מִי כָמְוֹךָ אַב הָרַחֲמִים
זוֹכֵר יְצוּרָיו לְחַיִּים בְּרַחֲמִים.

וְנֶאֱמָן אַתָּה לְהַחֲיוֹת מֵתִים.
בָּרוּךְ אַתָּה יהוה, מְחַיֵּה הַמֵּתִים.

When saying the עמידה silently, continue with אַתָּה קָדוֹשׁ on the next page.

קדושה

During the חזרת הש״ץ, the following is said standing with feet together, rising on the toes at the words indicated by ⁺.

קהל then ש״ץ: נְקַדֵּשׁ אֶת שִׁמְךָ בָּעוֹלָם, כְּשֵׁם שֶׁמַּקְדִּישִׁים אוֹתוֹ בִּשְׁמֵי מָרוֹם
כַּכָּתוּב עַל יַד נְבִיאֶךָ: וְקָרָא זֶה אֶל־זֶה וְאָמַר — ישעיה ו

קהל then ש״ץ: ⁺קָדוֹשׁ, ⁺קָדוֹשׁ, ⁺קָדוֹשׁ, יהוה צְבָאוֹת, מְלֹא כָל־הָאָרֶץ כְּבוֹדוֹ:
לְעֻמָּתָם בָּרוּךְ יֹאמֵרוּ

קהל then ש״ץ: ⁺בָּרוּךְ כְּבוֹד־יהוה מִמְּקוֹמוֹ: — יחזקאל ג
וּבְדִבְרֵי קָדְשְׁךָ כָּתוּב לֵאמֹר

קהל then ש״ץ: ⁺יִמְלֹךְ יהוה לְעוֹלָם, אֱלֹהַיִךְ צִיּוֹן לְדֹר וָדֹר, הַלְלוּיָהּ: — תהלים קמו

ש״ץ: לְדוֹר וָדוֹר נַגִּיד גָּדְלֶךָ, וּלְנֵצַח נְצָחִים קְדֻשָּׁתְךָ נַקְדִּישׁ
וְשִׁבְחֲךָ אֱלֹהֵינוּ מִפִּינוּ לֹא יָמוּשׁ לְעוֹלָם וָעֶד
כִּי אֵל מֶלֶךְ גָּדוֹל וְקָדוֹשׁ אָתָּה.
בָּרוּךְ אַתָּה יהוה, הָאֵל הַקָּדוֹשׁ./ בעשרת ימי תשובה: הַמֶּלֶךְ הַקָּדוֹשׁ./

The שליח ציבור continues with אַתָּה חוֹנֵן on the next page.

HOLINESS

אַתָּה קָדוֹשׁ You are holy and Your name is holy,
and holy ones praise You daily, Selah!
Blessed are You, LORD,
the holy God. / *Between Rosh HaShana & Yom Kippur:* the holy King./
(*If forgotten, repeat the Amida.*)

KNOWLEDGE

אַתָּה חוֹנֵן You grace humanity with knowledge
and teach mortals understanding.
Grace us with the knowledge, understanding
and discernment that come from You.
Blessed are You, LORD,
who graciously grants knowledge.

REPENTANCE

הֲשִׁיבֵנוּ Bring us back, our Father, to Your Torah.
Draw us near, our King, to Your service.
Lead us back to You in perfect repentance.
Blessed are You, LORD,
who desires repentance.

FORGIVENESS

Strike the left side of the chest at °.

סְלַח לָנוּ Forgive us, our Father,
for we have °sinned.
Pardon us, our King,
for we have °transgressed;
for You pardon and forgive.
Blessed are You, LORD,
the gracious One who repeatedly forgives.

REDEMPTION

רְאֵה Look on our affliction, plead our cause,
and redeem us soon for Your name's sake,
for You are a powerful Redeemer.
Blessed are You, LORD,
the Redeemer of Israel.

קדושת השם

אַתָּה קָדוֹשׁ וְשִׁמְךָ קָדוֹשׁ

וּקְדוֹשִׁים בְּכָל יוֹם יְהַלְלוּךָ סֶּלָה.

בָּרוּךְ אַתָּה יהוה

הָאֵל הַקָּדוֹשׁ./ בעשרת ימי תשובה: הַמֶּלֶךְ הַקָּדוֹשׁ./

(*If forgotten, repeat the* עמידה.)

דעת

אַתָּה חוֹנֵן לְאָדָם דַּעַת, וּמְלַמֵּד לֶאֱנוֹשׁ בִּינָה.

חָנֵּנוּ מֵאִתְּךָ דֵּעָה בִּינָה וְהַשְׂכֵּל.

בָּרוּךְ אַתָּה יהוה, חוֹנֵן הַדָּעַת.

תשובה

הֲשִׁיבֵנוּ אָבִינוּ לְתוֹרָתֶךָ, וְקָרְבֵנוּ מַלְכֵּנוּ לַעֲבוֹדָתֶךָ

וְהַחֲזִירֵנוּ בִּתְשׁוּבָה שְׁלֵמָה לְפָנֶיךָ.

בָּרוּךְ אַתָּה יהוה, הָרוֹצֶה בִּתְשׁוּבָה.

סליחה

Strike the left side of the chest at °.

סְלַח לָנוּ אָבִינוּ כִּי °חָטָאנוּ

מְחַל לָנוּ מַלְכֵּנוּ כִּי °פָשָׁעְנוּ

כִּי מוֹחֵל וְסוֹלֵחַ אָתָּה.

בָּרוּךְ אַתָּה יהוה, חַנּוּן הַמַּרְבֶּה לִסְלֹחַ.

גאולה

רְאֵה בְעָנְיֵנוּ, וְרִיבָה רִיבֵנוּ

וּגְאָלֵנוּ מְהֵרָה לְמַעַן שְׁמֶךָ

כִּי גוֹאֵל חָזָק אָתָּה.

בָּרוּךְ אַתָּה יהוה, גּוֹאֵל יִשְׂרָאֵל.

HEALING

רְפָאֵנוּ Heal us, LORD, and we shall be healed.
Save us and we shall be saved,
for You are our praise.
Bring complete recovery for all our ailments,

The following prayer for a sick person may be said here:
May it be Your will, O LORD my God and God of my ancestors, that You speedily send a complete recovery from heaven, a healing of both soul and body, to the patient (*name*), son/daughter of (*mother's name*) among the other afflicted of Israel.

---

for You, God, King, are a faithful and compassionate Healer.
Blessed are You, LORD, Healer of the sick of His people Israel.

PROSPERITY

The phrase "Grant dew and rain as a blessing" is said from December 5th (in the year before a civil leap year, December 6th) until Pesaḥ. In Israel, it is said from the 7th of Marḥeshvan. The phrase "Grant blessing" is said from Ḥol HaMo'ed Pesaḥ until December 4th (in the year before a civil leap year, December 5th). In Israel it is said through the 6th of Marḥeshvan.

בָּרֵךְ Bless this year for us, LORD our God,
and all its types of produce for good.

In winter: Grant dew and rain as a blessing
In other seasons: Grant blessing

on the face of the earth,
and from its goodness satisfy us,
blessing our year as the best of years.
Blessed are You, LORD, who blesses the years.

INGATHERING OF EXILES

תְּקַע Sound the great shofar for our freedom,
raise high the banner to gather our exiles,
and gather us together
from the four quarters of the earth.
Blessed are You, LORD,
who gathers the dispersed of His people Israel.

רפואה

רְפָאֵנוּ יהוה וְנֵרָפֵא, הוֹשִׁיעֵנוּ וְנִוָּשֵׁעָה, כִּי תְהִלָּתֵנוּ אָתָּה וְהַעֲלֵה רְפוּאָה שְׁלֵמָה לְכָל מַכּוֹתֵינוּ

The following prayer for a sick person may be said here:

יְהִי רָצוֹן מִלְּפָנֶיךָ יהוה אֱלֹהַי וֵאלֹהֵי אֲבוֹתַי, שֶׁתִּשְׁלַח מְהֵרָה רְפוּאָה שְׁלֵמָה מִן הַשָּׁמַיִם רְפוּאַת הַנֶּפֶשׁ וּרְפוּאַת הַגּוּף לַחוֹלֶה/לַחוֹלָה *name of patient* בֶּן/בַּת *mother's name* בְּתוֹךְ שְׁאָר חוֹלֵי יִשְׂרָאֵל.

כִּי אֵל מֶלֶךְ רוֹפֵא נֶאֱמָן וְרַחֲמָן אָתָּה.
בָּרוּךְ אַתָּה יהוה, רוֹפֵא חוֹלֵי עַמּוֹ יִשְׂרָאֵל.

ברכת השנים

The phrase וְתֵן טַל וּמָטָר לִבְרָכָה *is said from December 5th (in the year before a civil leap year, December 6th) until* פסח. *In* ארץ ישראל, *it is said from* ז׳ מרחשון. *The phrase* וְתֵן בְּרָכָה *is said from* חול המועד פסח *until December 4th (in the year before a civil leap year, December 5th). In* ארץ ישראל *it is said through* ו׳ מרחשון.

בָּרֵךְ עָלֵינוּ יהוה אֱלֹהֵינוּ אֶת הַשָּׁנָה הַזֹּאת
וְאֶת כָּל מִינֵי תְבוּאָתָהּ, לְטוֹבָה
בחורף: וְתֵן טַל וּמָטָר לִבְרָכָה / בקיץ: וְתֵן בְּרָכָה
עַל פְּנֵי הָאֲדָמָה, וְשַׂבְּעֵנוּ מִטּוּבָהּ
וּבָרֵךְ שְׁנָתֵנוּ כַּשָּׁנִים הַטּוֹבוֹת.
בָּרוּךְ אַתָּה יהוה, מְבָרֵךְ הַשָּׁנִים.

קבוץ גלויות

תְּקַע בְּשׁוֹפָר גָּדוֹל לְחֵרוּתֵנוּ
וְשָׂא נֵס לְקַבֵּץ גָּלֻיּוֹתֵינוּ
וְקַבְּצֵנוּ יַחַד מֵאַרְבַּע כַּנְפוֹת הָאָרֶץ.
בָּרוּךְ אַתָּה יהוה
מְקַבֵּץ נִדְחֵי עַמּוֹ יִשְׂרָאֵל.

JUSTICE

הָשִׁיבָה Restore our judges as at first
and our counselors as at the beginning,
and remove from us sorrow and sighing.
May You alone, LORD,
reign over us with loving-kindness and compassion,
and vindicate us in justice.
Blessed are You, LORD,
the King who loves righteousness and justice.
/*Between Rosh HaShana & Yom Kippur, end the blessing:* the King of justice./

AGAINST INFORMERS

וְלַמַּלְשִׁינִים For the slanderers
let there be no hope,
and may all wickedness perish in an instant.
May all Your people's enemies swiftly be cut down.
May You swiftly uproot, crush, cast down
and humble the arrogant swiftly in our days.
Blessed are You, LORD,
who destroys enemies and humbles the arrogant.

THE RIGHTEOUS

עַל הַצַּדִּיקִים To the righteous, the pious,
the elders of Your people the house of Israel,
the remnant of their scholars,
the righteous converts, and to us,
may Your compassion be aroused, LORD our God.
Grant a good reward
to all who sincerely trust in Your name
Set our lot with them,
so that we may never be ashamed,
for in You we trust
Blessed are You, LORD,
who is the support and trust of the righteous.

השבת המשפט

הָשִׁיבָה שׁוֹפְטֵינוּ כְּבָרִאשׁוֹנָה
וְיוֹעֲצֵינוּ כְּבַתְּחִלָּה
וְהָסֵר מִמֶּנּוּ יָגוֹן וַאֲנָחָה
וּמְלֹךְ עָלֵינוּ אַתָּה יהוה לְבַדְּךָ בְּחֶסֶד וּבְרַחֲמִים
וְצַדְּקֵנוּ בַּמִּשְׁפָּט.
בָּרוּךְ אַתָּה יהוה
מֶלֶךְ אוֹהֵב צְדָקָה וּמִשְׁפָּט. / בעשרת ימי תשובה: הַמֶּלֶךְ הַמִּשְׁפָּט./

ברכת המינים

וְלַמַּלְשִׁינִים אַל תְּהִי תִקְוָה
וְכָל הָרִשְׁעָה כְּרֶגַע תֹּאבֵד
וְכָל אוֹיְבֵי עַמְּךָ מְהֵרָה יִכָּרֵתוּ
וְהַזֵּדִים מְהֵרָה תְעַקֵּר וּתְשַׁבֵּר וּתְמַגֵּר וְתַכְנִיעַ בִּמְהֵרָה בְיָמֵינוּ.
בָּרוּךְ אַתָּה יהוה, שׁוֹבֵר אוֹיְבִים וּמַכְנִיעַ זֵדִים.

על הצדיקים

עַל הַצַּדִּיקִים וְעַל הַחֲסִידִים
וְעַל זִקְנֵי עַמְּךָ בֵּית יִשְׂרָאֵל
וְעַל פְּלֵיטַת סוֹפְרֵיהֶם
וְעַל גֵּרֵי הַצֶּדֶק, וְעָלֵינוּ
יֶהֱמוּ רַחֲמֶיךָ יהוה אֱלֹהֵינוּ
וְתֵן שָׂכָר טוֹב לְכָל הַבּוֹטְחִים בְּשִׁמְךָ בֶּאֱמֶת
וְשִׂים חֶלְקֵנוּ עִמָּהֶם
וּלְעוֹלָם לֹא נֵבוֹשׁ כִּי בְךָ בָטָחְנוּ.
בָּרוּךְ אַתָּה יהוה, מִשְׁעָן וּמִבְטָח לַצַּדִּיקִים.

REBUILDING JERUSALEM

וְלִירוּשָׁלַיִם To Jerusalem, Your city,
may You return in compassion,
and may You dwell in it as You promised.
May You rebuild it rapidly in our days
as an everlasting structure,
and install within it soon the throne of David.
Blessed are You, LORD, who builds Jerusalem.

KINGDOM OF DAVID

אֶת צֶמַח May the offshoot
of Your servant David soon flower,
and may his pride be raised high by Your salvation,
for we wait for Your salvation all day.
Blessed are You, LORD, who makes the glory of salvation flourish.

RESPONSE TO PRAYER

שְׁמַע קוֹלֵנוּ Listen to our voice, LORD our God.
Spare us and have compassion on us,
and in compassion and favor accept our prayer,
for You, God, listen to prayers and pleas.
Do not turn us away, O our King,
empty-handed from Your presence,*
for You listen with compassion
to the prayer of Your people Israel.
Blessed are You, LORD, who listens to prayer.

TEMPLE SERVICE

רְצֵה Find favor, LORD our God,
in Your people Israel and their prayer.
Restore the service to Your most holy House,
and accept in love and favor
the fire-offerings of Israel and their prayer.
May the service of Your people Israel always find favor with You.

אֱלֹהֵינוּ Our God and God of our ancestors, may there rise, come, reach, appear, be favored, heard, regarded and remembered before You, our recollection and remembrance, as well as the remembrance of our ancestors, and

בניין ירושלים

וְלִירוּשָׁלַיִם עִירְךָ בְּרַחֲמִים תָּשׁוּב
וְתִשְׁכֹּן בְּתוֹכָהּ כַּאֲשֶׁר דִּבַּרְתָּ
וּבְנֵה אוֹתָהּ בְּקָרוֹב בְּיָמֵינוּ בִּנְיַן עוֹלָם
וְכִסֵּא דָוִד מְהֵרָה לְתוֹכָהּ תָּכִין.
בָּרוּךְ אַתָּה יהוה, בּוֹנֵה יְרוּשָׁלָיִם.

משיח בן דוד

אֶת צֶמַח דָּוִד עַבְדְּךָ מְהֵרָה תַצְמִיחַ
וְקַרְנוֹ תָּרוּם בִּישׁוּעָתֶךָ, כִּי לִישׁוּעָתְךָ קִוִּינוּ כָּל הַיּוֹם.
בָּרוּךְ אַתָּה יהוה, מַצְמִיחַ קֶרֶן יְשׁוּעָה.

שומע תפילה

שְׁמַע קוֹלֵנוּ יהוה אֱלֹהֵינוּ
חוּס וְרַחֵם עָלֵינוּ
וְקַבֵּל בְּרַחֲמִים וּבְרָצוֹן אֶת תְּפִלָּתֵנוּ
כִּי אֵל שׁוֹמֵעַ תְּפִלּוֹת וְתַחֲנוּנִים אָתָּה
וּמִלְּפָנֶיךָ מַלְכֵּנוּ רֵיקָם אַל תְּשִׁיבֵנוּ*
כִּי אַתָּה שׁוֹמֵעַ תְּפִלַּת עַמְּךָ יִשְׂרָאֵל בְּרַחֲמִים.
בָּרוּךְ אַתָּה יהוה, שׁוֹמֵעַ תְּפִלָּה.

עבודה

רְצֵה יהוה אֱלֹהֵינוּ בְּעַמְּךָ יִשְׂרָאֵל וּבִתְפִלָּתָם
וְהָשֵׁב אֶת הָעֲבוֹדָה לִדְבִיר בֵּיתֶךָ
וְאִשֵּׁי יִשְׂרָאֵל וּתְפִלָּתָם בְּאַהֲבָה תְקַבֵּל בְּרָצוֹן
וּתְהִי לְרָצוֹן תָּמִיד עֲבוֹדַת יִשְׂרָאֵל עַמֶּךָ.

אֱלֹהֵינוּ וֵאלֹהֵי אֲבוֹתֵינוּ, יַעֲלֶה וְיָבוֹא וְיַגִּיעַ, וְיֵרָאֶה וְיֵרָצֶה וְיִשָּׁמַע, וְיִפָּקֵד וְיִזָּכֵר זִכְרוֹנֵנוּ וּפִקְדוֹנֵנוּ וְזִכְרוֹן אֲבוֹתֵינוּ, וְזִכְרוֹן מָשִׁיחַ בֶּן דָּוִד

of the Messiah son of David Your servant, and of Jerusalem Your holy city, and of all Your people the house of Israel – for deliverance and well-being, grace, loving-kindness and compassion, life and peace, on this day of:

On Rosh Ḥodesh: Rosh Ḥodesh.
On Pesaḥ: the Festival of Matzot.
On Sukkot: the Festival of Sukkot.

On it remember us, LORD our God, for good; recollect us for blessing, and deliver us for life. In accord with Your promise of salvation and compassion, spare us and be gracious to us; have compassion on us and deliver us, for our eyes are turned to You because You, God, are a gracious and compassionate King.

וְתֶחֱזֶינָה And may our eyes witness Your return to Zion in compassion. Blessed are You, LORD, who restores His Presence to Zion.

THANKSGIVING

Bow at the first nine words.

מוֹדִים We give thanks to You,
for You are the LORD our God
and God of our ancestors
for ever and all time.
You are the Rock of our lives,
Shield of our salvation
from generation to generation.
We will thank You and
declare Your praise for our lives,
which are entrusted into Your hand;
for our souls,
which are placed in Your charge;
for Your miracles
which are with us every day;
and for Your wonders and favors
at all times, evening, morning and midday.
You are good –
for Your compassion never fails.
You are compassionate –
for Your loving-kindnesses never cease.
We have always placed our hope in You.

During the Leader's Repetition, the congregation says quietly:

מוֹדִים We give thanks to You,
for You are the LORD our God
and God of our ancestors,
God of all flesh,
who formed us
and formed the universe.
Blessings and thanks
are due to Your great
and holy name for giving us
life and sustaining us.
May You continue
to give us life and sustain us;
and may You gather our
exiles to Your holy courts,
to keep Your decrees,
do Your will and serve You
with a perfect heart,
for it is for us to give You thanks.
Blessed be God to whom
thanksgiving is due.

עַבְדֶּךָ, וְזִכְרוֹן יְרוּשָׁלַיִם עִיר קָדְשֶׁךָ, וְזִכְרוֹן כָּל עַמְּךָ בֵּית יִשְׂרָאֵל, לְפָנֶיךָ, לִפְלֵיטָה לְטוֹבָה, לְחֵן וּלְחֶסֶד וּלְרַחֲמִים, לְחַיִּים וּלְשָׁלוֹם בְּיוֹם

בראש חודש: רֹאשׁ הַחֹדֶשׁ / בפסח: חַג הַמַּצּוֹת / בסוכות: חַג הַסֻּכּוֹת

הַזֶּה. זָכְרֵנוּ יהוה אֱלֹהֵינוּ בּוֹ לְטוֹבָה, וּפָקְדֵנוּ בוֹ לִבְרָכָה, וְהוֹשִׁיעֵנוּ בוֹ לְחַיִּים. וּבִדְבַר יְשׁוּעָה וְרַחֲמִים, חוּס וְחָנֵּנוּ וְרַחֵם עָלֵינוּ וְהוֹשִׁיעֵנוּ, כִּי אֵלֶיךָ עֵינֵינוּ, כִּי אֵל מֶלֶךְ חַנּוּן וְרַחוּם אָתָּה.

וְתֶחֱזֶינָה עֵינֵינוּ בְּשׁוּבְךָ לְצִיּוֹן בְּרַחֲמִים.
בָּרוּךְ אַתָּה יהוה, הַמַּחֲזִיר שְׁכִינָתוֹ לְצִיּוֹן.

הודאה

Bow at the first five words.

ˈמוֹדִים אֲנַחְנוּ לָךְ
שָׁאַתָּה הוּא יהוה אֱלֹהֵינוּ
וֵאלֹהֵי אֲבוֹתֵינוּ לְעוֹלָם וָעֶד.
צוּר חַיֵּינוּ, מָגֵן יִשְׁעֵנוּ
אַתָּה הוּא לְדוֹר וָדוֹר.
נוֹדֶה לְּךָ וּנְסַפֵּר תְּהִלָּתֶךָ
עַל חַיֵּינוּ הַמְּסוּרִים בְּיָדֶךָ
וְעַל נִשְׁמוֹתֵינוּ הַפְּקוּדוֹת לָךְ
וְעַל נִסֶּיךָ שֶׁבְּכָל יוֹם עִמָּנוּ
וְעַל נִפְלְאוֹתֶיךָ וְטוֹבוֹתֶיךָ
שֶׁבְּכָל עֵת, עֶרֶב וָבֹקֶר וְצָהֳרָיִם.
הַטּוֹב, כִּי לֹא כָלוּ רַחֲמֶיךָ
וְהַמְרַחֵם, כִּי לֹא תַמּוּ חֲסָדֶיךָ
מֵעוֹלָם קִוִּינוּ לָךְ.

During the חזרת הש״ץ*, the* קהל *says quietly:*

ˈמוֹדִים אֲנַחְנוּ לָךְ
שָׁאַתָּה הוּא יהוה אֱלֹהֵינוּ
וֵאלֹהֵי אֲבוֹתֵינוּ
אֱלֹהֵי כָל בָּשָׂר
יוֹצְרֵנוּ, יוֹצֵר בְּרֵאשִׁית.
בְּרָכוֹת וְהוֹדָאוֹת
לְשִׁמְךָ הַגָּדוֹל וְהַקָּדוֹשׁ
עַל שֶׁהֶחֱיִיתָנוּ וְקִיַּמְתָּנוּ.
כֵּן תְּחַיֵּנוּ וּתְקַיְּמֵנוּ
וְתֶאֱסֹף גָּלֻיּוֹתֵינוּ
לְחַצְרוֹת קָדְשֶׁךָ
לִשְׁמֹר חֻקֶּיךָ וְלַעֲשׂוֹת רְצוֹנֶךָ
וּלְעָבְדְּךָ בְּלֵבָב שָׁלֵם
עַל שֶׁאֲנַחְנוּ מוֹדִים לָךְ.
בָּרוּךְ אֵל הַהוֹדָאוֹת.

On Ḥanukka:

עַל הַנִּסִּים [We thank You also] for the miracles, the redemption, the mighty deeds, and the victories in battle which You performed for our ancestors in those days, at this time.

בִּימֵי מַתִּתְיָהוּ In the days of Mattityahu, son of Yoḥanan, the High Priest, the Hasmonean, and his sons, the wicked Greek kingdom rose up against Your people Israel to make them forget Your Torah and to force them to transgress the statutes of Your will. It was then that You in Your great compassion stood by them in the time of their distress. You championed their cause, judged their claim, and avenged their wrong. You delivered the strong into the hands of the weak, the many into the hands of the few, the impure into the hands of the pure, the wicked into the hands of the righteous, and the arrogant into the hands of those who were engaged in the study of Your Torah. You made for Yourself great and holy renown in Your world, and for Your people Israel You performed a great salvation and redemption as of this very day. Your children then entered the holiest part of Your House, cleansed Your Temple, purified Your Sanctuary, kindled lights in Your holy courts, and designated these eight days of Ḥanukka for giving thanks and praise to Your great name.

Continue with "For all these things."

On Purim:

עַל הַנִּסִּים [We thank You also] for the miracles, the redemption, the mighty deeds, and the victories in battle which You performed for our ancestors in those days, at this time.

בִּימֵי מָרְדְּכַי In the days of Mordekhai and Esther, in Shushan the capital, the
wicked Haman rose up against them and sought to destroy, slay and exterminate *Esther 3*
all the Jews, young and old, children and women, on one day, the thirteenth day of the twelfth month, which is the month of Adar, and to plunder their possessions. Then You in Your great compassion thwarted his counsel, frustrated his plans, and caused his scheme to recoil on his own head, so that they hanged him and his sons on the gallows.

Continue with "For all these things."

וְעַל כֻּלָּם For all these things may Your name be blessed and exalted, our King, continually, for ever and all time.

Between Rosh HaShana & Yom Kippur: And write, for a good life,
all the children of Your covenant.

Let all that lives thank You, Selah! and praise Your name in truth,
God, our Savior and Help, Selah!
▾Blessed are You, Lord, whose name is "the Good"
and to whom thanks are due.

בחנוכה:

עַל הַנִּסִּים וְעַל הַפֻּרְקָן וְעַל הַגְּבוּרוֹת וְעַל הַתְּשׁוּעוֹת וְעַל הַמִּלְחָמוֹת שֶׁעָשִׂיתָ לַאֲבוֹתֵינוּ בַּיָּמִים הָהֵם בַּזְּמַן הַזֶּה.

בִּימֵי מַתִּתְיָהוּ בֶּן יוֹחָנָן כֹּהֵן גָּדוֹל חַשְׁמוֹנַאי וּבָנָיו, כְּשֶׁעָמְדָה מַלְכוּת יָוָן הָרְשָׁעָה עַל עַמְּךָ יִשְׂרָאֵל לְהַשְׁכִּיחָם תּוֹרָתֶךָ וּלְהַעֲבִירָם מֵחֻקֵּי רְצוֹנֶךָ, וְאַתָּה בְּרַחֲמֶיךָ הָרַבִּים עָמַדְתָּ לָהֶם בְּעֵת צָרָתָם, רַבְתָּ אֶת רִיבָם, דַּנְתָּ אֶת דִּינָם, נָקַמְתָּ אֶת נִקְמָתָם, מָסַרְתָּ גִבּוֹרִים בְּיַד חַלָּשִׁים, וְרַבִּים בְּיַד מְעַטִּים, וּטְמֵאִים בְּיַד טְהוֹרִים, וּרְשָׁעִים בְּיַד צַדִּיקִים, וְזֵדִים בְּיַד עוֹסְקֵי תוֹרָתֶךָ, וּלְךָ עָשִׂיתָ שֵׁם גָּדוֹל וְקָדוֹשׁ בְּעוֹלָמֶךָ, וּלְעַמְּךָ יִשְׂרָאֵל עָשִׂיתָ תְּשׁוּעָה גְדוֹלָה וּפֻרְקָן כְּהַיּוֹם הַזֶּה. וְאַחַר כֵּן בָּאוּ בָנֶיךָ לִדְבִיר בֵּיתֶךָ, וּפִנּוּ אֶת הֵיכָלֶךָ, וְטִהֲרוּ אֶת מִקְדָּשֶׁךָ, וְהִדְלִיקוּ נֵרוֹת בְּחַצְרוֹת קָדְשֶׁךָ, וְקָבְעוּ שְׁמוֹנַת יְמֵי חֲנֻכָּה אֵלּוּ, לְהוֹדוֹת וּלְהַלֵּל לְשִׁמְךָ הַגָּדוֹל.

Continue with וְעַל כֻּלָּם.

בפורים:

עַל הַנִּסִּים וְעַל הַפֻּרְקָן וְעַל הַגְּבוּרוֹת וְעַל הַתְּשׁוּעוֹת וְעַל הַמִּלְחָמוֹת שֶׁעָשִׂיתָ לַאֲבוֹתֵינוּ בַּיָּמִים הָהֵם בַּזְּמַן הַזֶּה.

בִּימֵי מָרְדְּכַי וְאֶסְתֵּר בְּשׁוּשַׁן הַבִּירָה, כְּשֶׁעָמַד עֲלֵיהֶם הָמָן הָרָשָׁע, בִּקֵּשׁ לְהַשְׁמִיד לַהֲרֹג וּלְאַבֵּד אֶת־כָּל־הַיְּהוּדִים מִנַּעַר וְעַד־זָקֵן טַף וְנָשִׁים בְּיוֹם אסתר ג
אֶחָד, בִּשְׁלוֹשָׁה עָשָׂר לְחֹדֶשׁ שְׁנֵים־עָשָׂר, הוּא־חֹדֶשׁ אֲדָר, וּשְׁלָלָם לָבוֹז: וְאַתָּה בְּרַחֲמֶיךָ הָרַבִּים הֵפַרְתָּ אֶת עֲצָתוֹ, וְקִלְקַלְתָּ אֶת מַחֲשַׁבְתּוֹ, וַהֲשֵׁבוֹתָ לּוֹ גְּמוּלוֹ בְּרֹאשׁוֹ, וְתָלוּ אוֹתוֹ וְאֶת בָּנָיו עַל הָעֵץ.

Continue with וְעַל כֻּלָּם.

וְעַל כֻּלָּם יִתְבָּרַךְ וְיִתְרוֹמַם שִׁמְךָ מַלְכֵּנוּ תָּמִיד לְעוֹלָם וָעֶד.

בעשרת ימי תשובה: וּכְתֹב לְחַיִּים טוֹבִים כָּל בְּנֵי בְרִיתֶךָ.

וְכֹל הַחַיִּים יוֹדוּךָ סֶּלָה, וִיהַלְלוּ אֶת שִׁמְךָ בֶּאֱמֶת הָאֵל יְשׁוּעָתֵנוּ וְעֶזְרָתֵנוּ סֶלָה.

בָּרוּךְ אַתָּה יהוה, הַטּוֹב שִׁמְךָ וּלְךָ נָאֶה לְהוֹדוֹת.

PEACE

שָׁלוֹם רָב Grant great peace
to Your people Israel for ever,
for You are the sovereign LORD of all peace;
and may it be good in Your eyes
to bless Your people Israel
at every time, at every hour, with Your peace.

Between Rosh HaShana & Yom Kippur: In the book of life, blessing, peace and prosperity,
may we and all Your people the house of Israel be remembered
and written before You for a good life, and for peace.*

Blessed are You, LORD,
who blesses His people Israel with peace.

**Between Rosh HaShana and Yom Kippur in the Diaspora, many end the blessing:*

Blessed are You, LORD, who makes peace.

The following verse concludes the Leader's Repetition of the Amida. Some also say it here as part of the silent Amida.

May the words of my mouth and the meditation of my heart *Ps. 19*
find favor before You, LORD, my Rock and Redeemer.

אֱלֹהַי My God, *Berakhot 17a*
guard my tongue from evil and my lips from deceitful speech.
To those who curse me, let my soul be silent;
may my soul be to all like the dust.
Open my heart to Your Torah and let my soul
pursue Your commandments. As for all who plan evil against me,
swiftly thwart their counsel and frustrate their plans.
Act for the sake of Your name; act for the sake of Your right hand;
act for the sake of Your holiness; act for the sake of Your Torah.
That Your beloved ones may be delivered, *Ps. 60*
save with Your right hand and answer me.
*May the words of my mouth and the meditation of my heart *Ps. 19*
find favor before You, LORD, my Rock and Redeemer.

Bow, take three steps back, then bow, first left, then right, then center, while saying:

May He who makes peace in His high places,
make peace for us and all Israel – and say: Amen.

ברכת שלום

שָׁלוֹם רָב עַל יִשְׂרָאֵל עַמְּךָ תָּשִׂים לְעוֹלָם
כִּי אַתָּה הוּא מֶלֶךְ אָדוֹן לְכָל הַשָּׁלוֹם.
וְטוֹב בְּעֵינֶיךָ לְבָרֵךְ אֶת עַמְּךָ יִשְׂרָאֵל
בְּכָל עֵת וּבְכָל שָׁעָה בִּשְׁלוֹמֶךָ.

בעשרת ימי תשובה: **בְּסֵפֶר חַיִּים, בְּרָכָה וְשָׁלוֹם, וּפַרְנָסָה טוֹבָה**
נִזָּכֵר וְנִכָּתֵב לְפָנֶיךָ, אֲנַחְנוּ וְכָל עַמְּךָ בֵּית יִשְׂרָאֵל
לְחַיִּים טוֹבִים וּלְשָׁלוֹם.*

בָּרוּךְ אַתָּה יהוה, הַמְבָרֵךְ אֶת עַמּוֹ יִשְׂרָאֵל בַּשָּׁלוֹם.

**During the* עשרת ימי תשובה *in* חוץ לארץ, *many end the blessing:*

בָּרוּךְ אַתָּה יהוה, עוֹשֵׂה הַשָּׁלוֹם.

The following verse concludes the חזרת הש״ץ.
Some also say it here as part of the silent עמידה.

יִהְיוּ לְרָצוֹן אִמְרֵי־פִי וְהֶגְיוֹן לִבִּי לְפָנֶיךָ, יהוה צוּרִי וְגֹאֲלִי: תהלים יט

אֱלֹהַי ברכות יז.

נְצֹר לְשׁוֹנִי מֵרָע וּשְׂפָתַי מִדַּבֵּר מִרְמָה
וְלִמְקַלְלַי נַפְשִׁי תִדֹּם, וְנַפְשִׁי כֶּעָפָר לַכֹּל תִּהְיֶה.
פְּתַח לִבִּי בְּתוֹרָתֶךָ, וּבְמִצְוֹתֶיךָ תִּרְדֹּף נַפְשִׁי.
וְכָל הַחוֹשְׁבִים עָלַי רָעָה
מְהֵרָה הָפֵר עֲצָתָם וְקַלְקֵל מַחֲשַׁבְתָּם.
עֲשֵׂה לְמַעַן שְׁמֶךָ, עֲשֵׂה לְמַעַן יְמִינֶךָ
עֲשֵׂה לְמַעַן קְדֻשָּׁתֶךָ, עֲשֵׂה לְמַעַן תּוֹרָתֶךָ.
לְמַעַן יֵחָלְצוּן יְדִידֶיךָ, הוֹשִׁיעָה יְמִינְךָ וַעֲנֵנִי: תהלים ס
***יִהְיוּ לְרָצוֹן אִמְרֵי־פִי וְהֶגְיוֹן לִבִּי לְפָנֶיךָ, יהוה צוּרִי וְגֹאֲלִי:** תהלים יט

Bow, take three steps back, then bow, first left, then right, then center, while saying:

עֹשֶׂה שָׁלוֹם/ בעשרת ימי תשובה: **הַשָּׁלוֹם/ בִּמְרוֹמָיו**
הוּא יַעֲשֶׂה שָׁלוֹם עָלֵינוּ וְעַל כָּל יִשְׂרָאֵל, וְאִמְרוּ אָמֵן.

יְהִי רָצוֹן May it be Your will, Lord our God and God of our ancestors,
that the Temple be rebuilt speedily in our days,
and grant us a share in Your Torah.
And there we will serve You with reverence,
as in the days of old and as in former years.
Then the offering of Judah and Jerusalem will be pleasing to the Lord *Mal. 3*
as in the days of old and as in former years.

The Leader says Full Kaddish below.

FULL KADDISH

Leader: יִתְגַּדַּל Magnified and sanctified may His great name be,
in the world He created by His will.
May He establish His kingdom
in your lifetime and in your days,
and in the lifetime of all the house of Israel,
swiftly and soon – and say: Amen.

All: May His great name be blessed for ever and all time.

Leader: Blessed and praised, glorified and exalted,
raised and honored,
uplifted and lauded
be the name of the Holy One,
blessed be He,
beyond any blessing,
song, praise and consolation
uttered in the world – and say: Amen.

May the prayers and pleas of all Israel
be accepted by their Father in heaven – and say: Amen.

May there be great peace from heaven,
and life for us and all Israel – and say: Amen.

Bow, take three steps back, as if taking leave of the Divine Presence, then bow, first left, then right, then center, while saying:

May He who makes peace in His high places,
make peace for us and all Israel – and say: Amen.

יְהִי רָצוֹן מִלְּפָנֶיךָ יהוה אֱלֹהֵינוּ וֵאלֹהֵי אֲבוֹתֵינוּ
שֶׁיִּבָּנֶה בֵּית הַמִּקְדָּשׁ בִּמְהֵרָה בְיָמֵינוּ, וְתֵן חֶלְקֵנוּ בְּתוֹרָתֶךָ
וְשָׁם נַעֲבָדְךָ בְּיִרְאָה כִּימֵי עוֹלָם וּכְשָׁנִים קַדְמֹנִיּוֹת.
וְעָרְבָה לַיהוה מִנְחַת יְהוּדָה וִירוּשָׁלָםִ כִּימֵי עוֹלָם וּכְשָׁנִים קַדְמֹנִיּוֹת: מלאכי ג

The שליח ציבור *says* קדיש שלם *below.*

קדיש שלם

ש״ץ: יִתְגַּדַּל וְיִתְקַדַּשׁ שְׁמֵהּ רַבָּא (קהל: אָמֵן)
בְּעָלְמָא דִּי בְרָא כִרְעוּתֵהּ
וְיַמְלִיךְ מַלְכוּתֵהּ
בְּחַיֵּיכוֹן וּבְיוֹמֵיכוֹן וּבְחַיֵּי דְכָל בֵּית יִשְׂרָאֵל
בַּעֲגָלָא וּבִזְמַן קָרִיב, וְאִמְרוּ אָמֵן. (קהל: אָמֵן)

קהל וש״ץ: יְהֵא שְׁמֵהּ רַבָּא מְבָרַךְ לְעָלַם וּלְעָלְמֵי עָלְמַיָּא.

ש״ץ: יִתְבָּרַךְ וְיִשְׁתַּבַּח וְיִתְפָּאַר
וְיִתְרוֹמַם וְיִתְנַשֵּׂא וְיִתְהַדָּר וְיִתְעַלֶּה וְיִתְהַלָּל
שְׁמֵהּ דְּקֻדְשָׁא בְּרִיךְ הוּא (קהל: בְּרִיךְ הוּא)
לְעֵלָּא מִן כָּל בִּרְכָתָא
/בעשרת ימי תשובה: לְעֵלָּא לְעֵלָּא מִכָּל בִּרְכָתָא/
וְשִׁירָתָא, תֻּשְׁבְּחָתָא וְנֶחֱמָתָא
דַּאֲמִירָן בְּעָלְמָא, וְאִמְרוּ אָמֵן. (קהל: אָמֵן)

תִּתְקַבַּל צְלוֹתְהוֹן וּבָעוּתְהוֹן דְּכָל יִשְׂרָאֵל
קֳדָם אֲבוּהוֹן דִּי בִשְׁמַיָּא, וְאִמְרוּ אָמֵן. (קהל: אָמֵן)

יְהֵא שְׁלָמָא רַבָּא מִן שְׁמַיָּא
וְחַיִּים, עָלֵינוּ וְעַל כָּל יִשְׂרָאֵל, וְאִמְרוּ אָמֵן. (קהל: אָמֵן)

Bow, take three steps back, as if taking leave of the Divine Presence, then bow, first left, then right, then center, while saying:

עֹשֶׂה שָׁלוֹם/בעשרת ימי תשובה: הַשָּׁלוֹם/ בִּמְרוֹמָיו
הוּא יַעֲשֶׂה שָׁלוֹם עָלֵינוּ וְעַל כָּל יִשְׂרָאֵל, וְאִמְרוּ אָמֵן. (קהל: אָמֵן)

Stand while saying Aleinu. Bow at ▾.

עָלֵינוּ It is our duty to praise the Master of all,
and ascribe greatness to the Author of creation,
who has not made us like the nations of the lands
nor placed us like the families of the earth;
who has not made our portion like theirs,
nor our destiny like all their multitudes.
(For they worship vanity and emptiness,
and pray to a god who cannot save.)
▾But we bow in worship
and thank the Supreme King of kings,
the Holy One, blessed be He,
who extends the heavens and establishes the earth,
whose throne of glory is in the heavens above,
and whose power's Presence is in the highest of heights.
He is our God; there is no other.
Truly He is our King, there is none else,
as it is written in His Torah:
"You shall know and take to heart this day that the Lord is God, *Deut. 4*
in heaven above and on earth below. There is no other."

Therefore, we place our hope in You, Lord our God,
that we may soon see the glory of Your power,
when You will remove abominations from the earth,
and idols will be utterly destroyed,
when the world will be perfected
under the sovereignty of the Almighty,
when all humanity will call on Your name,
to turn all the earth's wicked toward You.
All the world's inhabitants will realize and know
that to You every knee must bow and every tongue swear loyalty.
Before You, Lord our God, they will kneel and bow down
and give honor to Your glorious name.
They will all accept the yoke of Your kingdom,
and You will reign over them soon and for ever.
For the kingdom is Yours, and to all eternity You will reign in glory,

Stand while saying עָלֵינוּ*. Bow at* ˅.

עָלֵינוּ לְשַׁבֵּחַ לַאֲדוֹן הַכֹּל, לָתֵת גְּדֻלָּה לְיוֹצֵר בְּרֵאשִׁית
שֶׁלֹּא עָשָׂנוּ כְּגוֹיֵי הָאֲרָצוֹת, וְלֹא שָׂמָנוּ כְּמִשְׁפְּחוֹת הָאֲדָמָה
שֶׁלֹּא שָׂם חֶלְקֵנוּ כָּהֶם וְגוֹרָלֵנוּ כְּכָל הֲמוֹנָם.
(שֶׁהֵם מִשְׁתַּחֲוִים לְהֶבֶל וָרִיק וּמִתְפַּלְלִים אֶל אֵל לֹא יוֹשִׁיעַ.)
˅וַאֲנַחְנוּ כּוֹרְעִים וּמִשְׁתַּחֲוִים וּמוֹדִים
לִפְנֵי מֶלֶךְ מַלְכֵי הַמְּלָכִים, הַקָּדוֹשׁ בָּרוּךְ הוּא
שֶׁהוּא נוֹטֶה שָׁמַיִם וְיוֹסֵד אָרֶץ
וּמוֹשַׁב יְקָרוֹ בַּשָּׁמַיִם מִמַּעַל, וּשְׁכִינַת עֻזּוֹ בְּגָבְהֵי מְרוֹמִים.
הוּא אֱלֹהֵינוּ, אֵין עוֹד.
אֱמֶת מַלְכֵּנוּ, אֶפֶס זוּלָתוֹ
כַּכָּתוּב בְּתוֹרָתוֹ
וְיָדַעְתָּ הַיּוֹם וַהֲשֵׁבֹתָ אֶל־לְבָבֶךָ דברים ד
כִּי יהוה הוּא הָאֱלֹהִים בַּשָּׁמַיִם מִמַּעַל וְעַל־הָאָרֶץ מִתָּחַת,
אֵין עוֹד:

עַל כֵּן נְקַוֶּה לְּךָ יהוה אֱלֹהֵינוּ, לִרְאוֹת מְהֵרָה בְּתִפְאֶרֶת עֻזֶּךָ
לְהַעֲבִיר גִּלּוּלִים מִן הָאָרֶץ, וְהָאֱלִילִים כָּרוֹת יִכָּרֵתוּן
לְתַקֵּן עוֹלָם בְּמַלְכוּת שַׁדַּי.
וְכָל בְּנֵי בָשָׂר יִקְרְאוּ בִשְׁמֶךָ לְהַפְנוֹת אֵלֶיךָ כָּל רִשְׁעֵי אָרֶץ.
יַכִּירוּ וְיֵדְעוּ כָּל יוֹשְׁבֵי תֵבֵל
כִּי לְךָ תִּכְרַע כָּל בֶּרֶךְ, תִּשָּׁבַע כָּל לָשׁוֹן.
לְפָנֶיךָ יהוה אֱלֹהֵינוּ יִכְרְעוּ וְיִפֹּלוּ, וְלִכְבוֹד שִׁמְךָ יְקָר יִתֵּנוּ
וִיקַבְּלוּ כֻלָּם אֶת עֹל מַלְכוּתֶךָ
וְתִמְלֹךְ עֲלֵיהֶם מְהֵרָה לְעוֹלָם וָעֶד.

as it is written in Your Torah:
"The LORD will reign for ever and ever." *Ex. 15*
▸ And it is said: "Then the LORD shall be King over all the earth; *Zech. 14*
on that day the LORD shall be One and His name One."

Some add:
Have no fear of sudden terror or of the ruin when it overtakes the wicked. *Prov. 3*
Devise your strategy, but it will be thwarted; *Is. 8*
propose your plan, but it will not stand, for God is with us.
When you grow old, I will still be the same. *Is. 46*
When your hair turns gray, I will still carry you.
I made you, I will bear you, I will carry you, and I will rescue you.

MOURNER'S KADDISH

The following prayer requires the presence of a minyan.
A transliteration can be found on page 199.

Mourner: יִתְגַּדַּל Magnified and sanctified
may His great name be,
in the world He created by His will.
May He establish His kingdom
in your lifetime and in your days,
and in the lifetime of all the house of Israel,
swiftly and soon – and say: Amen.

All: May His great name be blessed for ever and all time.

Mourner: Blessed and praised, glorified and exalted,
raised and honored,
uplifted and lauded
be the name of the Holy One,
blessed be He,
beyond any blessing,
song, praise and consolation
uttered in the world – and say: Amen.

May there be great peace from heaven,
and life for us and all Israel – and say: Amen.

Bow, take three steps back, as if taking leave of the Divine Presence,
then bow, first left, then right, then center, while saying:
May He who makes peace in His high places,
make peace for us and all Israel – and say: Amen.

כִּי הַמַּלְכוּת שֶׁלְּךָ הִיא וּלְעוֹלְמֵי עַד תִּמְלֹךְ בְּכָבוֹד
כַּכָּתוּב בְּתוֹרָתֶךָ, יהוה יִמְלֹךְ לְעֹלָם וָעֶד: שמות טו
◂ וְנֶאֱמַר, וְהָיָה יהוה לְמֶלֶךְ עַל־כָּל־הָאָרֶץ זכריה יד
בַּיּוֹם הַהוּא יִהְיֶה יהוה אֶחָד וּשְׁמוֹ אֶחָד:

Some add:

אַל־תִּירָא מִפַּחַד פִּתְאֹם וּמִשֹּׁאַת רְשָׁעִים כִּי תָבֹא: משלי ג
עֻצוּ עֵצָה וְתֻפָר, דַּבְּרוּ דָבָר וְלֹא יָקוּם, כִּי עִמָּנוּ אֵל: ישעיה ח
וְעַד־זִקְנָה אֲנִי הוּא, וְעַד־שֵׂיבָה אֲנִי אֶסְבֹּל ישעיה מו
אֲנִי עָשִׂיתִי וַאֲנִי אֶשָּׂא וַאֲנִי אֶסְבֹּל וַאֲמַלֵּט:

קדיש יתום

The following prayer requires the presence of a מנין.
A transliteration can be found on page 199.

אבל: יִתְגַּדַּל וְיִתְקַדַּשׁ שְׁמֵהּ רַבָּא (קהל: אָמֵן)
בְּעָלְמָא דִּי בְרָא כִרְעוּתֵהּ, וְיַמְלִיךְ מַלְכוּתֵהּ
בְּחַיֵּיכוֹן וּבְיוֹמֵיכוֹן וּבְחַיֵּי דְכָל בֵּית יִשְׂרָאֵל
בַּעֲגָלָא וּבִזְמַן קָרִיב, וְאִמְרוּ אָמֵן. (קהל: אָמֵן)

קהל ואבל: יְהֵא שְׁמֵהּ רַבָּא מְבָרַךְ לְעָלַם וּלְעָלְמֵי עָלְמַיָּא.

אבל: יִתְבָּרַךְ וְיִשְׁתַּבַּח וְיִתְפָּאַר וְיִתְרוֹמַם וְיִתְנַשֵּׂא
וְיִתְהַדָּר וְיִתְעַלֶּה וְיִתְהַלָּל
שְׁמֵהּ דְּקֻדְשָׁא בְּרִיךְ הוּא (קהל: בְּרִיךְ הוּא)
לְעֵלָּא מִן כָּל בִּרְכָתָא
/בעשרת ימי תשובה: לְעֵלָּא לְעֵלָּא מִכָּל בִּרְכָתָא/
וְשִׁירָתָא, תֻּשְׁבְּחָתָא וְנֶחֱמָתָא
דַּאֲמִירָן בְּעָלְמָא, וְאִמְרוּ אָמֵן. (קהל: אָמֵן)

יְהֵא שְׁלָמָא רַבָּא מִן שְׁמַיָּא
וְחַיִּים, עָלֵינוּ וְעַל כָּל יִשְׂרָאֵל, וְאִמְרוּ אָמֵן. (קהל: אָמֵן)

Bow, take three steps back, as if taking leave of the Divine Presence, then bow, first left, then right, then center, while saying:

עֹשֶׂה שָׁלוֹם/בעשרת ימי תשובה: הַשָּׁלוֹם/ בִּמְרוֹמָיו
הוּא יַעֲשֶׂה שָׁלוֹם עָלֵינוּ וְעַל כָּל יִשְׂרָאֵל, וְאִמְרוּ אָמֵן. (קהל: אָמֵן)

EIRUV TEḤUMIN

On Shabbat and Yom Tov it is forbidden to walk more than 2000 cubits (about 3000 feet) beyond the boundary (teḥum) of the town where you live or are staying when the day begins. By placing food sufficient for two meals, before nightfall, at a point within 2000 cubits from the town limits, you confer on that place the status of a dwelling for the next day, and are then permitted to walk 2000 cubits from there.

בָּרוּךְ Blessed are You, LORD our God, King of the Universe,
who has made us holy through His commandments,
and has commanded us about the mitzva of Eiruv.

By this Eiruv may we be permitted to walk from this place, two thousand cubits in any direction.

EIRUV ḤATZEROT

On Shabbat it is forbidden to carry objects from one private domain to another, or from a private domain into space shared by others, such as a communal staircase, corridor or courtyard. An Eiruv Ḥatzerot is created when each of the Jewish households in a court or apartment block, before Shabbat, places a loaf of bread or matza in one of the homes. The entire court or block then becomes a single private domain within which it is permitted to carry.

בָּרוּךְ Blessed are You, LORD our God, King of the Universe,
who has made us holy through His commandments,
and has commanded us about the mitzva of Eiruv.

By this Eiruv may we be permitted to move, carry out and carry in from the houses to the courtyard, or from the courtyard to the houses, or from house to house, for all the houses within the courtyard.

---

binic prohibition against carrying in a courtyard. "Said R. Yehoshua ben Levi: On what account do they prepare an *eiruv* of courtyards? It is for the sake of peace. There was the case of a woman who was in conflict with her neighbor. She sent her contribution to the *eiruv* with her son. The neighbor took him and hugged and kissed him. He went and told his mother this. She said, 'Is this how she loved me, and I did not know about it!' They thus became friends once again." (*Eiruvin* 3:2, 20d) (YS)

עירוב תחומין

On שבת and יום טוב it is forbidden to walk more than 2000 cubits (about 3000 feet) beyond the boundary (תחום) of the town where you live or are staying when the day begins. By placing food sufficient for two meals, before nightfall, at a point within 2000 cubits from the town limits, you confer on that place the status of a dwelling for the next day, and are then permitted to walk 2000 cubits from there.

בָּרוּךְ אַתָּה יהוה אֱלֹהֵינוּ מֶלֶךְ הָעוֹלָם
אֲשֶׁר קִדְּשָׁנוּ בְּמִצְוֹתָיו וְצִוָּנוּ עַל מִצְוַת עֵרוּב.

בְּדֵין עֵרוּבָא יְהֵא שְׁרֵא לִי לְמֵיזַל מֵאַתְרָא הָדֵין תְּרֵין אַלְפִּין אַמִּין לְכָל רוּחָא.

עירוב חצרות

On שבת it is forbidden to carry objects from one private domain to another, or from a private domain into space shared by others, such as a communal staircase, corridor or courtyard. An עירוב חצרות is created when each of the Jewish households in a court or apartment block, before שבת, places a loaf of bread or matza in one of the homes. The entire court or block then becomes a single private domain within which it is permitted to carry.

בָּרוּךְ אַתָּה יהוה אֱלֹהֵינוּ מֶלֶךְ הָעוֹלָם
אֲשֶׁר קִדְּשָׁנוּ בְּמִצְוֹתָיו וְצִוָּנוּ עַל מִצְוַת עֵרוּב.

בְּדֵין עֵרוּבָא יְהֵא שְׁרֵא לָנָא לְטַלְטוֹלֵי וּלְאַפּוֹקֵי וּלְעַיּוֹלֵי מִן הַבָּתִּים לֶחָצֵר וּמִן הֶחָצֵר לַבָּתִּים וּמִבַּיִת לְבַיִת לְכָל הַבָּתִּים שֶׁבֶּחָצֵר.

In the Talmud, the word "Eiruv" refers to bread which is set aside by neighbors who share the same courtyard and wish to carry in it. Typically, transporting an item from a home to a courtyard or from a courtyard to a home would violate a Rabbinic prohibition against carrying. By contributing flour or money to baking a common bread, the neighbors "domesticate" the entire courtyard, rendering it one home. The Jerusalem Talmud wonders why the Rabbis instituted the *Eiruv* instead of simply limiting or disarming the Rab-

CANDLE LIGHTING

Cover the eyes with the hands after lighting the candles, and say:

בָּרוּךְ Blessed are You, LORD our God, King of the Universe,
who has made us holy through His commandments,
and has commanded us to light the Sabbath light.

Baruch ata Adonai Eloheinu melech ha'olam asher
ki'deshanu bemitzvotav, vetzivanu lehadlik ner shel shabat.

Some add:

יְהִי May it be Your will, LORD our God and God of our ancestors, that the Temple be speedily rebuilt in our days, and grant us our share in Your Torah. And may we serve You there in reverence, as in the days of old and as in former years.

Prayer after candlelighting (add the words in parentheses as appropriate):

יְהִי May it be Your will, LORD my God and God of my forebears, that You give me grace – me (and my husband/and my father/and my mother/and my sons and my daughters) and all those close to me, and give us and all Israel good and long lives. And remember us with a memory that brings goodness and blessing; come to us with compassion and bless us with great blessings. Build our homes until they are complete, and allow Your Presence to live among us. And may I merit to raise children and grandchildren, each one wise and understanding, loving the LORD and in awe of God, people of truth, holy children, who will cling on to the LORD and light up the world with Torah and with good actions, and with all the kinds of work that serve the Creator. Please, hear my pleading at this time, by the merit of Sarah and Rebecca, Rachel and Leah our mothers, and light our candle that it should never go out, and light up Your face, so that we shall be saved, Amen.

The ancient custom is for women to perform this commandment since they are the primary guardians of the home. Our custom is to light two candles, representing the two dimensions of Shabbat: *shamor,* "guarding," observing the prohibitions of Shabbat, and *zakhor,* "remembering," keeping its positive commandments.

Normally we make a blessing over a commandment *before* performing it. In the case of Shabbat lights, however, the blessing is made afterward, so that the lighting precedes mental acceptance of the day and its prohibitions. The blessing is made while covering one's eyes, so that the blessing follows the act but precedes its benefit.

הדלקת נרות

Cover the eyes with the hands after lighting the candles, and say:

בָּרוּךְ אַתָּה יהוה אֱלֹהֵינוּ מֶלֶךְ הָעוֹלָם
אֲשֶׁר קִדְּשָׁנוּ בְּמִצְוֹתָיו, וְצִוָּנוּ לְהַדְלִיק נֵר שֶׁל שַׁבָּת.

Some add:

יְהִי רָצוֹן מִלְּפָנֶיךָ יהוה אֱלֹהֵינוּ וֵאלֹהֵי אֲבוֹתֵינוּ, שֶׁיִּבָּנֶה בֵּית הַמִּקְדָּשׁ בִּמְהֵרָה בְיָמֵינוּ, וְתֵן חֶלְקֵנוּ בְּתוֹרָתֶךָ, וְשָׁם נַעֲבָדְךָ בְּיִרְאָה כִּימֵי עוֹלָם וּכְשָׁנִים קַדְמֹנִיּוֹת.
וְעָרְבָה לַיהוה מִנְחַת יְהוּדָה וִירוּשָׁלָםִ כִּימֵי עוֹלָם וּכְשָׁנִים קַדְמֹנִיּוֹת: מלאכי ג

Prayer after candlelighting (add the words in parentheses as appropriate):

יְהִי רָצוֹן מִלְּפָנֶיךָ יהוה אֱלֹהַי וֵאלֹהֵי אֲבוֹתַי, שֶׁתְּחוֹנֵן אוֹתִי (וְאֶת אִישִׁי/ וְאֶת אָבִי/ וְאֶת אִמִּי/ וְאֶת בָּנַי וְאֶת בְּנוֹתַי) וְאֶת כָּל קְרוֹבַי, וְתִתֶּן לָנוּ וּלְכָל יִשְׂרָאֵל חַיִּים טוֹבִים וַאֲרֻכִּים, וְתִזְכְּרֵנוּ בְּזִכְרוֹן טוֹבָה וּבְרָכָה, וְתִפְקְדֵנוּ בִּפְקֻדַּת יְשׁוּעָה וְרַחֲמִים, וּתְבָרְכֵנוּ בְּרָכוֹת גְּדוֹלוֹת, וְתַשְׁלִים בָּתֵּינוּ וְתַשְׁכֵּן שְׁכִינָתְךָ בֵּינֵינוּ. וְזַכֵּנִי לְגַדֵּל בָּנִים וּבְנֵי בָנִים חֲכָמִים וּנְבוֹנִים, אוֹהֲבֵי יהוה יִרְאֵי אֱלֹהִים, אַנְשֵׁי אֱמֶת זֶרַע קֹדֶשׁ, בַּיהוה דְּבֵקִים וּמְאִירִים אֶת הָעוֹלָם בַּתּוֹרָה וּבְמַעֲשִׂים טוֹבִים וּבְכָל מְלֶאכֶת עֲבוֹדַת הַבּוֹרֵא. אָנָּא שְׁמַע אֶת תְּחִנָּתִי בָּעֵת הַזֹּאת בִּזְכוּת שָׂרָה וְרִבְקָה וְרָחֵל וְלֵאָה אִמּוֹתֵינוּ, וְהָאֵר נֵרֵנוּ שֶׁלֹּא יִכְבֶּה לְעוֹלָם וָעֶד, וְהָאֵר פָּנֶיךָ וְנִוָּשֵׁעָה. אָמֵן.

CANDLE LIGHTING

Lighting candles is a positive rabbinic commandment, symbolizing *shalom bayit*, domestic peace. By creating peace in the home, we are helping to make peace in the world.

The Shabbat candles also symbolize the light of the Divine Presence, which illuminates relationships within the home. Rabbi Akiva noted that the Hebrew words for man (*ish*) and woman (*isha*) both contain the letters of *esh*, "fire." Each contains one extra letter – *yod* in the case of man, *heh* in the case of woman, and these two letters together spell one of the names of God. He concluded: "When husband and wife are worthy, the Divine Presence dwells between them" (*Sotah* 17a).

The service starts with Minḥa on page 2.
Most congregations sing "Beloved of the soul" before the Kabbalat Shabbat service.
On Yom Tov or Motza'ei Yom Tov falling on Shabbat, or on Shabbat Ḥol HaMo'ed, the service begins with Psalm 92 on page 65.

יְדִיד Beloved of the soul, Father of compassion,
draw Your servant close to Your will.
Like a deer will Your servant run
and fall prostrate before Your beauty.
To him Your love is sweeter
than honey from the comb, than any taste.

הָדוּר Glorious, beautiful, radiance of the world,
my soul is sick with love for You.
Please, God, heal her now
by showing her Your tender radiance.
Then she will recover her strength and be healed,
Be Your servant for eternity.

וָתִיק Ancient of Days, let Your mercy be aroused;
please have pity on Your beloved child.
How long have I yearned
to see the glory of Your strength.
Please, my God, my heart's desire –
hasten; do not hide Yourself.

הִגָּלֵה Reveal Yourself, beloved, and spread over me
the tabernacle of Your peace.
Let the earth shine with Your glory,
let us be overjoyed and rejoice in You.
Hurry, beloved, for the appointed time has come,
and be gracious to me as in the times of old.

The service starts with מנחה *on page 3.*
Most congregations sing יְדִיד נֶפֶשׁ *at this point before* קבלת שבת.
On יום טוב *or* מוצאי יום טוב *falling on* שבת, *or on* שבת חול המועד,
the service begins with מִזְמוֹר שִׁיר *on page 65.*

יְדִיד נֶפֶשׁ, אָב הָרַחֲמָן, מְשֹׁךְ עַבְדְּךָ אֶל רְצוֹנָךְ
יָרוּץ עַבְדְּךָ כְּמוֹ אַיָּל, יִשְׁתַּחֲוֶה מוּל הֲדָרָךְ
כִּי יֶעֱרַב לוֹ יְדִידוּתָךְ, מִנֹּפֶת צוּף וְכָל טָעַם.

הָדוּר, נָאֶה, זִיו הָעוֹלָם, נַפְשִׁי חוֹלַת אַהֲבָתָךְ
אָנָּא, אֵל נָא, רְפָא נָא לָהּ, בְּהַרְאוֹת לָהּ נֹעַם זִיוָךְ
אָז תִּתְחַזֵּק וְתִתְרַפֵּא, וְהָיְתָה לָךְ שִׁפְחַת עוֹלָם.

וָתִיק, יֶהֱמוּ רַחֲמֶיךָ, וְחוּס נָא עַל בֵּן אוֹהֲבָךְ
כִּי זֶה כַּמָּה נִכְסֹף נִכְסַף לִרְאוֹת בְּתִפְאֶרֶת עֻזָּךְ
אָנָּא, אֵלִי, מַחְמַד לִבִּי, חוּשָׁה נָּא, וְאַל תִּתְעַלָּם.

הִגָּלֶה נָא וּפְרֹשׂ, חָבִיב, עָלַי אֶת סֻכַּת שְׁלוֹמָךְ
תָּאִיר אֶרֶץ מִכְּבוֹדָךְ, נָגִילָה וְנִשְׂמְחָה בָךְ.
מַהֵר, אָהוּב, כִּי בָא מוֹעֵד, וְחָנֵּנִי כִּימֵי עוֹלָם.

יְדִיד נֶפֶשׁ *Beloved of the soul:* A song of passionate intensity, composed by the Safed kabbalist Rabbi Elazar Azikri (1533–1600). In language reminiscent of Song of Songs, it speaks of Israel's yearning for God: Azikri himself called it "a prayer for union and the desire of love." The text here, differing in a number of details from that found in some other siddurim, is based on the original manuscript in the author's own hand. The initial letters of the four verses spell God's holiest name. **וְאַל תִּתְעַלָּם** *Do not hide Yourself:* refers to Israel's exile. The poet calls for God to reveal Himself at *the appointed time* of redemption, **כִּי בָא מוֹעֵד**.

תהלים צג מִקּוֹלוֹת מַיִם רַבִּים
אַדִּירִים מִשְׁבְּרֵי־יָם
אַדִּיר בַּמָּרוֹם יהוה:

שַׁבָּת, שַׁבָּת
שַׁבָּת, שַׁבָּת
שַׁבָּת הַיּוֹם לַה׳, שַׁבָּת הַיּוֹם לַה׳

אִלּוּ הָיָה לִי כֹּחַ
הָיִיתִי יוֹצֵא לַשּׁוּק
הָיִיתִי מַכְרִיז
וְאוֹמֵר שַׁבָּת הַיּוֹם לַה׳

שַׁבָּת, שַׁבָּת
שַׁבָּת, שַׁבָּת
שַׁבָּת הַיּוֹם לַה׳, שַׁבָּת הַיּוֹם לַה׳

Mightier than the noise of many waters, Ps. 93
than the mighty waves of the sea is the Lord on high.

Shabbat, Shabbat / Shabbat, Shabbat,
Shabbat is the day of the Lord! Shabbat is the day of the Lord!

Had I but strength, I would go out to the market place;
I would cry out there, "Shabbat is the day of the Lord!"

Shabbat, Shabbat / Shabbat, Shabbat,
Shabbat is the day of the Lord! Shabbat is the day of the Lord!

Mikolot mayim rabim / adirim mishberei-yam, adir bamarom Adonai.

Shabat, Shabat / Shabat, Shabat,
Shabat ha'yom la'Hashem, Shabat ha'yom la'Hashem.

Ilu haya li ko'ach, hayiti yotzeh lashuk,
hayiti machriz ve'omer:
"Shabat ha'yom la'Hashem."

Shabat, Shabat / Shabat, Shabat,
Shabat ha'yom la'Hashem, Shabat ha'yom la'Hashem.

וועןאיך וואָלט געהאַט כּוח
וואָלט איך געלאָפֿן אין די גאַסן
און איך וואָלט געשריגן הויך
שבת, הליגע שבת!
שבת, שבת, הליגע שבת!
שבת, שבת, הליגע שבת!
שבת היום לה׳

Ven ikh volt gehat koyekh
Volt ikh gelofn in di gasn
un ikh volt geshrign hoykh
shabbos, heylige shabbos!
shabbos, shabbos, heylige shabbos!
shabbos, shabbos, heylige shabbos!
shabbos hayom lashem

The singing of *Mikolot Mayim Rabim* and *Ilu Haya Li Ko'aḥ* on Erev Shabbat begins with Rabbi Aharon HaGadol of Karlin, a student of the Maggid of Mezheritch. The original words presented above, were sung in Yiddish on Friday nights by his Ḥassidim. The Hebrew text was adapted by HaRav Yeshayahu Shapiro, also known as the Admor HeḤalutz. He was a leader of the Religious Zionist Labor Movement and one of the founders of the Hapoel Mizraḥi movement. He believed in a return to an agrarian, labor-minded Judaism and ultimately fulfilled his yearnings by becoming a farmer later in life. Singing *Mikolot*, he envisioned a farmer entering a synagogue on Friday night exhausted but satisfied, having labored the entire week, without an ounce of physical energy left. At that very moment he breaks into song emerging from the depths of an exhausted yearning: "If I only had strength, I would go out into the market place and proclaim, 'Shabbat is the day of the Lord!'" (YR)

קבלת שבת
KABBALAT SHABBAT

Already in Talmudic times Shabbat was seen as a bride, and the day itself as a wedding. "Rabbi Ḥanina robed himself and stood on the eve of Shabbat at sunset and said, 'Come, let us go and welcome Shabbat the queen.' Rabbi Yanai donned his robes and said, 'Come O bride, come O bride'" (*Shabbat* 119a).

In the late sixteenth century, this idea was developed with fresh intensity by a remarkable group of Jewish mystics in Safed. They included Rabbi Moses Cordovero who developed the custom of saying special psalms to greet the incoming Shabbat; his brother-in-law Rabbi Shlomo Alkabets, composer of the song *Lekha Dodi* ("Come, my Beloved"); Rabbi Elazar Azikri, author of *Yedid Nefesh* ("Beloved of the Soul"); and Rabbi Isaac Luria (known as the "Ari" or "Arizal"), greatest of the Safed mystics, whose thought brought new depth to our understanding of prayer and observance of Shabbat as acts that help heal the spiritual fractures of the world.

By the twelfth century, the custom existed to say Psalm 92 as a song of welcome to Shabbat. The Safed kabbalists did more. Dressed in white, they would go out into the fields as the sun set, singing psalms and songs to the Shabbat bride. That is the origin of the custom (first mentioned by Rabbi Moshe ben Yehuda Makhir, *Seder HaYom*) to recite the six extra psalms (95–99, 29) prior to *Lekha Dodi*. A further reminder of the original custom is our practice of turning round to face west at the last verse of the song, facing, as they did, the setting sun, to welcome the incoming bride. To emphasize the non-statutory character of Kabbalat Shabbat, the custom in some synagogues is for the Leader to recite it from the bima rather than the amud (lectern) at the front of the synagogue.

The six psalms said before *Lekha Dodi* represent the six days of the week. The first five appear sequentially in the book of Psalms (95–99). They speak of the song creation sings to its Creator. These are followed by Psalm 29, understood by some as a description of the Giving of the Torah at Mount Sinai. *Lekha Dodi* looks forward to future redemption, and Psalms 92 and 93 envision the end of days. Thus the entire sequence is structured around the movement from creation to revelation to redemption.

לְכוּ נְרַנְּנָה לַיהוה, נָרִיעָה לְצוּר יִשְׁעֵנוּ: נְקַדְּמָה פָנָיו בְּתוֹדָה, בִּזְמִרוֹת תהלים צה
נָרִיעַ לוֹ: כִּי אֵל גָּדוֹל יהוה, וּמֶלֶךְ גָּדוֹל עַל־כָּל־אֱלֹהִים: אֲשֶׁר בְּיָדוֹ
מֶחְקְרֵי־אָרֶץ, וְתוֹעֲפוֹת הָרִים לוֹ: אֲשֶׁר־לוֹ הַיָּם וְהוּא עָשָׂהוּ, וְיַבֶּשֶׁת יָדָיו
יָצָרוּ: בֹּאוּ נִשְׁתַּחֲוֶה וְנִכְרָעָה, נִבְרְכָה לִפְנֵי־יהוה עֹשֵׂנוּ: כִּי הוּא אֱלֹהֵינוּ,
וַאֲנַחְנוּ עַם מַרְעִיתוֹ וְצֹאן יָדוֹ, הַיּוֹם אִם־בְּקֹלוֹ תִשְׁמָעוּ: אַל־תַּקְשׁוּ לְבַבְכֶם
כִּמְרִיבָה, כְּיוֹם מַסָּה בַּמִּדְבָּר: אֲשֶׁר נִסּוּנִי אֲבוֹתֵיכֶם, בְּחָנוּנִי גַּם רָאוּ פָעֳלִי:
‣ אַרְבָּעִים שָׁנָה אָקוּט בְּדוֹר, וָאֹמַר עַם תֹּעֵי לֵבָב הֵם, וְהֵם לֹא־יָדְעוּ
דְרָכָי: אֲשֶׁר־נִשְׁבַּעְתִּי בְאַפִּי, אִם־יְבֹאוּן אֶל מְנוּחָתִי:

Ps. 95 לְכוּ נְרַנְּנָה Come, let us sing for joy to the LORD, let us shout aloud to the Rock of our salvation. Let us greet Him with thanksgiving, shout aloud to Him with songs of praise. For the LORD is the great God, the King great above all powers. In His hand are the depths of the earth, and the mountain peaks are His. The sea is His, for He made it; the dry land too, for His hands formed it. Come, let us bow in worship and bend the knee before the LORD our Maker. For He is our God, and we are the people of His pasture, the flock He tends – today, if you would heed His voice. Do not harden your hearts as you did at Meribah, as you did that day at Massah in the desert, when your ancestors tested and tried Me though they had seen My deeds. ‣ For forty years I strove with that generation. I said, "They are a people whose hearts go astray, who have not understood My ways." So I swore in My anger, "They shall not enter My place of rest."

Lechu neranena l'Adonai, nariya letzur yish'enu. Nekadema fanav betoda, bizmirot nariya lo. Ki el gadol Adonai, umelech gadol al-kol-elohim. Asher beyado mechkerei-aretz, veto'afot harim lo. Asher-lo hayam vehu asahu, veyabeshet yadav yatzaru. Bo'u nishtachaveh venichra'a, nivrecha lifnei-Adonai osenu. Ki hu Eloheinu, va'anachnu am mari'to vetzon yado, hayom im bekolo tishma'u. Al-takshu levavchem kimriva, keyom masa bamidbar. Asher nisuni avoteichem, bechanuni gam ra'u po'oli. ‣ *Arba'im shana akut bedor, va'omar am to'ei levav hem, vehem lo-yade'u derachai. Asher-nishba'ti ve'api, im-yevo'un el menuchati.*

תהלים צו
שִׁירוּ לַיהוה שִׁיר חָדָשׁ, שִׁירוּ לַיהוה כׇּל־הָאָרֶץ: שִׁירוּ לַיהוה, בָּרְכוּ שְׁמוֹ, בַּשְּׂרוּ מִיּוֹם־לְיוֹם יְשׁוּעָתוֹ: סַפְּרוּ בַגּוֹיִם כְּבוֹדוֹ, בְּכׇל־הָעַמִּים נִפְלְאוֹתָיו: כִּי גָדוֹל יהוה וּמְהֻלָּל מְאֹד, נוֹרָא הוּא עַל־כׇּל־אֱלֹהִים: כִּי כׇּל־אֱלֹהֵי הָעַמִּים אֱלִילִים, וַיהוה שָׁמַיִם עָשָׂה: הוֹד־וְהָדָר לְפָנָיו, עֹז וְתִפְאֶרֶת בְּמִקְדָּשׁוֹ: הָבוּ לַיהוה מִשְׁפְּחוֹת עַמִּים, הָבוּ לַיהוה כָּבוֹד וָעֹז: הָבוּ לַיהוה כְּבוֹד שְׁמוֹ, שְׂאוּ־מִנְחָה וּבֹאוּ לְחַצְרוֹתָיו: הִשְׁתַּחֲווּ לַיהוה בְּהַדְרַת־קֹדֶשׁ, חִילוּ מִפָּנָיו כׇּל־הָאָרֶץ: אִמְרוּ בַגּוֹיִם יהוה מָלָךְ, אַף־תִּכּוֹן תֵּבֵל בַּל־תִּמּוֹט, יָדִין עַמִּים בְּמֵישָׁרִים: ◂ יִשְׂמְחוּ הַשָּׁמַיִם וְתָגֵל הָאָרֶץ, יִרְעַם הַיָּם וּמְלֹאוֹ: יַעֲלֹז שָׂדַי וְכׇל־אֲשֶׁר־בּוֹ, אָז יְרַנְּנוּ כׇּל־עֲצֵי־יָעַר: לִפְנֵי יהוה כִּי בָא, כִּי בָא לִשְׁפֹּט הָאָרֶץ, יִשְׁפֹּט־תֵּבֵל בְּצֶדֶק, וְעַמִּים בֶּאֱמוּנָתוֹ:

Ps. 96 שִׁירוּ Sing to the LORD a new song; sing to the LORD all the earth. Sing to the LORD, bless His name; proclaim his deliverance day after day. Declare His glory among the nations, His marvels among all peoples. For great is the LORD and greatly to be praised; He is awesome beyond all heavenly powers. For all the gods of the peoples are mere idols: it was the LORD who made the heavens. Before Him are majesty and splendor; there are strength and beauty in His holy place. Render to the LORD, O families of the peoples; render to the LORD glory and might. Render to the LORD the glory due to His name; bring an offering and come into His courts. Bow down to the LORD in the splendor of holiness. Tremble before Him, all the earth. Say among the nations, "The LORD is King." The world stands firm, it will not be shaken. He will judge the peoples with equity. ▸ Let the heavens rejoice and the earth be glad. Let the sea roar, and all that is in it; let the fields be jubilant, and all they contain. Then the trees of the forest will sing for joy before the LORD, for He is coming to judge the earth. He will judge the world with justice, and the peoples with His faithfulness.

Shiru l'Adonai shir chadash, shiru l'Adonai kol-ha'aretz. Shiru l'Adonai, barechu shemo, baseru mi'yom-le'yom yeshu'ato. Saperu vagoyim kevodo, bechol-ha'amim nifle'otav. Ki gadol Adonai umhulal me'od, nora hu al-kol-elohim. Ki kol-elohei ha'amim elilim, v'Adonai shamayim asa. Hod-ve'hadar lefanav, oz vetiferet bemikdasho. Havu l'Adonai mishpechot amim, havu l'Adonai kavod va'oz. Havu l'Adonai kevod shemo, se'u-mincha u'vo'u lechatzrotav. Hishtachavu l'Adonai behadrat-kodesh, chilu mipanav kol-ha'aretz. Imru vagoyim Adonai malach, af-tikon tevel bal-timot, yadin amim bemeisharim. ▸ Yismechu hashamayim vetagel ha'aretz, yir'am hayam um'lo'o. Ya'aloz sadai vechol-asher-bo, az yeranenu kol-atzei-ya'ar. Lifnei Adonai ki va, ki va lishpot ha'aretz, yishpot-tevel betzedek, ve'amim be'emunato.

יהוה מָלָךְ תָּגֵל הָאָרֶץ, יִשְׂמְחוּ אִיִּים רַבִּים: עָנָן וַעֲרָפֶל סְבִיבָיו, צֶדֶק תהלים צז
וּמִשְׁפָּט מְכוֹן כִּסְאוֹ: אֵשׁ לְפָנָיו תֵּלֵךְ, וּתְלַהֵט סָבִיב צָרָיו: הֵאִירוּ בְרָקָיו
תֵּבֵל, רָאֲתָה וַתָּחֵל הָאָרֶץ: הָרִים כַּדּוֹנַג נָמַסּוּ מִלִּפְנֵי יהוה, מִלִּפְנֵי אֲדוֹן
כָּל־הָאָרֶץ: הִגִּידוּ הַשָּׁמַיִם צִדְקוֹ, וְרָאוּ כָל־הָעַמִּים כְּבוֹדוֹ: יֵבֹשׁוּ כָּל־עֹבְדֵי
פֶסֶל הַמִּתְהַלְלִים בָּאֱלִילִים, הִשְׁתַּחֲווּ־לוֹ כָּל־אֱלֹהִים: שָׁמְעָה וַתִּשְׂמַח
צִיּוֹן, וַתָּגֵלְנָה בְּנוֹת יְהוּדָה, לְמַעַן מִשְׁפָּטֶיךָ יהוה: כִּי־אַתָּה יהוה עֶלְיוֹן
עַל־כָּל־הָאָרֶץ, מְאֹד נַעֲלֵיתָ עַל־כָּל־אֱלֹהִים: ‣ אֹהֲבֵי יהוה שִׂנְאוּ רָע,
שֹׁמֵר נַפְשׁוֹת חֲסִידָיו, מִיַּד רְשָׁעִים יַצִּילֵם: אוֹר זָרֻעַ לַצַּדִּיק, וּלְיִשְׁרֵי־לֵב
שִׂמְחָה: שִׂמְחוּ צַדִּיקִים בַּיהוה, וְהוֹדוּ לְזֵכֶר קָדְשׁוֹ:

Ps. 97 יהוה מָלָךְ The Lord reigns, let the earth be glad. Let the many islands rejoice. Clouds and thick darkness surround Him; righteousness and justice are the foundation of His throne. Fire goes ahead of Him, consuming His enemies on every side. His lightning lights up the world; the earth sees and trembles. Mountains melt like wax before the Lord, before the Lord of all the earth. The heavens proclaim His righteousness, and all the peoples see His glory. All who worship images and boast in idols are put to shame. Bow down to Him, all you heavenly powers. Zion hears and rejoices, and the towns of Judah are glad because of Your judgments, Lord. For You, Lord, are supreme over all the earth; You are exalted far above all heavenly powers. ‣ Let those who love the Lord hate evil, for He protects the lives of his devoted ones, delivering them from the hand of the wicked. Light is sown for the righteous, and joy for the upright in heart. Rejoice in the Lord, you who are righteous, and give thanks to His holy name.

Adonai malach tagel ha'aretz, yismechu i'yim rabim. Anan va'arafel sevivav, tzedek umishpat mechon kiso. Esh lefanav telech, ut'lahet saviv tzarav. He'iru verakav tevel, ra'ata vatachel ha'aretz. Harim kadonag namasu milifnei Adonai, milifnei adon kol-ha'aretz. Higidu hashamayim tzidko, vera'u kol-ha'amim kevodo. Yevoshu kol-ovedei fesel hamit'halelim ba'elilim, hishtachavu-lo kol-elohim. Shame'a vatismach tziyon, vatagelna benot Yehuda, lema'an mishpatecha Adonai. Ki-ata Adonai elyon al-kol-ha'aretz, me'od na'aleita al-kol-elohim. ‣ Ohavei Adonai sinu ra, shomer nafshot chasidav, miyad resha'im yatzilem. Or zaru'a latzadik, ulyishrei-lev simcha. Simchu tzadikim b'Adonai, vehodu lezecher kodsho.

מִזְמוֹר, שִׁירוּ לַיהוה שִׁיר חָדָשׁ, כִּי־נִפְלָאוֹת עָשָׂה, הוֹשִׁיעָה־לּוֹ יְמִינוֹ תהלים צח
וּזְרוֹעַ קָדְשׁוֹ: הוֹדִיעַ יהוה יְשׁוּעָתוֹ, לְעֵינֵי הַגּוֹיִם גִּלָּה צִדְקָתוֹ: זָכַר
חַסְדּוֹ וֶאֱמוּנָתוֹ לְבֵית יִשְׂרָאֵל, רָאוּ כָל־אַפְסֵי־אָרֶץ אֵת יְשׁוּעַת אֱלֹהֵינוּ:
הָרִיעוּ לַיהוה כָּל־הָאָרֶץ, פִּצְחוּ וְרַנְּנוּ וְזַמֵּרוּ: זַמְּרוּ לַיהוה בְּכִנּוֹר, בְּכִנּוֹר
וְקוֹל זִמְרָה: בַּחֲצֹצְרוֹת וְקוֹל שׁוֹפָר, הָרִיעוּ לִפְנֵי הַמֶּלֶךְ יהוה: ◂ יִרְעַם
הַיָּם וּמְלֹאוֹ, תֵּבֵל וְיֹשְׁבֵי בָהּ: נְהָרוֹת יִמְחֲאוּ־כָף, יַחַד הָרִים יְרַנֵּנוּ:
לִפְנֵי יהוה כִּי בָא לִשְׁפֹּט הָאָרֶץ, יִשְׁפֹּט־תֵּבֵל בְּצֶדֶק, וְעַמִּים בְּמֵישָׁרִים:

Ps. 98 מִזְמוֹר A Psalm. Sing a new song to the LORD, for He has done wondrous things; He has saved by His right hand and His holy arm. The LORD has made His salvation known; He has displayed His righteousness in the sight of the nations. He remembered His loving-kindness and faithfulness to the house of Israel; all the ends of the earth have seen the victory of our LORD. Shout for joy to the LORD, all the earth; burst into song, sing with joy, play music. Play music to the LORD on the harp – on the harp with the sound of singing. With trumpets and the sound of the shofar, shout for joy before the LORD, the King. ▸ Let the sea and all that is in it thunder, the world and all who live in it. Let the rivers clap their hands, the mountains sing together for joy – before the LORD, for He is coming to judge the earth. He will judge the world with justice, and the peoples with equity.

Mizmor, shiru l'Adonai shir chadash, ki nifla'ot asu, hoshiya-lo yemino uzro'a kodsho. Hodiya Adonai yeshu'ato, le'einei hagoyim gila tzidkato. Zachar chasdo ve'emunato leveit Yisrael, ra'u kol-afesei-aretz et yeshu'at Eloheinu. Hariyu l'Adonai kol-ha'aretz, pitzechu veranenu vezameru. Zameru l'Adonai bechinor, bechinor vekol zimra. Bachatzotzerot vekol shofar, hariyu lifnei hamelech Adonai. ▸ *Yir'am hayam umlo'o, tevel veyoshevei va. Neharot yimcha'u-chaf, yachad harim yeranenu. Lifnei Adonai ki va lishpot ha'aretz, yishpot-tevel betzedek, ve'amim bemeisharim.*

תהלים צט
יהוה מָלָךְ יִרְגְּזוּ עַמִּים, יֹשֵׁב כְּרוּבִים תָּנוּט הָאָרֶץ: יהוה בְּצִיּוֹן גָּדוֹל, וְרָם הוּא עַל־כָּל־הָעַמִּים: יוֹדוּ שִׁמְךָ גָּדוֹל וְנוֹרָא קָדוֹשׁ הוּא: וְעֹז מֶלֶךְ מִשְׁפָּט אָהֵב, אַתָּה כּוֹנַנְתָּ מֵישָׁרִים, מִשְׁפָּט וּצְדָקָה בְּיַעֲקֹב אַתָּה עָשִׂיתָ: רוֹמְמוּ יהוה אֱלֹהֵינוּ, וְהִשְׁתַּחֲווּ לַהֲדֹם רַגְלָיו, קָדוֹשׁ הוּא: מֹשֶׁה וְאַהֲרֹן בְּכֹהֲנָיו, וּשְׁמוּאֵל בְּקֹרְאֵי שְׁמוֹ, קֹרְאִים אֶל־יהוה וְהוּא יַעֲנֵם: ◂ בְּעַמּוּד עָנָן יְדַבֵּר אֲלֵיהֶם, שָׁמְרוּ עֵדֹתָיו וְחֹק נָתַן־לָמוֹ: יהוה אֱלֹהֵינוּ אַתָּה עֲנִיתָם, אֵל נֹשֵׂא הָיִיתָ לָהֶם, וְנֹקֵם עַל־עֲלִילוֹתָם: רוֹמְמוּ יהוה אֱלֹהֵינוּ, וְהִשְׁתַּחֲווּ לְהַר קָדְשׁוֹ, כִּי־קָדוֹשׁ יהוה אֱלֹהֵינוּ:

Ps. 99 יהוה מָלָךְ The LORD reigns, let the peoples tremble. He sits enthroned on the Cherubim, let the earth quake. Great is the LORD in Zion, He is exalted over all the peoples. Let them praise Your name, O great and awesome One: He is holy! The King in His might loves justice. You have established equity. The justice and righteousness in Jacob is Your doing. Exalt the LORD our God, and bow at His footstool: He is holy! Moses and Aaron were among His priests; Samuel was among those who called on His name. They called on the LORD and He answered them. ▸ He spoke to them in a pillar of cloud; they observed His testimonies and the statute He gave them. LORD our God, You answered them. You were for them a forgiving God, though You punished their misdeeds. Exalt the LORD our God and bow at His holy mountain, for the LORD our God is holy.

Adonai malach yirgezu amim, yoshev keruvim tanut ha'aretz. Adonai betziyon gadol, veram hu al-kol-ha'amim. Yodu shimcha gadol venora kadosh hu. Veoz melech mishpat ahev, ata konanta meisharim, mishpat utzdaka be'ya'akov ata asita. Romemu Adonai Eloheinu, vehishtachavu lahadom raglav, kadosh hu. Moshe ve'aharon bechohanav, ushmu'el bekore'ei shemo, korim el-Adonai vehu ya'anem. ▸ Be'amud anan yedaber aleihem, shameru edotav vechok natan-lamo. Adonai Eloheinu ata anitam, el noseh hayita lahem, venokem al-alilotam. Romemu Adonai Eloheinu, vehishtachavu lehar kodsho, ki-kadosh Adonai Eloheinu.

The following psalm is said standing:

מִזְמוֹר לְדָוִד, הָבוּ לַיהוה בְּנֵי אֵלִים, הָבוּ לַיהוה כָּבוֹד וָעֹז: הָבוּ לַיהוה כְּבוֹד שְׁמוֹ, הִשְׁתַּחֲווּ לַיהוה בְּהַדְרַת־קֹדֶשׁ: קוֹל יהוה עַל הַמָּיִם, אֵל־הַכָּבוֹד הִרְעִים, יהוה עַל־מַיִם רַבִּים: קוֹל־יהוה בַּכֹּחַ, קוֹל יהוה בֶּהָדָר: קוֹל יהוה שֹׁבֵר אֲרָזִים, וַיְשַׁבֵּר יהוה אֶת־אַרְזֵי הַלְּבָנוֹן: וַיַּרְקִידֵם כְּמוֹ־עֵגֶל, לְבָנוֹן וְשִׂרְיוֹן כְּמוֹ בֶן־רְאֵמִים: קוֹל־יהוה חֹצֵב לַהֲבוֹת אֵשׁ: קוֹל יהוה יָחִיל מִדְבָּר, יָחִיל יהוה מִדְבַּר קָדֵשׁ: ‣ קוֹל יהוה יְחוֹלֵל אַיָּלוֹת וַיֶּחֱשֹׂף יְעָרוֹת, וּבְהֵיכָלוֹ, כֻּלּוֹ אֹמֵר כָּבוֹד: יהוה לַמַּבּוּל יָשָׁב, וַיֵּשֶׁב יהוה מֶלֶךְ לְעוֹלָם: יהוה עֹז לְעַמּוֹ יִתֵּן, יהוה יְבָרֵךְ אֶת־עַמּוֹ בַשָּׁלוֹם: תהלים כט

The following psalm is said standing:

Ps. 29 מִזְמוֹר לְדָוִד A psalm of David. Render to the Lord, you angelic powers, render to the Lord glory and might. Render to the Lord the glory due to His name. Bow to the Lord in the beauty of holiness. The Lord's voice echoes over the waters; the God of glory thunders; the Lord is over the mighty waters. The Lord's voice in power, the Lord's voice in beauty, the Lord's voice breaks cedars, the Lord shatters the cedars of Lebanon. He makes Lebanon skip like a calf, Sirion like a young wild ox. The Lord's voice cleaves flames of fire. The Lord's voice makes the desert quake, the Lord shakes the desert of Kadesh. ‣ The Lord's voice makes hinds calve and strips the forests bare, and in His temple all say: "Glory!" The Lord sat enthroned at the Flood, the Lord sits enthroned as King for ever. The Lord will give strength to His people; the Lord will bless His people with peace.

Mizmor ledavid, havu l'Adonai benei elim, havu l'Adonai kavod va'oz. Havu l'Adonai kevod shemo, hishtachavu l'Adonai behadrat-kodesh. Kol Adonai al hamayim, el-hakavod hir'im, Adonai al-mayim rabim. Kol-Adonai bako'ach, kol-Adonai behadar. Kol Adonai shover arazim, vay'shaber Adonai et-arzei halevanon. Vayarkidem kemo-egel, levanon vesiryon kemo ven-re'emim. Kol-Adonai chotzev lahavot esh. Kol Adonai yachil midbar, yachil Adonai midbar kadesh. ‣ Kol Adonai yecholel ayalot vayechesof ye'arot, uv'heichalo, kulo omer kavod. Adonai lamabul yashav, va'yeshev Adonai melech le'olam. Adonai oz le'amo yiten, Adonai yevarech et-amo vashalom.

The following is said in some congregations:

Please, by the power of Your great right hand,
set the captive nation free.
Accept Your people's prayer. Strengthen us, purify us,
You who are revered.
Please, mighty One, guard like the pupil of the eye
those who seek Your unity.
Bless them, cleanse them, have compassion on them,
grant them your righteousness always.
Mighty One, holy One, in Your great goodness
guide Your congregation.
Only One, exalted One, turn to Your people,
who proclaim Your holiness.
Accept our plea and heed our cry,
You who know all secret thoughts.

Blessed be the name of His glorious kingdom for
ever and all time.

Ana, becho'ach gedulat yeminecha, tatir tzerura.
Kabel rinat amecha, sagevenu, taharenu, nora.
Na gibor, doreshei yichudecha kevavat shomrem.
Barechem, taharem, rachamem, tzidkatecha tamid gomlem.
Chasin kadosh, berov tuvecha nahel adatecha.
Yachid ge'eh, le'amecha feneh, zocherei kedushatecha.
Shav'atenu kabel ushma tza'akatenu yode'a ta'alumot.
Baruch shem kevod malchuto le'olam va'ed.

The following is said in some congregations:

אָנָּא, בְּכֹחַ גְּדֻלַּת יְמִינְךָ, תַּתִּיר צְרוּרָה.
קַבֵּל רִנַּת עַמְּךָ, שַׂגְּבֵנוּ, טַהֲרֵנוּ, נוֹרָא.
נָא גִבּוֹר, דּוֹרְשֵׁי יִחוּדְךָ כְּבָבַת שָׁמְרֵם.
בָּרְכֵם, טַהֲרֵם, רַחֲמֵם, צִדְקָתְךָ תָּמִיד גָּמְלֵם.
חֲסִין קָדוֹשׁ, בְּרֹב טוּבְךָ נַהֵל עֲדָתֶךָ.
יָחִיד גֵּאֶה, לְעַמְּךָ פְּנֵה, זוֹכְרֵי קְדֻשָּׁתֶךָ.
שַׁוְעָתֵנוּ קַבֵּל וּשְׁמַע צַעֲקָתֵנוּ, יוֹדֵעַ תַּעֲלוּמוֹת.
בָּרוּךְ שֵׁם כְּבוֹד מַלְכוּתוֹ לְעוֹלָם וָעֶד.

לְכָה דוֹדִי לִקְרַאת כַּלָּה, פְּנֵי שַׁבָּת נְקַבְּלָה.

לְכָה דוֹדִי לִקְרַאת כַּלָּה, פְּנֵי שַׁבָּת נְקַבְּלָה.

שָׁמוֹר וְזָכוֹר בְּדִבּוּר אֶחָד, הִשְׁמִיעָנוּ אֵל הַמְיֻחָד
יהוה אֶחָד וּשְׁמוֹ אֶחָד, לְשֵׁם וּלְתִפְאֶרֶת וְלִתְהִלָּה.

לְכָה דוֹדִי לִקְרַאת כַּלָּה, פְּנֵי שַׁבָּת נְקַבְּלָה.

לִקְרַאת שַׁבָּת לְכוּ וְנֵלְכָה, כִּי הִיא מְקוֹר הַבְּרָכָה
מֵרֹאשׁ מִקֶּדֶם נְסוּכָה, סוֹף מַעֲשֶׂה בְּמַחֲשָׁבָה תְּחִלָּה.

לְכָה דוֹדִי לִקְרַאת כַּלָּה, פְּנֵי שַׁבָּת נְקַבְּלָה.

לְכָה דוֹדִי Come, my Beloved, to greet the bride;
let us welcome the Sabbath.
Come, my Beloved, to greet the bride;
let us welcome the Sabbath.

שָׁמוֹר "Observe" and "Remember" in one act of speech,
the One and Only God made us hear.
The LORD is One and His name is One,
for renown, for splendor, and for praise.
Come, my Beloved…

לִקְרַאת To greet the Sabbath, come let us go,
for of blessing, she is the source.
From the outset, as of old, ordained:
last in deed, first in thought.
Come, my Beloved…

Lecha dodi likrat kala, penei shabat nekabela.
Lecha dodi likrat kala, penei shabat nekabela.

Shamor vezachor bedibur echad, Hishmiyanu El hameyuchad
Adonai echad ushmo echad, Leshem ultiferet velit'hila.
Lecha dodi likrat kala, penei shabat nekabela.

Likrat shabat lechu venelecha, Ki hi mekor haberacha
Merosh mikedem nesucha, Sof ma'aseh bemachashava techila.
Lecha dodi likrat kala, penei shabat nekabela.

מִקְדַּשׁ מֶלֶךְ עִיר מְלוּכָה, קוּמִי צְאִי מִתּוֹךְ הַהֲפֵכָה
רַב לָךְ שֶׁבֶת בְּעֵמֶק הַבָּכָא, וְהוּא יַחֲמֹל עָלַיִךְ חֶמְלָה.
לְכָה דוֹדִי לִקְרַאת כַּלָּה, פְּנֵי שַׁבָּת נְקַבְּלָה.

הִתְנַעֲרִי, מֵעָפָר קוּמִי, לִבְשִׁי בִּגְדֵי תִפְאַרְתֵּךְ עַמִּי
עַל יַד בֶּן יִשַׁי בֵּית הַלַּחְמִי, קָרְבָה אֶל נַפְשִׁי, גְּאָלָהּ.
לְכָה דוֹדִי לִקְרַאת כַּלָּה, פְּנֵי שַׁבָּת נְקַבְּלָה.

הִתְעוֹרְרִי הִתְעוֹרְרִי, כִּי בָא אוֹרֵךְ קוּמִי אוֹרִי
עוּרִי עוּרִי, שִׁיר דַּבֵּרִי, כְּבוֹד יהוה עָלַיִךְ נִגְלָה.
לְכָה דוֹדִי לִקְרַאת כַּלָּה, פְּנֵי שַׁבָּת נְקַבְּלָה.

מִקְדַּשׁ Sanctuary of the King, royal city,
arise, go forth from your ruined state.
Too long have you dwelt in the valley of tears.
He will shower compassion on you.
Come, my Beloved…

הִתְנַעֲרִי Shake yourself off, arise from the dust!
Put on your clothes of glory, My people.
Through the son of Jesse the Bethlehemite,
draw near to my soul and redeem it.
Come, my Beloved…

הִתְעוֹרְרִי Wake up, wake up,
for your light has come: rise, shine!
Awake, awake, break out in song,
for the Lord's glory is revealed on you.
Come, my Beloved…

Mikdash melech ir melucha, Kumi tze'i mitoch hahafecha
Rav lach shevet be'emek habacha, Vehu yachamol alayich chemla.
Lecha dodi likrat kala, penei shabat nekabela.

Hitna'ari, me'afar kumi, Livshi bigdei tifartech ami
Al yad ben yishai beit halachmi, Korva el nafshi, ge'ala.
Lecha dodi likrat kala, penei shabat nekabela.

Hitoreri hitoreri, Ki va orech kumi ori
Uri uri, shir daberi, Kevod Adonai alayich nigla.
Lecha dodi likrat kala, penei shabat nekabela.

לֹא תֵבֹשִׁי וְלֹא תִכָּלְמִי, מַה תִּשְׁתּוֹחֲחִי וּמַה תֶּהֱמִי
בָּךְ יֶחֱסוּ עֲנִיֵּי עַמִּי, וְנִבְנְתָה עִיר עַל תִּלָּהּ.
לְכָה דוֹדִי לִקְרַאת כַּלָּה, פְּנֵי שַׁבָּת נְקַבְּלָה.

וְהָיוּ לִמְשִׁסָּה שֹׁאסָיִךְ, וְרָחֲקוּ כָּל מְבַלְּעָיִךְ
יָשִׂישׂ עָלַיִךְ אֱלֹהָיִךְ, כִּמְשׂוֹשׂ חָתָן עַל כַּלָּה.
לְכָה דוֹדִי לִקְרַאת כַּלָּה, פְּנֵי שַׁבָּת נְקַבְּלָה.

יָמִין וּשְׂמֹאל תִּפְרֹצִי, וְאֶת יהוה תַּעֲרִיצִי
עַל יַד אִישׁ בֶּן פַּרְצִי, וְנִשְׂמְחָה וְנָגִילָה.
לְכָה דוֹדִי לִקְרַאת כַּלָּה, פְּנֵי שַׁבָּת נְקַבְּלָה.

לֹא תֵבֹשִׁי Do not be ashamed, do not be confounded.
Why be downcast? Why do you mourn?
In you the needy of My people find shelter,
and the city shall be rebuilt on its hill.
Come, my Beloved…

וְהָיוּ Those who despoiled you shall be despoiled,
and all who devoured you shall be far away.
Your God will rejoice over you
as a bridegroom rejoices over his bride.
Come, my Beloved…

יָמִין Right and left you shall spread out,
and God you will revere.
Through the descendant of Peretz,
we shall rejoice and we shall be glad.
Come, my Beloved…

Lo tevoshi velo tikalemi, Ma tishtochachi uma tehemi
Bach yechesu aniyei ami, Venivneta ir al tila.
Lecha dodi likrat kala, penei shabat nekabela.

Vehayu limshisa shosayich, Verachaku kol mevale'ayich
Yasis alayich Elohayich, Kimsos chatan al kala.
Lecha dodi likrat kala, penei shabat nekabela.

Yamin usmol tifrotzi, Ve'et Adonai ta'aritzi
Al yad ish ben partzi, Venismecha venagila.
Lecha dodi likrat kala, penei shabat nekabela.

Stand and turn to face the rear (usually western side) of the בית כנסת*,*
as if to greet the incoming bride, bowing at the words בּוֹאִי כַלָּה*, then turn forward.*

בּוֹאִי בְשָׁלוֹם עֲטֶרֶת בַּעְלָהּ, גַּם בְּשִׂמְחָה וּבְצָהֳלָה
תּוֹךְ אֱמוּנֵי עַם סְגֻלָּה, בּוֹאִי כַלָּה, בּוֹאִי כַלָּה.
לְכָה דוֹדִי לִקְרַאת כַּלָּה, פְּנֵי שַׁבָּת נְקַבְּלָה.

Stand and turn to face the rear (usually western side) of the synagogue,
as if to greet the incoming bride, bowing at the words "Enter, O bride!," then turn forward.

בּוֹאִי Come in peace, O crown of her husband;
come with joy and jubilation,
among the faithful of the treasured people.
Enter, O bride! Enter, O bride!
Come, my Beloved…

Bo'i veshalom ateret ba'la, Gam besmicha uv'tzohola
Toch emunei am segula, Bo'i chala, bo'i chala.
Lecha dodi likrat kala, penei shabat nekabela.

Mourners during the week of שבעה *return to the* בית כנסת *at this point.*
They are greeted with the following words of consolation:

הַמָּקוֹם יְנַחֵם אֶתְכֶם בְּתוֹךְ שְׁאָר אֲבֵלֵי צִיּוֹן וִירוּשָׁלָיִם.

Mourners during the week of Shiva return to the synagogue at this point.
They are greeted with the following words of consolation:

הַמָּקוֹם May the Almighty comfort you
among the other mourners of Zion and Jerusalem.

Hamakom yenachem etchem betoch she'ar avelei tziyon virushalayim.

On Yom Tov, Motza'ei Yom Tov or Shabbat Ḥol HaMo'ed, Kabbalat Shabbat begins here.

מִזְמוֹר שִׁיר לְיוֹם הַשַּׁבָּת: טוֹב לְהֹדוֹת לַיהוה, וּלְזַמֵּר לְשִׁמְךָ עֶלְיוֹן: לְהַגִּיד תהלים צב
בַּבֹּקֶר חַסְדֶּךָ, וֶאֱמוּנָתְךָ בַּלֵּילוֹת: עֲלֵי־עָשׂוֹר וַעֲלֵי־נָבֶל, עֲלֵי הִגָּיוֹן בְּכִנּוֹר:
כִּי שִׂמַּחְתַּנִי יהוה בְּפָעֳלֶךָ, בְּמַעֲשֵׂי יָדֶיךָ אֲרַנֵּן: מַה־גָּדְלוּ מַעֲשֶׂיךָ יהוה, מְאֹד
עָמְקוּ מַחְשְׁבֹתֶיךָ: אִישׁ־בַּעַר לֹא יֵדָע, וּכְסִיל לֹא־יָבִין אֶת־זֹאת: בִּפְרֹחַ
רְשָׁעִים כְּמוֹ עֵשֶׂב, וַיָּצִיצוּ כָּל־פֹּעֲלֵי אָוֶן, לְהִשָּׁמְדָם עֲדֵי־עַד: וְאַתָּה מָרוֹם
לְעֹלָם יהוה: כִּי הִנֵּה אֹיְבֶיךָ יהוה, כִּי־הִנֵּה אֹיְבֶיךָ יֹאבֵדוּ, יִתְפָּרְדוּ כָּל־פֹּעֲלֵי
אָוֶן: וַתָּרֶם כִּרְאֵים קַרְנִי, בַּלֹּתִי בְּשֶׁמֶן רַעֲנָן: וַתַּבֵּט עֵינִי בְּשׁוּרָי, בַּקָּמִים עָלַי
מְרֵעִים תִּשְׁמַעְנָה אָזְנָי: ◂ צַדִּיק כַּתָּמָר יִפְרָח, כְּאֶרֶז בַּלְּבָנוֹן יִשְׂגֶּה: שְׁתוּלִים
בְּבֵית יהוה, בְּחַצְרוֹת אֱלֹהֵינוּ יַפְרִיחוּ: עוֹד יְנוּבוּן בְּשֵׂיבָה, דְּשֵׁנִים וְרַעֲנַנִּים
יִהְיוּ: לְהַגִּיד כִּי־יָשָׁר יהוה, צוּרִי, וְלֹא־עַוְלָתָה בּוֹ:

Ps. 92 מִזְמוֹר A psalm. A song for the Sabbath day. It is good to thank the LORD and sing psalms to Your name, Most High – to tell of Your loving-kindness in the morning and Your faithfulness at night, to the music of the ten-stringed lyre and the melody of the harp. For You have made me rejoice by Your work, O LORD; I sing for joy at the deeds of Your hands. How great are Your deeds, LORD, and how very deep Your thoughts. A boor cannot know, nor can a fool understand, that though the wicked spring up like grass and all evildoers flourish, it is only that they may be destroyed for ever. But You, LORD, are eternally exalted. For behold Your enemies, LORD, behold Your enemies will perish; all evildoers will be scattered. You have raised my pride like that of a wild ox; I am anointed with fresh oil. My eyes shall look in triumph on my adversaries, my ears shall hear the downfall of the wicked who rise against me. ▸ The righteous will flourish like a palm tree and grow tall like a cedar in Lebanon. Planted in the LORD's House, blossoming in our God's courtyards, they will still bear fruit in old age, and stay vigorous and fresh, proclaiming that the LORD is upright: He is my Rock, in whom there is no wrong.

Mizmor shir leyom hashabat. Tov lehodot l'Adonai, ul'zamer leshimcha elyon. Le'hagid baboker chasdecha, ve'emunatecha baleilot. Alei-asor va'alei-na'vel, alei higayon bechinor. Ki simachtani Adonai befo'olecha, bema'asei yadecha aranen. Ma gadelu ma'asecha Adonai, me'od ameku machshevotecha. Ish ba'ar lo yeda, uch'sil lo-yavin et-zot. Bifroach resha'im kemo esev, vayatzitzu kol po'alei a'ven, lehishmedam adei-ad. Ve'ata marom le'olam Adonai. Ki hi'ne oyevecha Adonai, ki-hi'ne oyevecha yovedu, yitparedu kol-po'alei a'ven. Vatarem kireim karni, baloti beshemen ra'anan. Vatabet eini beshurai, bakamim alai mere'im tishma'na oznai. ▸ Tzadik katamar yifrach, ke'erez balevanon yisge. Shetulim beveit Adonai, bechatzrot Eloheinu yafrichu. Od yenuvun beseiva, deshenim vera'ananim yiyu. Lehagid ki-yashar Adonai, tzuri, velo-avlata bo.

תהלים צג יהוה מָלָךְ, גֵּאוּת לָבֵשׁ, לָבֵשׁ יהוה עֹז הִתְאַזָּר, אַף־תִּכּוֹן תֵּבֵל בַּל־תִּמּוֹט: נָכוֹן כִּסְאֲךָ מֵאָז, מֵעוֹלָם אָתָּה: נָשְׂאוּ נְהָרוֹת יהוה, נָשְׂאוּ נְהָרוֹת קוֹלָם, יִשְׂאוּ נְהָרוֹת דָּכְיָם: ◂ מִקֹּלוֹת מַיִם רַבִּים, אַדִּירִים מִשְׁבְּרֵי־יָם, אַדִּיר בַּמָּרוֹם יהוה: עֵדֹתֶיךָ נֶאֶמְנוּ מְאֹד, לְבֵיתְךָ נַאֲוָה־קֹדֶשׁ, יהוה לְאֹרֶךְ יָמִים:

Continue with Mourner's Kaddish (page 29).

Ps. 93 יהוה מָלָךְ The LORD reigns. He is robed in majesty. The LORD is robed, girded with strength. The world is firmly established; it cannot be moved. Your throne stands firm as of old; You are eternal. Rivers lift up, LORD, rivers lift up their voice, rivers lift up their crashing waves. ▸ Mightier than the noise of many waters, than the mighty waves of the sea is the LORD on high. Your testimonies are very sure; holiness adorns Your House, LORD, for evermore.

Adonai malach, ge'ut lavesh, lavesh Adonai oz hitazar, af-tikon tevel bal-timot. Nachon kisacha me'az, me'olam ata. Nase'u neharot Adonai, nase'u neharot kolam, yisu neharot doch'yam. ▸ Mikolot mayim rabim, adirim mishberei-yam, adir bamarom Adonai. Edotecha ne'emnu me'od, leveitecha na'ava-kodesh, Adonai le'orech yamim.

לימוד שבת

LIMMUD SHABBAT

For generations Torah study has been a part of the Friday evening service. One widespread custom is to study the second chapter of the Mishna tractate *Shabbat, Bameh Madlikin,* with the conclusion of Kabbalat Shabbat, though local customs differ on the order. In the German *Nusaḥ Ashkenaz, Bameh Madlikin* is recited at the conclusion of the evening services following *Magen Avot*. In *Nusaḥ Yehudi* of Morrocco, the custom is to recite *Bameh Madlikin* immediately before reciting *Lekha Dodi*. In American *Nusaḥ Ashkenaz,* the custom we have followed here, *Bameh Madlikin* comes between Kabbalat Shabbat and the evening service.

A second practice, reflected in *Nusaḥ Sepharad,* is to recite *KeGavna,* a section from the *Zohar* that describes the intensification of holiness that takes place with the approach of Shabbat.

A third tradition, following the Ari *z"l* (Rabbi Yitzḥak Luria), is to recite *Shir HaShirim*, Song of Songs, either before Kabbalat Shabbat or before the evening service.

Expanding upon this general custom of studying texts, we have included both versions of the Ten Commandments, which provide both the source as well as the rationale for the observance of the Shabbat. In addition, passages from the Talmud are included to provide the literary context ritual source of Kabbalat Shabbat.

Torah study and pursuit of knowledge is a central motif of Jewish practice and religion. Whether one adopts the custom to study texts from the Written Law (*Shir HaShirim*), the Oral Law (*Bameh Madlikin*), or Kabbala (*KeGavna*), the study of texts enlightens and enriches our Shabbat experience.

BL

THE TEN COMMANDMENTS, PARASHAT YITRO

I am the Lord your God, who has brought you out of the land of Egypt, out of the house of bondage. You shall have no other gods besides Me. You shall not make for yourself any carved idol, or any likeness of anything that is in heaven above, or that is in the earth beneath, or that is in the water under the earth: you shall not bow down to them, nor serve them: for I the Lord your God am a jealous God, punishing the iniquity of the fathers upon the children to the third and fourth generation of those that hate Me; but showing mercy to thousands of generations of those that love Me, and keep My commandments. You shall not take the name of the Lord your God in vain; for the Lord will not hold him guiltless that takes His name in vain. **Remember the Sabbath day, to keep it holy. Six days shall you labor, and do all your work: but the seventh day is a Sabbath to the Lord your God: in it you shall not do any work, you, nor your son, nor your daughter, your manservant, nor your maidservant, nor your cattle, nor your stranger that is within your gates: for in six days the Lord made heaven and earth, the sea, and all that is in them, and rested on the seventh day: therefore the Lord blessed the Sabbath day, and hallowed it.** Honor your father and your mother: that your days may be long in the land which the Lord your God gives you. You shall not murder. You shall not commit adultery. You shall not steal. You shall not bear false witness against your neighbor. You shall not covet your neighbor's house, You shall not covet your neighbor's wife, nor his manservant, nor his maidservant, nor his ox, nor his ass, nor anything that is your neighbor's.

The Torah records two versions of the Ten Commandments. In the first, Israel is commanded to "remember" (Ex. 20:8) the Sabbath; in the second, to "observe" (Deut. 5:12) it. According to the Sages, both were uttered at the same time. "Observe" refers to the negative commandment of Shabbat,

עשרת הדברות שבפרשת יתרו

בטעם העליון

אָנֹכִי֮ יְהוָ֣ה אֱלֹהֶ֒יךָ֒ אֲשֶׁ֧ר הוֹצֵאתִ֛יךָ
מֵאֶ֥רֶץ מִצְרַ֖יִם מִבֵּ֣ית עֲבָדִ֑ים לֹֽא־יִהְיֶ֥ה לְךָ֛ אֱלֹהִ֥ים אֲחֵרִ֖ים
עַל־פָּנַ֗י לֹ֣א תַעֲשֶׂ֨ה־לְךָ֥ פֶ֣סֶל ׀ וְכׇל־תְּמוּנָ֡ה אֲשֶׁ֣ר בַּשָּׁמַ֣יִם ׀ מִמַּ֡עַל
וַאֲשֶׁ֣ר בָּאָ֣רֶץ מִתַּ֔חַת וַאֲשֶׁ֥ר בַּמַּ֖יִם ׀ מִתַּ֣חַת לָאָ֑רֶץ לֹֽא־
תִשְׁתַּחֲוֶ֥ה לָהֶ֛ם וְלֹ֥א תָעׇבְדֵ֖ם כִּ֣י אָנֹכִ֞י יְהוָ֤ה אֱלֹהֶ֙יךָ֙ אֵ֣ל קַנָּ֔א
פֹּ֠קֵד עֲוֺ֨ן אָבֹ֧ת עַל־בָּנִ֛ים עַל־שִׁלֵּשִׁ֥ים וְעַל־רִבֵּעִ֖ים לְשֹׂנְאָ֑י
וְעֹ֥שֶׂה חֶ֙סֶד֙ לַאֲלָפִ֔ים לְאֹהֲבַ֖י וּלְשֹׁמְרֵ֥י מִצְוֺתָֽי׃ לֹ֥א
תִשָּׂ֛א אֶת־שֵֽׁם־יְהוָ֥ה אֱלֹהֶ֖יךָ לַשָּׁ֑וְא כִּ֣י לֹ֤א יְנַקֶּה֙ יְהוָ֔ה אֵ֛ת
אֲשֶׁר־יִשָּׂ֥א אֶת־שְׁמ֖וֹ לַשָּֽׁוְא׃
זָכ֛וֹר אֶת־י֥וֹם הַשַּׁבָּ֖ת לְקַדְּשׁ֑וֹ שֵׁ֤שֶׁת יָמִים֙ תַּעֲבֹ֔ד וְעָשִׂ֖יתָ כׇּל־
מְלַאכְתֶּֽךָ וְי֙וֹם֙ הַשְּׁבִיעִ֔י שַׁבָּ֖ת ׀ לַיהוָ֣ה אֱלֹהֶ֑יךָ לֹ֥א תַעֲשֶׂ֨ה כׇל־
מְלָאכָ֜ה אַתָּ֣ה ׀ וּבִנְךָ֣ וּבִתֶּ֗ךָ עַבְדְּךָ֤ וַאֲמָֽתְךָ֙ וּבְהֶמְתֶּ֔ךָ וְגֵרְךָ֖ אֲשֶׁ֥ר
בִּשְׁעָרֶֽיךָ כִּ֣י שֵֽׁשֶׁת־יָמִ֡ים עָשָׂ֣ה יְהוָה֩ אֶת־הַשָּׁמַ֨יִם וְאֶת־הָאָ֜רֶץ
אֶת־הַיָּם֙ וְאֶת־כׇּל־אֲשֶׁר־בָּ֔ם וַיָּ֖נַח בַּיּ֣וֹם הַשְּׁבִיעִ֑י עַל־כֵּ֗ן בֵּרַ֧ךְ
יְהוָ֛ה אֶת־י֥וֹם הַשַּׁבָּ֖ת וַֽיְקַדְּשֵֽׁהוּ׃ כַּבֵּ֥ד אֶת־אָבִ֖יךָ
וְאֶת־אִמֶּ֑ךָ לְמַ֙עַן֙ יַאֲרִכ֣וּן יָמֶ֔יךָ עַ֚ל הָאֲדָמָ֔ה אֲשֶׁר־יְהוָ֥ה אֱלֹהֶ֖יךָ
נֹתֵ֥ן לָֽךְ׃ לֹ֥א תִרְצָֽח׃ לֹ֖א
תִנְאָֽף׃ לֹ֖א תִגְנֹֽב׃ לֹֽא־
תַעֲנֶ֥ה בְרֵעֲךָ֖ עֵ֥ד שָֽׁקֶר׃ לֹ֥א
תַחְמֹ֖ד בֵּ֣ית רֵעֶ֑ךָ לֹֽא־
תַחְמֹ֞ד אֵ֣שֶׁת רֵעֶ֗ךָ וְעַבְדּ֤וֹ וַאֲמָתוֹ֙ וְשׁוֹר֣וֹ וַחֲמֹר֔וֹ וְכֹ֖ל אֲשֶׁ֥ר
לְרֵעֶֽךָ׃

THE TEN COMMANDMENTS, PARASHAT VA'ETHANAN

I am the LORD your God, who brought you out of the land of Egypt, from the house of bondage. You shall have no other gods besides Me. You shall not make for yourself any carved idol, or any likeness of anything that is in heaven above, or that is in the earth beneath, or that is in the waters beneath the earth: you shall not bow down to them, nor serve them: for I the LORD your God am a jealous God, punishing the iniquity of the fathers upon the children to the third and fourth generation of those who hate Me, and showing mercy to the thousandth generation of those who love Me and keep My commandments. You shall not take the name of the LORD your God in vain: for the LORD will not hold him guiltless that takes His name in vain. **Keep the Sabbath day to sanctify it, as the LORD your God has commanded you. Six days you shall labor, and do all your work: but the seventh day is the Sabbath of the LORD your God: on it you shall not do any work, you, nor your son, nor your daughter, nor your manservant, nor your maidservant, nor your ox, nor your ass, nor any of your cattle, nor your stranger that is within your gates; that your manservant and your maidservant may rest as well as you.** And remember that you were a slave in the land of Egypt, and that the LORD your God brought you out from there with a mighty hand and an outstretched arm: therefore the LORD your God commanded you to keep the Sabbath day. Honor your father and your mother, as the LORD your God has commanded you; that your days may be prolonged, and that it go well with you, in the land which the LORD your God gives you. You shall not murder. Neither shall you commit adultery. Neither shall you steal. Neither shall you bear false witness against your neighbor. Neither shall you covet your neighbor's wife, neither shall you desire your neighbor's house, his field, or his manservant, or his maidservant, his ox, or his ass, or anything that is your neighbor's.

---

spoken simultaneously teaches that the negative and positive aspects of holy time are inseparable. The prohibition against work creates space for rest and joy.

עשרת הדברות שבפרשת ואתחנן

בטעם העליון

אָנֹכִי֙ יְהוָ֣ה אֱלֹהֶ֔יךָ
אֲשֶׁ֧ר הוֹצֵאתִ֛יךָ מֵאֶ֥רֶץ מִצְרַ֖יִם מִבֵּ֣ית עֲבָדִ֑ים לֹ֣א יִהְיֶ֥ה לְךָ֛
אֱלֹהִ֥ים אֲחֵרִ֖ים עַל־פָּנַ֑י לֹ֣א תַעֲשֶׂה־לְךָ֥ פֶ֙סֶל֙ ׀ כָּל־תְּמוּנָ֔ה
אֲשֶׁ֤ר בַּשָּׁמַ֙יִם֙ ׀ מִמַּ֔עַל וַאֲשֶׁ֛ר בָּאָ֖רֶץ מִתַּ֑חַת וַאֲשֶׁ֥ר בַּמַּ֖יִם ׀
מִתַּ֥חַת לָאָֽרֶץ לֹֽא־תִשְׁתַּחֲוֶ֥ה לָהֶ֖ם וְלֹ֣א תָעָבְדֵ֑ם כִּ֣י אָנֹכִ֞י יְהוָ֤ה
אֱלֹהֶ֙יךָ֙ אֵ֣ל קַנָּ֔א פֹּ֠קֵד עֲוֺ֨ן אָב֧וֹת עַל־בָּנִ֛ים וְעַל־שִׁלֵּשִׁ֥ים
וְעַל־רִבֵּעִ֖ים לְשֹׂנְאָ֑י וְעֹ֤שֶׂה חֶ֙סֶד֙ לַאֲלָפִ֔ים לְאֹהֲבַ֖י וּלְשֹׁמְרֵ֥י
מצותו׃ לֹ֥א תִשָּׂ֛א אֶת־שֵֽׁם־יְהוָ֥ה אֱלֹהֶ֖יךָ לַשָּׁ֑וְא כִּ֣י לֹ֤א מִצְוֺתָֽי
יְנַקֶּה֙ יְהוָ֔ה אֵ֛ת אֲשֶׁר־יִשָּׂ֥א אֶת־שְׁמ֖וֹ לַשָּֽׁוְא׃ שָׁמ֛וֹר
אֶת־י֥וֹם הַשַּׁבָּ֖ת לְקַדְּשׁ֑וֹ כַּאֲשֶׁ֥ר צִוְּךָ֣ ׀ יְהוָ֣ה אֱלֹהֶ֔יךָ שֵׁ֤שֶׁת יָמִים֙
תַּֽעֲבֹ֔ד וְעָשִׂ֖יתָ כָּל־מְלַאכְתֶּֽךָ וְי֙וֹם֙ הַשְּׁבִיעִ֜י שַׁבָּ֣ת ׀ לַֽיהוָ֣ה
אֱלֹהֶ֗יךָ לֹ֣א תַעֲשֶׂ֣ה כָל־מְלָאכָ֡ה אַתָּ֣ה וּבִנְךָֽ־וּבִתֶּ֣ךָ וְֽעַבְדְּךָֽ־
וַ֠אֲמָתֶךָ וְשׁוֹרְךָ֨ וַחֲמֹרְךָ֜ וְכָל־בְּהֶמְתֶּ֗ךָ וְגֵרְךָ֙ אֲשֶׁ֣ר בִּשְׁעָרֶ֔יךָ לְמַ֗עַן יָנ֛וּחַ
עַבְדְּךָ֥ וַאֲמָתְךָ֖ כָּמ֑וֹךָ וְזָכַרְתָּ֞ כִּי־עֶ֣בֶד הָיִ֣יתָ ׀ בְּאֶ֣רֶץ מִצְרַ֗יִם וַיֹּצִאֲךָ֩
יְהוָ֨ה אֱלֹהֶ֤יךָ מִשָּׁם֙ בְּיָ֤ד חֲזָקָה֙ וּבִזְרֹ֣עַ נְטוּיָ֔ה עַל־כֵּ֗ן צִוְּךָ֙ יְהוָ֣ה אֱלֹהֶ֔יךָ
לַעֲשׂ֖וֹת אֶת־י֥וֹם הַשַּׁבָּֽת׃ כַּבֵּ֤ד
אֶת־אָבִ֙יךָ֙ וְאֶת־אִמֶּ֔ךָ כַּאֲשֶׁ֥ר צִוְּךָ֖ יְהוָ֣ה אֱלֹהֶ֑יךָ לְמַ֣עַן ׀ יַאֲרִיכֻ֣ן
יָמֶ֗יךָ וּלְמַ֙עַן֙ יִ֣יטַב לָ֔ךְ עַ֚ל הָאֲדָמָ֔ה אֲשֶׁר־יְהוָ֥ה אֱלֹהֶ֖יךָ נֹתֵ֥ן
לָֽךְ׃ לֹ֥א תִרְצָֽח׃ וְלֹ֣א
תִנְאָֽף׃ וְלֹ֣א תִגְנֹֽב׃ וְלֹֽא־
תַעֲנֶ֥ה בְרֵעֲךָ֖ עֵ֥ד שָֽׁוְא׃ וְלֹ֣א
תַחְמֹ֖ד אֵ֣שֶׁת רֵעֶ֑ךָ וְלֹ֣א
תִתְאַוֶּ֞ה בֵּ֣ית רֵעֶ֗ךָ שָׂדֵ֜הוּ וְעַבְדּ֣וֹ וַאֲמָתוֹ֙ שׁוֹר֣וֹ וַחֲמֹר֔וֹ וְכֹ֖ל אֲשֶׁ֥ר לְרֵעֶֽךָ׃

---

the prohibition against work, while "remember" refers to the positive commandment, to sanctify it in word and deed. The idea that both were

SHABBAT SIRENS

BABYLONIAN TALMUD *SHABBAT DAF* 35 *AMUD* A

The Sages taught in a *baraita*: **Six blasts are sounded on Shabbat eve** to herald the advent of Shabbat.

The *baraita* proceeds to detail the purpose of each blast:

The **first** is **to stop the people from** their **work in the fields.**

The **second** is **to stop** the people who are working in the **city, and** to close the **stores.**

The **third** is to inform them **to light the** Shabbat **candle,** this is **the statement of Rabbi Natan.**

Rabbi Yehuda HaNasi says: The **third** blast is to inform those donning phylacteries throughout the day **to remove** their **phylacteries,** as one does not don phylacteries on Shabbat.

And following the third blast, **he pauses** for an interval **as long as** it takes to **fry a small fish, or as long as** it takes **to stick bread to the** sides of the **oven,** in case someone remembered that he needs it for Shabbat,

and he sounds a *tekia* and a *terua* and a *tekia*, and he begins to **observe Shabbat** as at that point, Shabbat begins in every sense.

A GRAND ENTRANCE

BABYLONIAN TALMUD *SHABBAT DAF* 119 *AMUD* A

Rabbi Ḥanina would stand wrapped in his Shabbat garment **at nightfall on Shabbat eve and say: Come and we will go out and greet the Shabbat queen.**

Rabbi Yanai would **put on his garment on Shabbat eve and say: Come O bride, come O bride.**

---

greeting the Shabbat Queen. Yet, the true dichotomy of Kabbalat Shabbat is found in *Shabbat* 33b from the man carrying two bundles of myrtle and running at twilight. Twilight, on the one hand, is the instant in which one accepts the prohibitions and obligations of Shabbat, represented by "*shamor*" (safeguard) and "*zakhor*" (remember) respectively. On the other hand, the myrtle branches are collected to usher in the Shabbat Queen with a pleasant aroma. The dual fulfillment is what we seek during our own Kabbalat Shabbat. (BL)

שש תקיעות
תלמוד בבלי מסכת שבת דף לה עמוד ב

תנו רבנן, שש תקיעות תוקעין ערב שבת:
ראשונה – להבטיל את העם ממלאכה שבשדות
שניה – להבטיל עיר וחנויות
שלישית – להדליק את הנר
דברי רבי נתן.

רבי יהודה הנשיא אומר:
שלישית לחלוץ תפילין.
ושוהה כדי צליית דג קטן
או כדי להדביק פת בתנור
ותוקע ומריע ותוקע ושובת.

לקראת שבת המלכה
תלמוד בבלי מסכת שבת דף קיט עמוד א

רבי חנינא מיעטף וקאי אפניא דמעלי שבתא
אמר: בואו ונצא לקראת שבת המלכה.

רבי ינאי לביש מאניה מעלי שבת
ואמר: בואי כלה בואי כלה.

The words "Kabbalat Shabbat" are more than a title for a prayer; they indicate a deep state of mind we assume as Shabbat enters. Interestingly, "Kabbala" can either mean "to accept" or "to greet" which, in turn, allows for two distinctive approaches to the Shabbat preparations: *accepting* the prohibitions of Shabbat or *greeting* the Shabbat Queen.

These Talmudic passages enliven both definitions of Kabbalat Shabbat. In *Shabbat* 35a the Talmud attempts to define the precise moment at which a person accepts the prohibitions and obligations of Shabbat. In contrast, *Shabbat* 119a describes the preparations of Rabbi Ḥanina and Rabbi Yanai in

THE ALLEGORY OF THE CAVE

BABYLONIAN TALMUD *SHABBAT DAF* 30 *AMUD* B

He, Rabbi Shimon bar Yoḥai **and his son** Rabbi Elazar **went** and **hid in the study hall. Every day** Rabbi Shimon's **wife would bring them bread and a jug of water and they would eat. When the decree intensified,** Rabbi Shimon **said to his son: Women are easily impressionable** and therefore there is room for concern **lest** the authorities **will torture her and she will reveal our** whereabouts. **They went and they hid in a cave. A miracle occurred** and **a carob** tree **and a spring of water were created for them. They would remove their clothes and sit in sand up to their necks** for cover and **study** Torah **all day long. When it was time for prayer, they would dress and cover themselves and pray, and** then **they would again and remove their clothes so that they would not tatter. They sat in the cave for twelve years. Elijah** the Prophet **came and stood at the entrance to the cave** and **said: Who will inform Bar Yoḥai that** the **emperor died and his decree has been rescinded?**

They **emerged** from the cave, and **saw people who were plowing and sowing.** Rabbi Shimon bar Yoḥai **said:** These people **abandon eternal life** of Torah study **and engage in temporal life** for their own sustenance. The Gemara relates that **everywhere** Rabbi Shimon and his son Rabbi Elazar **directed their eyes** would **immediately burn. A divine voice emerged and said to them:** Did **you come out** of the cave in order **to destroy My world? Return to your cave. They returned** to the cave and **sat** there **for twelve months. They said: The judgment of the wicked in Gehinnom lasts** for **twelve months** and so surely our sins were pardoned during this period. **A divine voice emerged and said** to them: **Come out of your cave. They came out. Everywhere that Rabbi Elazar would strike** and cause harm, **Rabbi Shimon would heal.** Rabbi Shimon **said to him,** to his son Rabbi Elazar: **My son, you and I suffice for the** entire **world,** as the two of us are engaged in the study of Torah in the proper manner.

As Shabbat was approaching on Friday **they saw an elderly man, holding two bundles of myrtle branches and running at twilight. They said to him: Why do you have these** branches? **He said to them: In honor of Shabbat.** They said to him: **But does one suffice for you?** He answered them: **One** of them **corresponds to: "Remember** the Shabbat day, to keep it holy" (Exodus 20:8), **and** one of them **corresponds to: "Observe** the Shabbat day, to keep it holy" (Deuteronomy 5:12). **He** Rabbi Shimon **said to his son: See how beloved the mitzvot are to Israel. Their concerns were eased;** although the Jewish people did not live up to the expectations of Rabbi Shimon and his son in terms of Torah study, they were impressed by their devotion to mitzvot.

משל המערה

תלמוד בבלי מסכת שבת דף ל עמוד ב

אזל הוא ובריה טשו בי מדרשא.
כל יומא הוה מייתי להו דביתהו ריפתא וכוזא דמיא וכרכי.
כי תקיף גזירתא, אמר ליה לבריה:
נשים דעתן קלה עליהן, דילמא מצערי לה ומגליא לן.
אזלו טשו במערתא.
איתרחיש ניסא איברי להו חרובא ועינא דמיא.
והוו משלחי מנייהו, והוו יתבי עד צוארייהו בחלא,
כולי יומא גרסי, בעידן צלויי לבשו מיכסו ומצלו,
והדר משלחי מנייהו כי היכי דלא ליבלו.
איתבו תריסר שני במערתא.
אתא אליהו וקם אפיתחא דמערתא,
אמר: מאן לודעיה לבר יוחי דמית קיסר ובטיל גזרתיה?
נפקו. חזו אינשי דקא כרבי וזרעי,
אמר: מניחין חיי עולם ועוסקין בחיי שעה!
כל מקום שנותנין עיניהן – מיד נשרף.
יצתה בת קול ואמרה להם: להחריב עולמי יצאתם?
חיזרו למערתכם! הדור אזול.
איתיבו תריסר ירחי שתא.
אמרי: משפט רשעים בגיהנם – שנים עשר חדש.
יצתה בת קול ואמרה: צאו ממערתכם!
נפקו, כל היכא דהוה מחי רבי אלעזר – הוה מסי רבי שמעון.
אמר לו: בני, די לעולם אני ואתה.
בהדי פניא דמעלי שבתא חזו ההוא סבא דהוה נקיט תרי מדאני אסא,
ורהיט בין השמשות.
אמרו ליה: הני למה לך?
– אמר להו: לכבוד שבת.
– ותיסגי לך בחד?
– חד כנגד זכור, וחד כנגד שמור.
– אמר ליה לבריה: חזי כמה חביבין מצות על ישראל!
יתיב דעתייהו.

SHIR HASHIRIM – THE SONG OF SONGS

1:1 Solomon's Song of Songs.

2. *Would that he would kiss me with that mouth –*
   better than any wine is your love;

3. the fragrance of your oils, finer.
   Your very name flows forth like scented oil;
      what wonder then that young girls love you?

4. Come, draw me after you, let us run –
   the King has brought me into his chambers.
   In you our joy, our happiness:
   your love possesses us more than any wine;
      flowing freely falls this love.

5. I am dark yet fair,
   daughters of Jerusalem;
   black as the tents of Kedar,
   as Solomon's curtains.

6. Do not look at me, I am scorched black:
   the sun has stared at me.
   My mother's sons were furious.
   They made me a keeper of the vineyards;
      my own vineyard, I did not keep.

7. Tell me, you that I have loved,
   where will you pasture,
      where will you rest your flock at noon?
   Do not make me swathe my face and wander,
   among all the herds of your friends.

8. "If you do not know,
   most beautiful of women,
   then go out in the tracks of the flock;
   bring your own young goats to pasture
      where the shepherds' huts stand."

שיר השירים

א א שִׁיר הַשִּׁירִים אֲשֶׁר לִשְׁלֹמֹה: יִשָּׁקֵנִי מִנְּשִׁיקוֹת פִּיהוּ כִּי־טוֹבִים דֹּדֶיךָ
ב
ג מִיָּיִן: לְרֵיחַ שְׁמָנֶיךָ טוֹבִים שֶׁמֶן תּוּרַק שְׁמֶךָ עַל־כֵּן עֲלָמוֹת אֲהֵבוּךָ:
ד מָשְׁכֵנִי אַחֲרֶיךָ נָּרוּצָה הֱבִיאַנִי הַמֶּלֶךְ חֲדָרָיו נָגִילָה וְנִשְׂמְחָה בָּךְ
ה נַזְכִּירָה דֹדֶיךָ מִיַּיִן מֵישָׁרִים אֲהֵבוּךָ: שְׁחוֹרָה אֲנִי וְנָאוָה
ו בְּנוֹת יְרוּשָׁלִָם כְּאָהֳלֵי קֵדָר כִּירִיעוֹת שְׁלֹמֹה: אַל־תִּרְאוּנִי שֶׁאֲנִי
שְׁחַרְחֹרֶת שֶׁשֱּׁזָפַתְנִי הַשָּׁמֶשׁ בְּנֵי אִמִּי נִחֲרוּ־בִי שָׂמֻנִי נֹטֵרָה אֶת־
ז הַכְּרָמִים כַּרְמִי שֶׁלִּי לֹא נָטָרְתִּי: הַגִּידָה לִּי שֶׁאָהֲבָה נַפְשִׁי אֵיכָה
תִרְעֶה אֵיכָה תַּרְבִּיץ בַּצָּהֳרָיִם שַׁלָּמָה אֶהְיֶה כְּעֹטְיָה עַל עֶדְרֵי חֲבֵרֶיךָ:
ח אִם־לֹא תֵדְעִי לָךְ הַיָּפָה בַּנָּשִׁים צְאִי־לָךְ בְּעִקְבֵי הַצֹּאן וּרְעִי אֶת־
גְּדִיֹּתַיִךְ עַל מִשְׁכְּנוֹת הָרֹעִים:

As Shabbat enters, not only does a new day begin, but each individual is transformed by a *neshama yeteira*, an additional soul. Rav Kook, the first Chief Rabbi of Israel, says that receiving this Shabbat soul demands spiritual preparation, which comes through the recitation of Shir HaShirim, a book of the soul. Rabbi Akiva praises Shir HaShirim: "All the Writings are holy, but Shir HaShirim is the Holy of Holies" (*Yadayim* 3:5). Rav Kook believes that the hour of Kabbalat Shabbat is the "Holy of Holies" *of time*, since in this moment the additional light of the Shabbat holiness is revealed in each person. (YS)

9. "My mare among Pharaoh's chariots,
    that is what you are to me, my love,
10. your cheeks fair in their strings of beads,
    your neck, jewelled;
11. I would make you strings of solid gold –
    with silver grains."
12. As long as my king reclined to eat,
    my musk-root gave its scent;
13. my beloved a bundle of myrrh to me,
    resting between my breasts,
14. my beloved a cluster of henna to me,
    in the spice-beds of Ein Gedi.
15. "You are beautiful, my love,
    how beautiful, your eyes like doves."
16. How beautiful you are, beloved, and how good.
    Our bed is green, luscious.
17. Our house is roofed with cedars;
    its rafters are juniper trees.
2:1 I am a dune flower of the coast,
    I am a lily of the valleys.
2. "A lily among thorn weeds
    is my love among the girls."
3. Amid the forest, an apple tree
    is my beloved among men.
  I treasure his shade, there I rest –
    and his fruit fills my mouth with sweetness.
4. He has brought me to the wine house,
    and his flag flying over me is love.
5. Sustain me now with raisin cakes,
    spread a bed for me among apples –
      for I am sick with love.

ט י לְסֻסָתִי בְּרִכְבֵי פַרְעֹה דִּמִּיתִיךְ רַעְיָתִי׃ נָאווּ לְחָיַיִךְ בַּתֹּרִים
יא יב צַוָּארֵךְ בַּחֲרוּזִים׃ תּוֹרֵי זָהָב נַעֲשֶׂה־לָּךְ עִם נְקֻדּוֹת הַכָּסֶף׃ עַד־
יג שֶׁהַמֶּלֶךְ בִּמְסִבּוֹ נִרְדִּי נָתַן רֵיחוֹ׃ צְרוֹר הַמֹּר ׀ דּוֹדִי לִי בֵּין שָׁדַי יָלִין׃
יד טו אֶשְׁכֹּל הַכֹּפֶר ׀ דּוֹדִי לִי בְּכַרְמֵי עֵין גֶּדִי׃ הִנָּךְ יָפָה רַעְיָתִי
טז הִנָּךְ יָפָה עֵינַיִךְ יוֹנִים׃ הִנְּךָ יָפֶה דוֹדִי אַף נָעִים אַף־עַרְשֵׂנוּ רַעֲנָנָה׃
ב יז א קֹרוֹת בָּתֵּינוּ אֲרָזִים רחיטנו בְּרוֹתִים׃ אֲנִי חֲבַצֶּלֶת הַשָּׁרוֹן שׁוֹשַׁנַּת רָהִיטֵנוּ
ב ג הָעֲמָקִים׃ כְּשׁוֹשַׁנָּה בֵּין הַחוֹחִים כֵּן רַעְיָתִי בֵּין הַבָּנוֹת׃ כְּתַפּוּחַ בַּעֲצֵי
הַיַּעַר כֵּן דּוֹדִי בֵּין הַבָּנִים בְּצִלּוֹ חִמַּדְתִּי וְיָשַׁבְתִּי וּפִרְיוֹ מָתוֹק לְחִכִּי׃
ד ה הֱבִיאַנִי אֶל־בֵּית הַיָּיִן וְדִגְלוֹ עָלַי אַהֲבָה׃ סַמְּכוּנִי בָּאֲשִׁישׁוֹת רַפְּדוּנִי
בַּתַּפּוּחִים כִּי־חוֹלַת אַהֲבָה אָנִי׃

"A lily of the valleys" – שושנת העמקים *is identified with Narcissus tazetta, a wild relative of the daffodil, and is not the same as the* שושנה *(white lily) in the following verse.*
"A dune flower of the coast" – חבצלת השרון *– see page 97.*

"Thorn weeds" – חוחים *refers particularly to the species Scolymus maculatus, the spotted golden thistle.*

6. My head rests in his left hand;
his right arm is around me.

7. Swear to me, daughters of Jerusalem,
by the she-gazelles, by the does of the field,
swear that you will not waken, will not rouse
this love before its time.

8. The voice of my beloved – I hear him coming –
springing over the hills,
leaping the slopes;

9. he is like a gazelle, my beloved,
he is like a young deer –
here he stands, behind our wall,
gazing through the windows,
glimpsing through every gap.

10. My beloved, he spoke, he said to me,
"Come, rise,
my love, my beautiful one,
let us leave.

11. Winter is over.
The rains have passed
and left us.

12. On the land, buds have appeared.
The songbirds' time has come,
and the turtle-dove's call sounds over our land.

13. The fig has put out her young fruits,
and the flowering vines give scent –
so come, rise,
my love, my beautiful one,
let us leave."

ו ז שְׂמֹאלוֹ֙ תַּ֣חַת לְרֹאשִׁ֔י וִימִינ֖וֹ תְּחַבְּקֵֽנִי׃ הִשְׁבַּ֨עְתִּי אֶתְכֶ֜ם בְּנ֤וֹת
יְרוּשָׁלִַ֙ם֙ בִּצְבָא֔וֹת א֖וֹ בְּאַיְל֣וֹת הַשָּׂדֶ֑ה אִם־תָּעִ֧ירוּ ׀ וְֽאִם־תְּעֽוֹרְר֛וּ
ח אֶת־הָאַהֲבָ֖ה עַ֥ד שֶׁתֶּחְפָּֽץ׃ ק֣וֹל דּוֹדִ֔י הִנֵּה־זֶ֖ה בָּ֑א מְדַלֵּג֙
ט עַל־הֶ֣הָרִ֔ים מְקַפֵּ֖ץ עַל־הַגְּבָעֽוֹת׃ דּוֹמֶ֤ה דוֹדִי֙ לִצְבִ֔י א֖וֹ לְעֹ֣פֶר הָֽאַיָּלִ֑ים
הִנֵּה־זֶ֤ה עוֹמֵד֙ אַחַ֣ר כָּתְלֵ֔נוּ מַשְׁגִּ֙יחַ֙ מִן־הַֽחַלֹּנ֔וֹת מֵצִ֖יץ מִן־הַחֲרַכִּֽים׃
י יא עָנָ֥ה דוֹדִ֖י וְאָ֣מַר לִ֑י ק֥וּמִי לָ֛ךְ רַעְיָתִ֥י יָפָתִ֖י וּלְכִי־לָֽךְ׃ כִּֽי־הִנֵּ֥ה הַסְּתָ֖ו
יב עָבָ֑ר הַגֶּ֕שֶׁם חָלַ֖ף הָלַ֥ךְ לֽוֹ׃ הַנִּצָּנִים֙ נִרְא֣וּ בָאָ֔רֶץ עֵ֥ת הַזָּמִ֖יר הִגִּ֑יעַ
יג וְק֥וֹל הַתּ֖וֹר נִשְׁמַ֥ע בְּאַרְצֵֽנוּ׃ הַתְּאֵנָה֙ חָֽנְטָ֣ה פַגֶּ֔יהָ וְהַגְּפָנִ֥ים ׀ סְמָדַ֖ר
נָ֣תְנוּ רֵ֑יחַ ק֥וּמִי לכי רַעְיָתִ֥י יָפָתִ֖י וּלְכִי־לָֽךְ׃ לָֽךְ

"The fig has put out her young fruits" – פגיה – *What we consider the fruit of the fig tree is in fact a stem filled with flowers, which when pollinated develop into many tiny fruits. This early "inflorescence" develops in spring together with the leaves.*

14. "My dove, in the rock's cleft
    in the cliff's shadow
show me your face,
    let me hear your voice,
for it is lovely to me, your voice;
    your face so fair."

15. Catch the foxes,
    the little foxes,
ravaging the vineyards,
    just as our vineyard is in flower.

16. My beloved is my own and I am his,
    who pastures among lilies.

17. Until the day has breathed its light
    and the shadows have flown,
turn like a gazelle, my beloved,
    turn like a young deer,
        to the riven hills.

3:1 Upon my bed at night
    I search for the one I love;
        I search for him, I do not find him.

2. I shall rise, I shall go all around the town,
    through the streets, across the squares;
I am searching for the one I love –
    I search for him, I do not find him.

3. The guards find me, those who go around the town,
    The one that I love – have you seen him?

4. I have scarcely moved away from them
    when I find the one I love.
I catch hold of him, I will not let him go –
    until I have brought him to my mother's house,
        the chamber where I was conceived.

5. Swear to me, daughters of Jerusalem,
    by the she-gazelles, by the does of the field,
swear that you will not waken, will not rouse
    this love before its time.

יד יוֹנָתִי בְּחַגְוֵי הַסֶּלַע בְּסֵתֶר הַמַּדְרֵגָה הַרְאִינִי אֶת־מַרְאַיִךְ
טו הַשְׁמִיעִינִי אֶת־קוֹלֵךְ כִּי־קוֹלֵךְ עָרֵב וּמַרְאֵיךְ נָאוֶה׃ אֶחֱזוּ־
לָנוּ שׁוּעָלִים שֻׁעָלִים קְטַנִּים מְחַבְּלִים כְּרָמִים וּכְרָמֵינוּ סְמָדַר׃
טז יז דּוֹדִי לִי וַאֲנִי לוֹ הָרֹעֶה בַּשּׁוֹשַׁנִּים׃ עַד שֶׁיָּפוּחַ הַיּוֹם וְנָסוּ
הַצְּלָלִים סֹב דְּמֵה־לְךָ דוֹדִי לִצְבִי אוֹ לְעֹפֶר הָאַיָּלִים עַל־הָרֵי
ג א בָתֶר׃ עַל־מִשְׁכָּבִי בַּלֵּילוֹת בִּקַּשְׁתִּי אֵת שֶׁאָהֲבָה נַפְשִׁי
ב בִּקַּשְׁתִּיו וְלֹא מְצָאתִיו׃ אָקוּמָה נָּא וַאֲסוֹבְבָה בָעִיר בַּשְּׁוָקִים
וּבָרְחֹבוֹת אֲבַקְשָׁה אֵת שֶׁאָהֲבָה נַפְשִׁי בִּקַּשְׁתִּיו וְלֹא מְצָאתִיו׃
ג ד מְצָאוּנִי הַשֹּׁמְרִים הַסֹּבְבִים בָּעִיר אֵת שֶׁאָהֲבָה נַפְשִׁי רְאִיתֶם׃ כִּמְעַט
שֶׁעָבַרְתִּי מֵהֶם עַד שֶׁמָּצָאתִי אֵת שֶׁאָהֲבָה נַפְשִׁי אֲחַזְתִּיו וְלֹא אַרְפֶּנּוּ
ה עַד־שֶׁהֲבֵיאתִיו אֶל־בֵּית אִמִּי וְאֶל־חֶדֶר הוֹרָתִי׃ הִשְׁבַּעְתִּי אֶתְכֶם
בְּנוֹת יְרוּשָׁלִַם בִּצְבָאוֹת אוֹ בְּאַיְלוֹת הַשָּׂדֶה אִם־תָּעִירוּ ׀ וְאִם־תְּעוֹרְרוּ
אֶת־הָאַהֲבָה עַד שֶׁתֶּחְפָּץ׃

"To the riven hills" – It seems that the phrase הרי בתר *refers not to the location Betar, but to hills that are "riven" – sharply hewn, like these seen from the Jordan Valley.*

6. *"Who is this, rising from the desert*
like plumes of smoke,
perfumed with myrrh and frankincense,
and all the merchants' powders?"

7. Here stands Solomon's bed
sixty soldiers all around it,
heroes of Israel.

8. Each carrying his sword,
each learned in war,
each with his sword at his thigh
for very fear at night.

9. King Solomon built a palace
of Lebanon wood;

10. He plated the pillars with silver,
made the pillows of gold;
his couch is purple silk,
and all the space is lined with love
by the daughters of Jerusalem.

11. Go out and see,
daughters of Zion,
look at Solomon the King,
in the crown his mother gave to him
on this his wedding day,
on the day his heart rejoiced.

4:1 "How beautiful you are, my love,
how beautiful, your eyes like doves
seen through your tresses;
your hair like a flock of goats
flowing down Mount Gilead.

2. Your teeth are like a flock of sheep,
rising up from cleaning
each bearing twins, two and two,
not one among them lost.

ו מִי זֹאת עֹלָה מִן־הַמִּדְבָּר כְּתִימֲרוֹת עָשָׁן מְקֻטֶּרֶת מוֹר
ז וּלְבוֹנָה מִכֹּל אַבְקַת רוֹכֵל: הִנֵּה מִטָּתוֹ שֶׁלִּשְׁלֹמֹה שִׁשִּׁים גִּבֹּרִים
ח סָבִיב לָהּ מִגִּבֹּרֵי יִשְׂרָאֵל: כֻּלָּם אֲחֻזֵי חֶרֶב מְלֻמְּדֵי מִלְחָמָה אִישׁ
ט חַרְבּוֹ עַל־יְרֵכוֹ מִפַּחַד בַּלֵּילוֹת: אַפִּרְיוֹן עָשָׂה לוֹ הַמֶּלֶךְ
י שְׁלֹמֹה מֵעֲצֵי הַלְּבָנוֹן: עַמּוּדָיו עָשָׂה כֶסֶף רְפִידָתוֹ זָהָב מֶרְכָּבוֹ אַרְגָּמָן
יא תּוֹכוֹ רָצוּף אַהֲבָה מִבְּנוֹת יְרוּשָׁלָםִ: צְאֶינָה ׀ וּרְאֶינָה בְּנוֹת צִיּוֹן
בַּמֶּלֶךְ שְׁלֹמֹה בָּעֲטָרָה שֶׁעִטְּרָה־לּוֹ אִמּוֹ בְּיוֹם חֲתֻנָּתוֹ וּבְיוֹם שִׂמְחַת
א לִבּוֹ: הִנָּךְ יָפָה רַעְיָתִי הִנָּךְ יָפָה עֵינַיִךְ יוֹנִים מִבַּעַד לְצַמָּתֵךְ
ב שַׂעְרֵךְ כְּעֵדֶר הָעִזִּים שֶׁגָּלְשׁוּ מֵהַר גִּלְעָד: שִׁנַּיִךְ כְּעֵדֶר הַקְּצוּבוֹת
שֶׁעָלוּ מִן־הָרַחְצָה שֶׁכֻּלָּם מַתְאִימוֹת וְשַׁכֻּלָה אֵין בָּהֶם:

"A flock of goats… a flock of sheep"– The whiteness of clean sheep is a prized quality in teeth, while black goats rippling down the hills may recall curly hair. It is goatskin that makes "the tents of Kedar" black in 1:5.

3. Your lips are like a scarlet ribbon,
    and your speech is fair,
your forehead, like a pomegranate
    glowing through your tresses.
4. Your neck is like the Tower of David,
    built in splendor,
a thousand shields adorning it,
    the shields of all the heroes.
5. Your two breasts are like young
    twins of a she-gazelle,
        pasturing in lilies.
6. Until the day has breathed its light,
    and the shadows have flown,
I am going to the hill of myrrh,
    to the slopes of frankincense.
7. And all of you is beauty, my love,
    is flawless; wholly."
8. "Come with me from Lebanon, bride,
    come down with me from Lebanon;
from the peak of Amana, descend,
    from the peaks of Senir and Hermon,
        from the lions' haunts,
            the leopards' hills.
9. You have taken my heart, my sister, my bride;
    either one of your eyes would take my heart
        any strand of the necklace you wear.
10. How beautiful your love is, my sister, my bride,
    how much better than any wine your love,
        and finer than all perfumes the scent of your oils.
11. Your lips drip nectar, my bride;
    honey and milk lie under your tongue,
        and on your dress lingers
            Lebanon's scent."

ג כְּחוּט הַשָּׁנִי שִׂפְתוֹתַיִךְ וּמִדְבָּרֵיךְ נָאוֶה כְּפֶלַח הָרִמּוֹן רַקָּתֵךְ מִבַּעַד
ד לְצַמָּתֵךְ: כְּמִגְדַּל דָּוִיד צַוָּארֵךְ בָּנוּי לְתַלְפִּיּוֹת אֶלֶף הַמָּגֵן תָּלוּי עָלָיו
ה כֹּל שִׁלְטֵי הַגִּבּוֹרִים: שְׁנֵי שָׁדַיִךְ כִּשְׁנֵי עֳפָרִים תְּאוֹמֵי צְבִיָּה הָרוֹעִים
ו בַּשּׁוֹשַׁנִּים: עַד שֶׁיָּפוּחַ הַיּוֹם וְנָסוּ הַצְּלָלִים אֵלֶךְ לִי אֶל־הַר הַמּוֹר
ח וְאֶל־גִּבְעַת הַלְּבוֹנָה: כֻּלָּךְ יָפָה רַעְיָתִי וּמוּם אֵין בָּךְ: אִתִּי
מִלְּבָנוֹן כַּלָּה אִתִּי מִלְּבָנוֹן תָּבוֹאִי תָּשׁוּרִי ׀ מֵרֹאשׁ אֲמָנָה מֵרֹאשׁ
ט שְׂנִיר וְחֶרְמוֹן מִמְּעֹנוֹת אֲרָיוֹת מֵהַרְרֵי נְמֵרִים: לִבַּבְתִּנִי אֲחֹתִי כַלָּה
י לִבַּבְתִּנִי באחד מֵעֵינַיִךְ בְּאַחַד עֲנָק מִצַּוְּרֹנָיִךְ: מַה־יָּפוּ דֹדַיִךְ אֲחֹתִי בְּאַחַת
יא כַּלָּה מַה־טֹּבוּ דֹדַיִךְ מִיַּיִן וְרֵיחַ שְׁמָנַיִךְ מִכָּל־בְּשָׂמִים: נֹפֶת תִּטֹּפְנָה
שִׂפְתוֹתַיִךְ כַּלָּה דְּבַשׁ וְחָלָב תַּחַת לְשׁוֹנֵךְ וְרֵיחַ שַׂלְמֹתַיִךְ כְּרֵיחַ לְבָנוֹן:

"Until the day has breathed its light…"

12. "A locked garden is my sister, my bride,
a locked well, a spring sealed up –
13. Yet your dry ground
is a grove of pomegranates
of the sweetest fruits,
henna plants, musk-root;
14. musk-root and saffron,
calamus, cinnamon,
every kind of fragrant tree.
With myrrh plants and aloe,
with all the finest spices;
15. and a spring to water gardens,
a well of living waters,
waters flowing down from Lebanon."
16. Wake now, north wind, south wind, come:
breathe life into my garden, let its perfumes flow.
Let my beloved come to his garden,
and eat his sweetest fruits.
5:1 "I have come into my garden, my sister, my bride,
I have gathered my myrrh and my balsam,
I have eaten my honeycomb with honey,
I have drunk my wine with milk –"
Eat, loved ones, eat;
drink, drink deep of love.
2. I am asleep;
my heart is awake –
my beloved's voice, knocking –
"Open for me,
my sister, my love,
my dove, my perfection,
for my head is covered with dew,
my locks with fragments of the night."
3. *I have taken off my dress,*
how can I put it on again?
I have already washed my feet,
how can I dirty them?

יב יג גַּ֣ן ׀ נָע֖וּל אֲחֹתִ֣י כַלָּ֑ה גַּ֥ל נָע֖וּל מַעְיָ֥ן חָתֽוּם׃ שְׁלָחַ֙יִךְ֙ פַּרְדֵּ֣ס
יד רִמּוֹנִ֔ים עִ֖ם פְּרִ֣י מְגָדִ֑ים כְּפָרִ֖ים עִם־נְרָדִֽים׃ נֵ֣רְדְּ ׀ וְכַרְכֹּ֗ם קָנֶה֙ וְקִנָּמ֔וֹן
טו עִ֖ם כָּל־עֲצֵ֣י לְבוֹנָ֑ה מֹ֚ר וַאֲהָל֔וֹת עִ֖ם כָּל־רָאשֵׁ֥י בְשָׂמִֽים׃ מַעְיַ֣ן גַּנִּ֔ים
טז בְּאֵ֖ר מַ֣יִם חַיִּ֑ים וְנֹזְלִ֖ים מִן־לְבָנֽוֹן׃ ע֤וּרִי צָפוֹן֙ וּב֣וֹאִי תֵימָ֔ן הָפִ֥יחִי גַנִּ֖י
ה א יִזְּל֣וּ בְשָׂמָ֑יו יָבֹ֤א דוֹדִי֙ לְגַנּ֔וֹ וְיֹאכַ֖ל פְּרִ֥י מְגָדָֽיו׃ בָּ֣אתִי לְגַנִּי֮ אֲחֹתִ֣י כַלָּה֒
אָרִ֤יתִי מוֹרִי֙ עִם־בְּשָׂמִ֔י אָכַ֤לְתִּי יַעְרִי֙ עִם־דִּבְשִׁ֔י שָׁתִ֥יתִי יֵינִ֖י עִם־חֲלָבִ֑י
ב אִכְל֣וּ רֵעִ֔ים שְׁת֥וּ וְשִׁכְר֖וּ דּוֹדִֽים׃ אֲנִ֥י יְשֵׁנָ֖ה וְלִבִּ֣י עֵ֑ר ק֣וֹל ׀
דּוֹדִ֣י דוֹפֵ֗ק פִּתְחִי־לִ֞י אֲחֹתִ֤י רַעְיָתִי֙ יוֹנָתִ֣י תַמָּתִ֔י שֶׁרֹּאשִׁי֙ נִמְלָא־טָ֔ל
ג קְוֻצּוֹתַ֖י רְסִ֥יסֵי לָֽיְלָה׃ פָּשַׁ֙טְתִּי֙ אֶת־כֻּתָּנְתִּ֔י אֵיכָ֖כָה אֶלְבָּשֶׁ֑נָּה רָחַ֥צְתִּי
אֶת־רַגְלַ֖י אֵיכָ֥כָה אֲטַנְּפֵֽם׃

"Saffron" – The saffron crocus grows well in the land of Israel, while other species mentioned here (such as musk-root [spikenard] and calamus) were imported from distant countries.

4. My beloved stretches his hand through the door –
   and my being longs for him.

5. I rise to open the door for my beloved;
   my hands are dripping with myrrh,
   my fingers are streaming with myrrh oil,
   all over the handles of the latch.

6. I open for my beloved –
   he has slipped away; gone.
   I had fainted for him as he spoke –
   I search for him, I cannot find him;
   I call out, but he does not answer.

7. The guards find me,
   those who go around the town;
   they beat me, they wound me,
   they pull my scarf from me,
   those guardians of the walls.

8. Swear to me, daughters of Jerusalem;
   if you find my beloved,
   swear that you will tell him –
   tell him I am sick with love.

9. What makes your lover so much more than other lovers,
   you, most beautiful of women?
   What makes your lover so much more than other men
   that this is what you have us swear?

10. He is bright, my beloved, he is blooming;
    you would know him among ten thousand.

11. His face glows like gold, fine gold,
    his hair in locks like palm-flowers,
    raven black.

12. Yet his eyes are like doves,
    drinking at springs,
    washed in milk,
    at rest by the well.

ד ה דּוֹדִ֗י שָׁלַ֤ח יָדוֹ֙ מִן־הַחֹ֔ר וּמֵעַ֖י הָמ֥וּ עָלָֽיו׃ קַ֥מְתִּֽי אֲנִ֖י לִפְתֹּ֣חַ לְדוֹדִ֑י
ו וְיָדַ֣י נָֽטְפוּ־מ֗וֹר וְאֶצְבְּעֹתַי֙ מ֣וֹר עֹבֵ֔ר עַ֖ל כַּפּ֥וֹת הַמַּנְעֽוּל׃ פָּתַ֤חְתִּֽי אֲנִי֙
לְדוֹדִ֔י וְדוֹדִ֖י חָמַ֣ק עָבָ֑ר נַפְשִׁי֙ יָֽצְאָ֣ה בְדַבְּר֔וֹ בִּקַּשְׁתִּ֙יהוּ֙ וְלֹ֣א מְצָאתִ֔יהוּ
ז קְרָאתִ֖יו וְלֹ֥א עָנָֽנִי׃ מְצָאֻ֧נִי הַשֹּׁמְרִ֛ים הַסֹּבְבִ֥ים בָּעִ֖יר הִכּ֣וּנִי פְצָע֑וּנִי
ח נָשְׂא֤וּ אֶת־רְדִידִי֙ מֵעָלַ֔י שֹׁמְרֵ֖י הַחֹמֽוֹת׃ הִשְׁבַּ֥עְתִּי אֶתְכֶ֖ם בְּנ֣וֹת
יְרֽוּשָׁלָ֑ם אִֽם־תִּמְצְאוּ֙ אֶת־דּוֹדִ֔י מַה־תַּגִּ֣ידוּ ל֔וֹ שֶׁחוֹלַ֥ת אַהֲבָ֖ה אָֽנִי׃
ט מַה־דּוֹדֵ֣ךְ מִדּ֔וֹד הַיָּפָ֖ה בַּנָּשִׁ֑ים מַה־דּוֹדֵ֣ךְ מִדּ֔וֹד שֶׁכָּ֖כָה הִשְׁבַּעְתָּֽנוּ׃
י יא דּוֹדִי֙ צַח֙ וְאָד֔וֹם דָּג֖וּל מֵרְבָבָֽה׃ רֹאשׁ֖וֹ כֶּ֣תֶם פָּ֑ז קְוֻצּוֹתָיו֙ תַּלְתַּלִּ֔ים
יב שְׁחֹר֖וֹת כָּעוֹרֵֽב׃ עֵינָ֕יו כְּיוֹנִ֖ים עַל־אֲפִ֣יקֵי מָ֑יִם רֹֽחֲצוֹת֙ בֶּֽחָלָ֔ב יֹשְׁב֖וֹת
עַל־מִלֵּֽאת׃

"I search for him, I cannot find him."

13. His cheeks are like beds of balsam,
where perfume herbs are grown.
His lips smell like lilies,
flowing with myrrh oil.

14. His arms are like golden bars,
set with beryl stones.
His stomach is hewn like solid ivory,
inlaid with lapis lazuli.

15. His legs stand firm as marble pillars,
fixed on gold foundations.
Seeing him is like looking at Lebanon,
and he is as choice as its cedars.

16. His mouth is filled with sweetness,
for all of him, my longing.
This is my beloved, this is my love,
daughters of Jerusalem.

6:1 "Where has your beloved gone,
most beautiful of women?
Where has your beloved turned?
We shall search for him with you."

2. My beloved has gone to his garden,
down to the beds of balsam;
to pasture in the gardens,
to gather in lilies.

3. I am my beloved's – my beloved is my own,
who pastures among the lilies.

4. "My love, you are as beautiful as Tirzah,
as lovely as Jerusalem,
terrifying as the flagged armies.

5. "Turn your eyes from me
for they have overwhelmed me.
Your hair is like a flock of goats
streaming down from Gilead.

יג לְחָיָו כַּעֲרוּגַת הַבֹּשֶׂם מִגְדְּלוֹת מֶרְקָחִים שִׂפְתוֹתָיו שׁוֹשַׁנִּים נֹטְפוֹת
יד מוֹר עֹבֵר: יָדָיו גְּלִילֵי זָהָב מְמֻלָּאִים בַּתַּרְשִׁישׁ מֵעָיו עֶשֶׁת שֵׁן מְעֻלֶּפֶת
טו סַפִּירִים: שׁוֹקָיו עַמּוּדֵי שֵׁשׁ מְיֻסָּדִים עַל־אַדְנֵי־פָז מַרְאֵהוּ כַּלְּבָנוֹן
טז בָּחוּר כָּאֲרָזִים: חִכּוֹ מַמְתַקִּים וְכֻלּוֹ מַחֲמַדִּים זֶה דוֹדִי וְזֶה רֵעִי בְּנוֹת
ו א יְרוּשָׁלָם: אָנָה הָלַךְ דּוֹדֵךְ הַיָּפָה בַּנָּשִׁים אָנָה פָּנָה דוֹדֵךְ וּנְבַקְשֶׁנּוּ
ב עִמָּךְ: דּוֹדִי יָרַד לְגַנּוֹ לַעֲרֻגוֹת הַבֹּשֶׂם לִרְעוֹת בַּגַּנִּים וְלִלְקֹט שׁוֹשַׁנִּים:
ג אֲנִי לְדוֹדִי וְדוֹדִי לִי הָרֹעֶה בַּשּׁוֹשַׁנִּים:
ד ה יָפָה אַתְּ רַעְיָתִי כְּתִרְצָה נָאוָה כִּירוּשָׁלָם אֲיֻמָּה כַּנִּדְגָּלוֹת: הָסֵבִּי
עֵינַיִךְ מִנֶּגְדִּי שֶׁהֵם הִרְהִיבֻנִי שַׂעְרֵךְ כְּעֵדֶר הָעִזִּים שֶׁגָּלְשׁוּ מִן־הַגִּלְעָד:

"A dune flower of the coast" – חבצלת השרון *(2:1) is identified with the sand daffodil, Pancratium maritimum.*

6. Your teeth are like a flock of ewes
   rising up from cleaning;
each bears twins, two and two,
   not one among them lost.

7. Your forehead, like a pomegranate,
   glows through your tresses.

8. "Queens there are sixty; eighty concubines,
   and maids there are without number.

9. But my dove, my perfection, is one;
   one, unique to her mother –
      the shining one she bore.
Look at her, you girls, acknowledge she is blessed;
   look, queens and concubines – and praise her."

10. "Who is this, gazing out like morning,
   beautiful as the moon,
      shining like the sun,
         terrifying as the flagged armies?"

11. I went down to the nut-garden
   to see the plants of the stream;
      to see whether the vines were in flower,
         and if the pomegranate buds had burst.

12. I did not know myself – I found myself –
   amid the chariots of my princely people.

7:1 "Turn, turn back, Shulamite girl;
   turn back, turn, let us see you."
Why do you gaze at the Shulamite girl,
   as if she were a Maḥanaim dancer?

2. "How lovely are your steps
   in sandals, prince's daughter,
the turn of your thighs like jewelry,
   work of the artist's hands;

3. your navel a circular bowl –
   may it never lack wine;
your waist curved like baled wheat,
   bounded round with lilies.

ו שִׁנַּ֙יִךְ֙ כְּעֵ֣דֶר הָֽרְחֵלִ֔ים שֶׁעָל֖וּ מִן־הָֽרַחְצָ֑ה שֶׁכֻּלָּם֙ מַתְאִימ֔וֹת וְשַׁכֻּלָ֖ה
ז ח אֵ֥ין בָּהֶֽם׃ כְּפֶ֤לַח הָֽרִמּוֹן֙ רַקָּתֵ֔ךְ מִבַּ֖עַד לְצַמָּתֵֽךְ׃ שִׁשִּׁ֥ים הֵ֙מָּה֙ מְלָכ֔וֹת
ט וּשְׁמֹנִ֖ים פִּֽילַגְשִׁ֑ים וַעֲלָמ֖וֹת אֵ֥ין מִסְפָּֽר׃ אַחַ֥ת הִיא֙ יוֹנָתִ֣י תַמָּתִ֔י אַחַ֥ת
הִיא֙ לְאִמָּ֔הּ בָּרָ֥ה הִ֖יא לְיֽוֹלַדְתָּ֑הּ רָא֤וּהָ בָנוֹת֙ וַֽיְאַשְּׁר֔וּהָ מְלָכ֥וֹת
י וּפִֽילַגְשִׁ֖ים וַֽיְהַלְלֽוּהָ׃ מִי־זֹ֥את הַנִּשְׁקָפָ֖ה כְּמוֹ־שָׁ֑חַר יָפָ֣ה
יא כַלְּבָנָ֗ה בָּרָה֙ כַּֽחַמָּ֔ה אֲיֻמָּ֖ה כַּנִּדְגָּלֽוֹת׃ אֶל־גִּנַּ֤ת אֱגוֹז֙ יָרַ֔דְתִּי לִרְא֖וֹת
יב בְּאִבֵּ֣י הַנָּ֑חַל לִרְאוֹת֙ הֲפָֽרְחָ֣ה הַגֶּ֔פֶן הֵנֵ֖צוּ הָרִמֹּנִֽים׃ לֹ֣א יָדַ֔עְתִּי נַפְשִׁ֣י
ז א שָׂמַ֔תְנִי מַרְכְּב֖וֹת עַמִּ֥י נָדִֽיב׃ שׁ֤וּבִי שׁ֙וּבִי֙ הַשּֽׁוּלַמִּ֔ית שׁ֥וּבִי שׁ֖וּבִי
ב וְנֶחֱזֶה־בָּ֑ךְ מַֽה־תֶּחֱזוּ֙ בַּשּׁ֣וּלַמִּ֔ית כִּמְחֹלַ֖ת הַֽמַּחֲנָֽיִם׃ מַה־יָּפ֧וּ פְעָמַ֛יִךְ
ג בַּנְּעָלִ֖ים בַּת־נָדִ֑יב חַמּוּקֵ֣י יְרֵכַ֔יִךְ כְּמ֣וֹ חֲלָאִ֔ים מַעֲשֵׂ֖ה יְדֵ֥י אָמָּֽן׃ שָׁרְרֵךְ֙
אַגַּ֣ן הַסַּ֔הַר אַל־יֶחְסַ֖ר הַמָּ֑זֶג בִּטְנֵךְ֙ עֲרֵמַ֣ת חִטִּ֔ים סוּגָ֖ה בַּשּׁוֹשַׁנִּֽים׃

"If the pomegranate buds had burst."

4. Your two breasts are like young
twins of a she-gazelle;
5. your neck an ivory tower,
your eyes like pools in Ḥeshbon,
like pools by the Bat Rabbim Gate;
your nose like the Tower of Lebanon
gazing out to Damascus.
6. Your head rises from you like the Carmel,
its curls shine like purple silk –
a king is tangled up in its tresses.
7. How beautiful you are, how good;
my love, in all its joys."
8. "Your bearing is like a date palm,
your breasts its clustered fruits,
9. but I said, *I shall climb the date palm,*
I shall take hold of its stems,
and your breasts will be like clustered grapes,
your breath, the scent of apples.
10. And your mouth is like good wine, inside –"
It is for my beloved, flowing freely,
bringing words to sleeping lips.
11. I am my beloved's;
and his longing is for me.
12. Come, my beloved, let us go to the field,
let us lodge in the villages;
13. we will get up early and go to the vineyards,
to see if the vine has flowered,
whether its blossoms have opened out,
if the pomegranate buds have burst
and there shall I give you my love.
14. The mandrakes give their scent,
and on our own doorstep
the sweetest of fruits, new and old;
my beloved, I have hoarded them for you.

ד ה שְׁנֵי שָׁדַיִךְ כִּשְׁנֵי עֳפָרִים תָּאֳמֵי צְבִיָּה׃ צַוָּארֵךְ כְּמִגְדַּל הַשֵּׁן עֵינַיִךְ
בְּרֵכוֹת בְּחֶשְׁבּוֹן עַל־שַׁעַר בַּת־רַבִּים אַפֵּךְ כְּמִגְדַּל הַלְּבָנוֹן צוֹפֶה
ו פְּנֵי דַמָּשֶׂק׃ רֹאשֵׁךְ עָלַיִךְ כַּכַּרְמֶל וְדַלַּת רֹאשֵׁךְ כָּאַרְגָּמָן מֶלֶךְ אָסוּר
ז ח בָּרְהָטִים׃ מַה־יָּפִית וּמַה־נָּעַמְתְּ אַהֲבָה בַּתַּעֲנוּגִים׃ זֹאת קוֹמָתֵךְ
ט דָּמְתָה לְתָמָר וְשָׁדַיִךְ לְאַשְׁכֹּלוֹת׃ אָמַרְתִּי אֶעֱלֶה בְתָמָר אֹחֲזָה
י בְּסַנְסִנָּיו וְיִהְיוּ־נָא שָׁדַיִךְ כְּאֶשְׁכְּלוֹת הַגֶּפֶן וְרֵיחַ אַפֵּךְ כַּתַּפּוּחִים׃ וְחִכֵּךְ
יא כְּיֵין הַטּוֹב הוֹלֵךְ לְדוֹדִי לְמֵישָׁרִים דּוֹבֵב שִׂפְתֵי יְשֵׁנִים׃ אֲנִי לְדוֹדִי
יב יג וְעָלַי תְּשׁוּקָתוֹ׃ לְכָה דוֹדִי נֵצֵא הַשָּׂדֶה נָלִינָה בַּכְּפָרִים׃ נַשְׁכִּימָה
לַכְּרָמִים נִרְאֶה אִם־פָּרְחָה הַגֶּפֶן פִּתַּח הַסְּמָדַר הֵנֵצוּ הָרִמּוֹנִים שָׁם
יד אֶתֵּן אֶת־דֹּדַי לָךְ׃ הַדּוּדָאִים נָתְנוּ־רֵיחַ וְעַל־פְּתָחֵינוּ כָּל־מְגָדִים

"Like a date palm" – The sweet yellow dates grow on thickly bunched stems at the top of the tree; at the flowering stage these stems remind the woman of her beloved's curly hair (5:11).

8:1 If only you could have been my brother,
could have suckled at my mother's breast.
I would find you outside,
I would kiss you,
yet no one would shame me.

2. I would lead you,
I would bring you to my mother's house,
you would teach me.
I would give you to drink,
spiced wine, my pomegranate juice.

3. My head rests in his left hand,
and his right arm is around me.

4. Swear to me, daughters of Jerusalem, tell me,
why do you seek to waken, why to rouse
this love before its time?

5. *"Who is this, rising from the desert,*
leaning on her beloved?"
Beneath the apple tree I woke you;
where your mother bore you,
where in suffering she gave you birth.

6. Set me like a seal upon your heart,
like the seal upon your arm –
for love is as powerful as death itself
and jealousy as unyielding as the grave;
it burns with sparks of fire,
with the LORD's own flame.

7. Great waters cannot quench love,
nor torrents sweep it by.
If a man offered all his inheritance for love –
they would laugh him to shame.

ח א חֲדָשִׁים גַּם־יְשָׁנִים דּוֹדִי צָפַנְתִּי לָךְ: מִי יִתֶּנְךָ כְּאָח לִי יוֹנֵק שְׁדֵי
ב אִמִּי אֶמְצָאֲךָ בַחוּץ אֶשָּׁקְךָ גַּם לֹא־יָבֻזוּ לִי: אֶנְהָגֲךָ אֲבִיאֲךָ אֶל־
ג בֵּית אִמִּי תְּלַמְּדֵנִי אַשְׁקְךָ מִיַּיִן הָרֶקַח מֵעֲסִיס רִמֹּנִי: שְׂמֹאלוֹ תַּחַת
ד רֹאשִׁי וִימִינוֹ תְּחַבְּקֵנִי: הִשְׁבַּעְתִּי אֶתְכֶם בְּנוֹת יְרוּשָׁלִָם מַה־תָּעִירוּ ׀
ה וּמַה־תְּעֹרְרוּ אֶת־הָאַהֲבָה עַד שֶׁתֶּחְפָּץ: מִי זֹאת עֹלָה
מִן־הַמִּדְבָּר מִתְרַפֶּקֶת עַל־דּוֹדָהּ תַּחַת הַתַּפּוּחַ עוֹרַרְתִּיךָ שָׁמָּה
ו חִבְּלַתְךָ אִמֶּךָ שָׁמָּה חִבְּלָה יְלָדַתְךָ: שִׂימֵנִי כַחוֹתָם עַל־לִבֶּךָ כַּחוֹתָם
עַל־זְרוֹעֶךָ כִּי־עַזָּה כַמָּוֶת אַהֲבָה קָשָׁה כִשְׁאוֹל קִנְאָה רְשָׁפֶיהָ רִשְׁפֵּי
ז אֵשׁ שַׁלְהֶבֶתְיָה: מַיִם רַבִּים לֹא יוּכְלוּ לְכַבּוֹת אֶת־הָאַהֲבָה וּנְהָרוֹת
לֹא יִשְׁטְפוּהָ אִם־יִתֵּן אִישׁ אֶת־כָּל־הוֹן בֵּיתוֹ בָּאַהֲבָה בּוֹז יָבוּזוּ לוֹ:

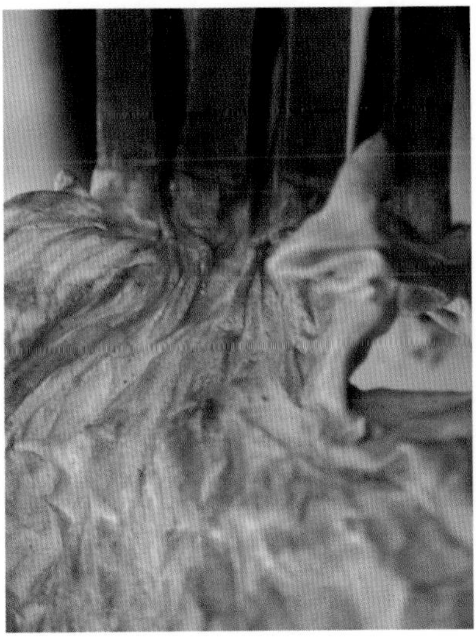

"Like the seal upon your arm"– Parchment phyllacteries at an early stage of production; the blocks will become the four chambers of the head tefillin. The binding of tefillin symbolizes man's love for God (Deut. 6:4–8).

8. “We have a little sister,
her breasts are not yet grown;
what shall we do for our sister
when a man comes for her?
9. If she were a wall
we would build a silver watchtower;
if a door,
then we would bar her up with cedar.”
10. But I am a wall.
My breasts are like towers.
It was when I was so
that I found peace
in his eyes.
11. Once, Solomon had a vineyard at Ba’al Hamon.
He gave the vineyard over to the keepers;
each keeper brought him in
a silver thousand from the fruits.
12. My vineyard stands before me, my own:
Solomon, keep your thousand; pay
two-hundred to each keeper of the vines.
13. “You who still sit in the gardens,
friends listen for your voice.
Have me hear.”
14. Away with you, my beloved,
like a gazelle,
or a young deer,
over perfumed hills.

ח אָחוֹת לָנוּ קְטַנָּה וְשָׁדַיִם אֵין לָהּ מַה־נַּעֲשֶׂה לַאֲחוֹתֵנוּ
ט בַּיּוֹם שֶׁיְּדֻבַּר־בָּהּ: אִם־חוֹמָה הִיא נִבְנֶה עָלֶיהָ טִירַת כָּסֶף וְאִם־
י דֶּלֶת הִיא נָצוּר עָלֶיהָ לוּחַ אָרֶז: אֲנִי חוֹמָה וְשָׁדַי כַּמִּגְדָּלוֹת אָז הָיִיתִי
יא בְעֵינָיו כְּמוֹצְאֵת שָׁלוֹם: כֶּרֶם הָיָה לִשְׁלֹמֹה בְּבַעַל הָמוֹן נָתַן אֶת־
יב הַכֶּרֶם לַנֹּטְרִים אִישׁ יָבִא בְּפִרְיוֹ אֶלֶף כָּסֶף: כַּרְמִי שֶׁלִּי לְפָנָי הָאֶלֶף
יג לְךָ שְׁלֹמֹה וּמָאתַיִם לְנֹטְרִים אֶת־פִּרְיוֹ: הַיּוֹשֶׁבֶת בַּגַּנִּים חֲבֵרִים
יד מַקְשִׁיבִים לְקוֹלֵךְ הַשְׁמִיעִנִי: בְּרַח ׀ דּוֹדִי וּדְמֵה־לְךָ לִצְבִי אוֹ לְעֹפֶר
הָאַיָּלִים עַל הָרֵי בְשָׂמִים:

"My vineyard… my own" – The Song opens and closes on the image of vineyards, and the question of who guards them. Like the garden, the vineyard partly symbolizes the woman herself.

במה מדליקין
HOW WE LIGHT

א בַּמֶּה מַדְלִיקִין וּבַמָּה אֵין מַדְלִיקִין. אֵין מַדְלִיקִין לֹא בְלֶכֶשׁ, וְלֹא בְחֹסֶן, וְלֹא בְכַלָּךְ, וְלֹא בִּפְתִילַת הָאִידָן, וְלֹא בִּפְתִילַת הַמִּדְבָּר, וְלֹא בִירוֹקָה שֶׁעַל פְּנֵי הַמָּיִם. וְלֹא בְזֶפֶת וְלֹא בְשַׁעֲוָה וְלֹא בְשֶׁמֶן קִיק וְלֹא בְשֶׁמֶן שְׂרֵפָה וְלֹא בְאַלְיָה וְלֹא בְחֵלֶב. נַחוּם הַמָּדִי אוֹמֵר: מַדְלִיקִין בְּחֵלֶב מְבֻשָּׁל, וַחֲכָמִים אוֹמְרִים: אֶחָד מְבֻשָּׁל וְאֶחָד שֶׁאֵינוֹ מְבֻשָּׁל, אֵין מַדְלִיקִין בּוֹ.

1. בַּמֶּה מַדְלִיקִין With what wicks may we light the Sabbath lamp and with what may we not light? We may not use a wick of cedar bast, or uncombed flax, or raw silk, or a wick made of willow bast or desert weed, or seaweed. [For oil] we may not use pitch, or wax, or cotton seed oil or [contaminated consecrated] oil that must be destroyed by burning, or fat from sheeps' tails, or tallow. Naḥum the Mede says: We may use boiled tallow. But the Sages say: Whether boiled or not boiled, we may not use it.

*1. **Ner with kik oil.** Samuel said: I asked all the seafarers about it, and they told me that there is a certain bird in the towns of the sea called kik. Rabbi Yitzḥak son of Rav Yehuda said: It is cottonseed oil; Resh Lakish said: Oil from Yonah's kikayon* (Shabbat *21a).*

In Bameh Madlikin, Rav Kook sees a parallel between oil and success, and between the wick and an individual. The loftier kind of success we seek is one which fills a person with inner happiness and raises one's life to a higher plane.

With what wicks may we light? This, the second chapter of the בַּמֶּה מַדְלִיקִין Mishna tractate *Shabbat*, was also added to prolong the service for the benefit of latecomers. Its recitation, however, is also related to an ancient controversy between those who accepted the Oral Law and those (Sadducees, and later, Karaites) who denied it. The latter held that the commandment, "Do not light a fire in any of your dwellings on the Sabbath day" (Ex. 35:3), precluded the use of any light; the former held that it excluded only the act of kindling itself, and not the use of a light that had been lit before Shabbat. Hence the study of the section of the Mishna, part of the Oral Law, that deals with Shabbat lights (*Sefer HaIttim*).

2. [Contaminated consecrated] oil that must be destroyed by burning may not be used for a festival lamp. Rabbi Yishmael says: We may not use tar out of respect for the honor due to the Sabbath. But the Sages permit all these oils: sesame oil, nut oil, radish oil, fish oil, gourd oil, tar or naphtha. Rabbi Tarfon, however, says: We may use only olive oil.

ב אֵין מַדְלִיקִין בְּשֶׁמֶן שְׂרֵפָה בְּיוֹם טוֹב. רַבִּי יִשְׁמָעֵאל אוֹמֵר: אֵין מַדְלִיקִין בְּעִטְרָן מִפְּנֵי כְּבוֹד הַשַּׁבָּת. וַחֲכָמִים מַתִּירִין בְּכָל הַשְּׁמָנִים, בְּשֶׁמֶן שֻׁמְשְׁמִין, בְּשֶׁמֶן אֱגוֹזִים, בְּשֶׁמֶן צְנוֹנוֹת, בְּשֶׁמֶן דָּגִים, בְּשֶׁמֶן פַּקֻּעוֹת, בְּעִטְרָן וּבְנֵפְט. רַבִּי טַרְפוֹן אוֹמֵר: אֵין מַדְלִיקִין אֶלָּא בְּשֶׁמֶן זַיִת בִּלְבָד.

3. No product from a tree may be used as a wick for the Sabbath lamp, except flax. Also no product of a tree can contract "tent" uncleanness, except flax. If a wick was made from a cloth that has been twisted but not singed, Rabbi Eliezer declares, it is susceptible to contamination and may not be used for a Sabbath lamp; but Rabbi Akiva says, it is not susceptible to contamination, and may be used for the Sabbath lamp.

ג כָּל הַיּוֹצֵא מִן הָעֵץ אֵין מַדְלִיקִין בּוֹ, אֶלָּא פִּשְׁתָּן. וְכָל הַיּוֹצֵא מִן הָעֵץ אֵינוֹ מִטַּמֵּא טֻמְאַת אֹהָלִים, אֶלָּא פִּשְׁתָּן. פְּתִילַת הַבֶּגֶד שֶׁקִּפְּלָהּ וְלֹא הִבְהֲבָהּ, רַבִּי אֱלִיעֶזֶר אוֹמֵר: טְמֵאָה הִיא, וְאֵין מַדְלִיקִין בָּהּ. רַבִּי עֲקִיבָא אוֹמֵר: טְהוֹרָה הִיא, וּמַדְלִיקִין בָּהּ.

4. One may not pierce an eggshell, fill it with oil, and put it over the mouth of a lamp so that the oil may drip from it into the lamp, even if the vessel is of earthenware, but Rabbi Yehuda permits it. If, however, the potter had originally attached it to the

This success is akin to the oil which is drawn through the extent of the wick, fully saturating it. Each Talmudic explanation of the term "kik" hints to a success which remains external to the individual.

First, the towns of the sea, though reputably prosperous, were known for their moral corruption. Anyone who pursues success there could be guaranteed that it would not penetrate their inner being nor bring them serenity. True happiness is not found on a distant island, but in the home of every Jew, in a life of modesty, humility and pure-heartedness. The love of family and the Torah awaken the holiest emotions of the heart by the light of the candles in one's home on Shabbat eve.

Second, the cotton plant resembles a grapevine in its form. The grapevine represents happiness, which appears to be internal, but in truth remains external to a person. Ultimately, the heart is empty.

lamp, it is permitted because it constitutes a single vessel. One may not fill a bowl with oil, put it beside a lamp, and put the end of the wick in it so that it draws oil from the bowl; but Rabbi Yehuda permits this.

5. One who extinguishes a lamp because he is afraid of heathens, robbers, or depression, or to enable a sick person to sleep, is not liable [for violating the Sabbath]. If he did it to spare the lamp, or the oil, or the wick, he is liable. Rabbi Yose absolves him in all these cases except that of sparing the wick, because he thereby turns it into charcoal.

ד לֹא יִקֹּב אָדָם שְׁפוֹפֶרֶת שֶׁל בֵּיצָה וִימַלְּאֶנָּה שֶׁמֶן וְיִתְּנֶנָּה עַל פִּי הַנֵּר, בִּשְׁבִיל שֶׁתְּהֵא מְנַטֶּפֶת, וַאֲפִילוּ הִיא שֶׁל חֶרֶס. וְרַבִּי יְהוּדָה מַתִּיר. אֲבָל אִם חִבְּרָהּ הַיּוֹצֵר מִתְּחִלָּה מֻתָּר, מִפְּנֵי שֶׁהוּא כְּלִי אֶחָד. לֹא יְמַלֵּא אָדָם אֶת הַקְּעָרָה שֶׁמֶן וְיִתְּנֶנָּה בְּצַד הַנֵּר וְיִתֵּן רֹאשׁ הַפְּתִילָה בְּתוֹכָהּ, בִּשְׁבִיל שֶׁתְּהֵא שׁוֹאֶבֶת. וְרַבִּי יְהוּדָה מַתִּיר.

ה הַמְכַבֶּה אֶת הַנֵּר מִפְּנֵי שֶׁהוּא מִתְיָרֵא מִפְּנֵי גוֹיִם, מִפְּנֵי לִסְטִים, מִפְּנֵי רוּחַ רָעָה, אוֹ בִּשְׁבִיל הַחוֹלֶה שֶׁיִּישַׁן, פָּטוּר. כְּחָס עַל הַנֵּר, כְּחָס עַל הַשֶּׁמֶן, כְּחָס עַל הַפְּתִילָה, חַיָּב. רַבִּי יוֹסֵי פּוֹטֵר בְּכֻלָּן חוּץ מִן הַפְּתִילָה, מִפְּנֵי שֶׁהוּא עוֹשָׂהּ פֶּחָם.

6. For three transgressions women may die in childbirth: for being careless in observing the laws of menstruation, separating challah [dough-offering], and lighting the Sabbath light.

7. One should say three things at home on the eve of the Sabbath just before dark:

Third, the kikayon of Yonah was here today and gone tomorrow. It highlights an ephemeral happiness, which dissipates all too soon. Because there is no inherent connection between material success and an individual, nothing can be harvested in the long term.

Rather, what our souls yearn for in earnest from Shabbat can only be acquired through hard work and a pure heart. This inherent happiness spreads naturally to the downhearted. This is the success we seek, and this is the oil we light.

2. Rabbi Tarfon says: We only light with olive oil. *The Shabbat lights allude to the enlightenment of the mind, which comes with the holiness of the day of rest. There are many kinds of oil, and there are many kinds of wisdom. Human wisdom can lead to character refinement and can prepare an individual to bring much good to the world. But the purest olive oil, the enlightenment of the Torah, is reserved for Shabbat. It is*

Have you tithed? Have you prepared the Eiruv? Light the Sabbath lamp. If there is doubt whether or not darkness has fallen, we may not tithe definitely untithed produce, nor immerse [unclean] vessels, nor light the Sabbath lamp. We may tithe produce about which there is a doubt whether it has been tithed or not, we may prepare an Eiruv, and insulate hot food.

It was taught, Rabbi Ḥanina said: One should examine his clothing on the eve of the Sabbath before nightfall [to ensure that one is not carrying anything], for one may forget and go out. Rav Yosef said: This is an important law about the Sabbath [for it is easy to forget, and thus inadvertently violate the holiness of the day].

Rabbi Elazar said in the name of Rabbi

ו עַל שָׁלֹשׁ עֲבֵרוֹת נָשִׁים מֵתוֹת בִּשְׁעַת לֵדָתָן, עַל שֶׁאֵינָן זְהִירוֹת בַּנִּדָּה, בְּחַלָּה וּבְהַדְלָקַת הַנֵּר.

ז שְׁלֹשָׁה דְבָרִים צָרִיךְ אָדָם לוֹמַר בְּתוֹךְ בֵּיתוֹ עֶרֶב שַׁבָּת עִם חֲשֵׁכָה: עִשַּׂרְתֶּם, עֵרַבְתֶּם, הַדְלִיקוּ אֶת הַנֵּר. סָפֵק חֲשֵׁכָה סָפֵק אֵינָהּ חֲשֵׁכָה, אֵין מְעַשְּׂרִין אֶת הַוַּדַּאי, וְאֵין מַטְבִּילִין אֶת הַכֵּלִים, וְאֵין מַדְלִיקִין אֶת הַנֵּרוֹת. אֲבָל מְעַשְּׂרִין אֶת הַדְּמַאי, וּמְעָרְבִין וְטוֹמְנִין אֶת הַחַמִּין.

תַּנְיָא, אָמַר רַבִּי חֲנִינָא: חַיָּב אָדָם לְמַשְׁמֵשׁ בְּגָדָיו בְּעֶרֶב שַׁבָּת עִם חֲשֵׁכָה, שֶׁמָּא יִשְׁכַּח וְיֵצֵא. אָמַר רַב יוֹסֵף: הִלְכְתָא רַבְּתָא לְשַׁבְּתָא.

אָמַר רַבִּי אֶלְעָזָר, אָמַר רַבִּי חֲנִינָא: תַּלְמִידֵי חֲכָמִים מַרְבִּים שָׁלוֹם בָּעוֹלָם, שֶׁנֶּאֱמַר: וְכָל־בָּנַיִךְ

impervious to confusion and evil intention. The holiest day is dedicated to the pursuit of the wisdom of the Torah.

6. ***For three transgressions women may die in childbirth.*** *Rav Kook explains that the moment of childbirth signifies the influx of divine energy into a person's home. To bring a new soul into this world, women must first prepare spiritually. The observance of Niddah represents the disruption of a natural animal pattern of sexual engagement in favor of a relationship built on ideals and lofty aspirations. Ḥallah, a portion of dough reserved for the Kohen, shows that a family accepts their interdependence with unique and holy individuals whom they hope will influence their home. The Shabbat lights demonstrate the inner light that a family seeks to reveal in its home through calm*

Ḥanina: The disciples of the Sages increase peace in the world, as it is said, "And all your children shall be taught of the Lord, and great shall be the peace of your children [*banayikh*]." Read not *banayikh*, "your children," but *bonayikh*, "your builders." Those who love Your Torah have great peace; there is no stumbling block for them. May there be peace within your ramparts, prosperity in your palaces. For the sake of my brothers and friends, I shall say, "Peace be within you." For the sake of the House of the Lord our God, I will seek your good. ▸ May the Lord grant strength to His people; may the Lord bless His people with peace.

לִמּוּדֵי יהוה, וְרַב שְׁלוֹם בָּנָיִךְ: אַל תִּקְרֵי בָּנָיִךְ, אֶלָּא בּוֹנָיִךְ. שָׁלוֹם רָב לְאֹהֲבֵי תוֹרָתֶךָ, וְאֵין־לָמוֹ מִכְשׁוֹל: יְהִי־שָׁלוֹם בְּחֵילֵךְ, שַׁלְוָה בְּאַרְמְנוֹתָיִךְ. לְמַעַן אַחַי וְרֵעָי אֲדַבְּרָה־נָּא שָׁלוֹם בָּךְ: לְמַעַן בֵּית־יהוה אֱלֹהֵינוּ אֲבַקְשָׁה טוֹב לָךְ: ◂ יהוה עֹז לְעַמּוֹ יִתֵּן, יהוה יְבָרֵךְ אֶת־עַמּוֹ בַשָּׁלוֹם:

interactions. Every heart rests from sadness and anxiety; every simple delight is sanctified and raised up. With these practices, a family is ready to receive the divine light and a new soul.

7. ***One should say three things at home on the eve of Sabbath.*** *Rav Kook emphasizes the importance of attaining certainty that the most important tasks in one's home have been fulfilled. As Shabbat enters and the holiness of Israel shines brightest, the soul which attains certainty that one's home is completely ready shall be engraved with its light.*

Rabbi Hanina said: One should examine his clothing. *According to Rav Kook, one of the fundamentals of Shabbat is comparing one's external life with one's inner life. The greater the distance is between the two, the greater the alienation one feels from one's true nature. In our external lives, we are constantly pulled by others in many different directions. Shabbat is a process not only of accentuating one's inner life, but also of bringing one's two lives in step with each other. Though one would not violate the spiritual dimension of Shabbat if his clothing are not examined, one would not have achieved a refocusing of one's external life, represented by one's clothing. Therefore, in addition to examining one's clothing, special Shabbat clothing are worn to demonstrate the realignment of one's external life.*

Adapted by Rabbi Sarna from Rav Kook, Olat Riya. *Rav Avraham Yitzḥak Kook, a renowned Halakhist, Kabbalist, and Jewish thinker was the first Chief Rabbi of Israel.*

THE RABBIS' KADDISH

The following prayer, said by mourners, requires the presence of a minyan. A transliteration can be found on page 198.

Mourner: יִתְגַּדַּל Magnified and sanctified
may His great name be,
in the world He created by His will.
May He establish His kingdom in your lifetime
and in your days, and in the lifetime of all the house of Israel,
swiftly and soon –
and say: Amen.

All: May His great name be blessed for ever and all time.

Mourner: Blessed and praised, glorified and exalted,
raised and honored, uplifted and lauded
be the name of the Holy One,
blessed be He, beyond any blessing,
song, praise and consolation
uttered in the world –
and say: Amen.

To Israel, to the teachers,
their disciples and their disciples' disciples,
and to all who engage in the study of Torah,
in this (*In Israel add:* holy) place or elsewhere,
may there come to them
and you great peace,
grace, kindness and compassion,
long life, ample sustenance and deliverance,
from their Father in Heaven –
and say: Amen.

May there be great peace from heaven,
and (good) life for us and all Israel –
and say: Amen.

Bow, take three steps back, as if taking leave of the Divine Presence, then bow, first left, then right, then center, while saying:

May He who makes peace in His high places,
in His compassion make peace for us and all Israel –
and say: Amen.

קדיש דרבנן

The following prayer, said by mourners, requires the presence of a מנין.
A transliteration can be found on page 198.

אבל: **יִתְגַּדַּל וְיִתְקַדַּשׁ שְׁמֵהּ רַבָּא** (קהל: אָמֵן)
בְּעָלְמָא דִּי בְרָא כִרְעוּתֵהּ, וְיַמְלִיךְ מַלְכוּתֵהּ
בְּחַיֵּיכוֹן וּבְיוֹמֵיכוֹן וּבְחַיֵּי דְכָל בֵּית יִשְׂרָאֵל
בַּעֲגָלָא וּבִזְמַן קָרִיב, וְאִמְרוּ אָמֵן. (קהל: אָמֵן)

קהל ואבל: **יְהֵא שְׁמֵהּ רַבָּא מְבָרַךְ לְעָלַם וּלְעָלְמֵי עָלְמַיָּא.**

אבל: **יִתְבָּרַךְ וְיִשְׁתַּבַּח וְיִתְפָּאַר וְיִתְרוֹמַם וְיִתְנַשֵּׂא**
וְיִתְהַדָּר וְיִתְעַלֶּה וְיִתְהַלָּל
שְׁמֵהּ דְּקֻדְשָׁא בְּרִיךְ הוּא (קהל: בְּרִיךְ הוּא)
לְעֵלָּא מִן כָּל בִּרְכָתָא
/בשבת שובה: **לְעֵלָּא לְעֵלָּא מִכָּל בִּרְכָתָא**/
וְשִׁירָתָא, תֻּשְׁבְּחָתָא וְנֶחֱמָתָא
דַּאֲמִירָן בְּעָלְמָא, וְאִמְרוּ אָמֵן. (קהל: אָמֵן)

עַל יִשְׂרָאֵל וְעַל רַבָּנָן
וְעַל תַּלְמִידֵיהוֹן וְעַל כָּל תַּלְמִידֵי תַלְמִידֵיהוֹן
וְעַל כָּל מָאן דְּעָסְקִין בְּאוֹרַיְתָא
דִּי בְּאַתְרָא (בארץ ישראל: **קַדִּישָׁא**) **הָדֵין, וְדִי בְּכָל אֲתַר וַאֲתַר**
יְהֵא לְהוֹן וּלְכוֹן שְׁלָמָא רַבָּא
חִנָּא וְחִסְדָּא, וְרַחֲמֵי, וְחַיֵּי אֲרִיכֵי, וּמְזוֹנֵי רְוִיחֵי
וּפֻרְקָנָא מִן קֳדָם אֲבוּהוֹן דִּי בִשְׁמַיָּא, וְאִמְרוּ אָמֵן. (קהל: אָמֵן)

יְהֵא שְׁלָמָא רַבָּא מִן שְׁמַיָּא
וְחַיִּים (טוֹבִים) עָלֵינוּ וְעַל כָּל יִשְׂרָאֵל, וְאִמְרוּ אָמֵן. (קהל: אָמֵן)

Bow, take three steps back, as if taking leave of the Divine Presence,
then bow, first left, then right, then center, while saying:

עֹשֶׂה שָׁלוֹם/בשבת שובה: **הַשָּׁלוֹם**/ **בִּמְרוֹמָיו**
הוּא יַעֲשֶׂה בְרַחֲמָיו שָׁלוֹם
עָלֵינוּ וְעַל כָּל יִשְׂרָאֵל, וְאִמְרוּ אָמֵן. (קהל: אָמֵן)

KEGAVNA

כְּגַוְנָא Just as the [six lower emanations of God] are unified in the higher world as One, so She [the Divine Presence] is unified below in the mystery of oneness, so that She can be with them above, one alongside One. The Holy One, blessed be He, who is One above, does not sit upon the throne of His glory until She has entered within the mystery of Oneness, like Him, to be one in One. And so we have established the secret of the phrase "the LORD shall be One and His name One" [He shall be One when His name too is One].

The mystery of Shabbat is that Shabbat is united with the mystery of the One so that the mystery of One may rest upon her. In the evening prayer of Shabbat, the holy throne of glory is made One in the mystery of Oneness, and thus made ready for the high and holy King to rest upon it. And when Shabbat enters, the Divine Presence becomes One and separates Herself from the Shadow Side, and She is released from all Her trials, and lingers in the Oneness of the holy light, and adorns Herself, crown upon crown, for the holy King. All the powers of rage and Her accusers flee and pass away from Her, and there is no other power in all the worlds [but Hers]. Then Her face shines with heavenly light, and the holy nation adorns Her here below, while each of its members adorn themselves with new souls. This is how this prayer begins, as they bless Her in joy, their faces shining.

An individual adds:

And they say, "Bless [*et*] the LORD, the blessed One," the word *et* referring to the eve of Shabbat. "Blessed is the LORD, the blessed One," indicates the stream of blessings from the source of life, from where water flows, bringing life to all things. And because it is the source – the mystery of the "sign" – we call it "the blessed," meaning, the outflowing of the well. And since they reach there, they become forever. That is what is meant by "Blessed is the LORD, the blessed One, forever."

---

of the Divine Presence, united with the Holy King who sits enthroned in glory, and a radiance spreads throughout the world, reflected in the shining faces and renewed souls of the community at prayer.

כגונא

זוהר פרשת תרומה

כְּגַוְנָא דְּאִנּוּן מִתְיַחֲדִין לְעֵלָּא בְּאֶחָד, אוֹף הָכִי אִיהִי אִתְיַחֲדַת לְתַתָּא בְּרָזָא דְאֶחָד, לְמֶהֱוֵי עִמְּהוֹן לְעֵלָּא חַד לָקֳבֵל חַד. קֻדְשָׁא בְּרִיךְ הוּא אֶחָד, לְעֵלָּא לָא יָתִיב עַל כֻּרְסְיָא דִיקָרֵיהּ עַד דְּאִיהִי אִתְעֲבִידַת בְּרָזָא דְאֶחָד כְּגַוְנָא דִילֵיהּ, לְמֶהֱוֵי אֶחָד בְּאֶחָד. וְהָא אוּקִימְנָא רָזָא דַיהוה אֶחָד וּשְׁמוֹ אֶחָד.

רָזָא דְשַׁבָּת אִיהִי שַׁבָּת דְּאִתְאַחֲדַת בְּרָזָא דְאֶחָד לְמִשְׁרֵי עֲלַהּ רָזָא דְאֶחָד. צְלוֹתָא דְמַעֲלֵי שַׁבַּתָּא, דְּהָא אִתְאַחֲדַת כֻּרְסְיָא יַקִּירָא קַדִּישָׁא בְּרָזָא דְאֶחָד, וְאִתְתַּקְּנַת לְמִשְׁרֵי עֲלַהּ מַלְכָּא קַדִּישָׁא עִלָּאָה. כַּד עַיִּל שַׁבַּתָּא אִיהִי אִתְיַחֲדַת וְאִתְפָּרְשַׁת מִסִּטְרָא אָחֳרָא, וְכָל דִּינִין מִתְעַבְּרִין מִנַּהּ, וְאִיהִי אִשְׁתְּאָרַת בְּיִחוּדָא דִנְהִירוּ קַדִּישָׁא וְאִתְעַטְּרַת בְּכַמָּה עִטְרִין לְגַבֵּי מַלְכָּא קַדִּישָׁא. וְכָל שֻׁלְטָנֵי רֻגְזִין וּמָארֵי דְדִינָא כֻּלְּהוּ עַרְקִין וְאִתְעַבְּרוּ מִנַּהּ, וְלֵית שֻׁלְטָנָא אָחֳרָא בְּכֻלְּהוּ עָלְמִין. וְאַנְפָּהָא נְהִירִין בִּנְהִירוּ עִלָּאָה וְאִתְעַטְּרַת לְתַתָּא בְּעַמָּא קַדִּישָׁא, וְכֻלְּהוֹן מִתְעַטְּרִין בְּנִשְׁמָתִין חַדְתִּין כְּדֵין שֵׁירוּתָא דִצְלוֹתָא לְבָרְכָא לַהּ בְּחֶדְוָה בִּנְהִירוּ דְאַנְפִּין.

An individual adds:

וְלוֹמַר בָּרְכוּ אֶת יהוה הַמְבֹרָךְ. אֶת דַּיְקָא דָא שַׁבָּת דְּמַעֲלֵי שַׁבַּתָּא. בָּרוּךְ יהוה הַמְבֹרָךְ. דָּא אַפִּיקוּ דְבִרְכָאן מִמְּקוֹרָא דְחַיֵּי וַאֲתַר דְּנָפִיק מִנֵּהּ כָּל שַׁקְיוּ לְאַשְׁקָאָה לְכֹלָּא וּבְגִין דְּאִיהוּ מְקוֹרָא בְּרָזָא דְאָת קַיָּמָא קָרֵינָן לֵיהּ הַמְבֹרָךְ אִיהוּ מַבּוּעָא דְבֵירָא וְכֵיוָן דִּמְטָאן הָתָם הָא כֻלְּהוּ לְעוֹלָם וָעֶד, וְדָא אִיהוּ בָּרוּךְ יהוה הַמְבֹרָךְ לְעוֹלָם וָעֶד.

This mystical passage, taken from the *Zohar* (II: 134–135), describes the ultimate unity at the heart of diversity, a unity that transcends normal categories of thought, and is thus a "mystery," but one to which we aspire in prayer and the life of the commands, as we try to mend the fractures of a still-broken world. A sense of this unity is especially evident on Shabbat when harmony below mirrors the harmony above. As Shabbat begins, all negative and fractious forces fade. The spirit of Shabbat enters, personified as the female figure

ליל שבת

LEIL SHABBAT

Ma'ariv for Shabbat

BLESSINGS OF THE SHEMA

The Leader says the following, bowing at "Bless," standing straight at "the LORD." The congregation, followed by the Leader, responds, bowing at "Bless," standing straight at "the LORD."

Leader: **BLESS**
the LORD, the blessed One.

Congregation: Bless the LORD, the blessed One,
for ever and all time.

Leader: Bless the LORD, the blessed One,
for ever and all time.

בָּרוּךְ Blessed are You, LORD our God, King of the Universe,
who by His word brings on evenings,
by His wisdom opens the gates of heaven,
with understanding makes time change and the seasons rotate,
and by His will orders the stars in their constellations in the sky.
He creates day and night,
rolling away the light before the darkness,
and darkness before the light.
▸ He makes the day pass and brings on night,
distinguishing day from night:
the LORD of hosts is His name.
May the living and forever enduring God rule over us for all time.
Blessed are You, LORD, who brings on evenings.

אֲשֶׁר בִּדְבָרוֹ מַעֲרִיב עֲרָבִים *Who by His word brings on evenings:* The three key Jewish beliefs are creation (that God made the universe), revelation (that God speaks to mankind), and redemption (that God rescues humanity,

מעריב לשבת

קריאת שמע וברכותיה

The שליח ציבור *says the following, bowing at* בָּרְכוּ*, standing straight at* ה׳*.*
The קהל*, followed by the* שליח ציבור*, responds, bowing at* בָּרוּךְ*, standing straight at* ה׳*.*

ש״ץ: **בָּרְכוּ**
אֶת יהוה הַמְבֹרָךְ.

קהל: בָּרוּךְ יהוה הַמְבֹרָךְ לְעוֹלָם וָעֶד.

ש״ץ: בָּרוּךְ יהוה הַמְבֹרָךְ לְעוֹלָם וָעֶד.

בָּרוּךְ אַתָּה יהוה אֱלֹהֵינוּ מֶלֶךְ הָעוֹלָם
אֲשֶׁר בִּדְבָרוֹ מַעֲרִיב עֲרָבִים
בְּחָכְמָה פּוֹתֵחַ שְׁעָרִים
וּבִתְבוּנָה מְשַׁנֶּה עִתִּים וּמַחֲלִיף אֶת הַזְּמַנִּים
וּמְסַדֵּר אֶת הַכּוֹכָבִים בְּמִשְׁמְרוֹתֵיהֶם בָּרָקִיעַ כִּרְצוֹנוֹ.
בּוֹרֵא יוֹם וָלַיְלָה, גּוֹלֵל אוֹר מִפְּנֵי חֹשֶׁךְ וְחֹשֶׁךְ מִפְּנֵי אוֹר
◂ וּמַעֲבִיר יוֹם וּמֵבִיא לַיְלָה
וּמַבְדִּיל בֵּין יוֹם וּבֵין לַיְלָה
יהוה צְבָאוֹת שְׁמוֹ.
אֵל חַי וְקַיָּם תָּמִיד, יִמְלֹךְ עָלֵינוּ לְעוֹלָם וָעֶד.
בָּרוּךְ אַתָּה יהוה, הַמַּעֲרִיב עֲרָבִים.

אַהֲבַת עוֹלָם With everlasting love
have You loved Your people, the house of Israel.
You have taught us Torah and commandments,
decrees and laws of justice.
Therefore, Lord our God, when we lie down and when we rise up
we will speak of Your decrees, rejoicing in the words of Your Torah
and Your commandments for ever.
▸ For they are our life and the length of our days;
on them will we meditate day and night.
May You never take away Your love from us.
Blessed are You, Lord, who loves His people Israel.

The Shema must be said with intense concentration.
When not with a minyan, say:
God, faithful King!

The following verse should be said aloud, while covering the eyes with the right hand:

Listen, Israel: the Lord is our God, the Lord is One.

Deut. 6

Quietly: Blessed be the name of His glorious kingdom for ever and all time.

וְאָהַבְתָּ Love the Lord your God with all your heart, with all your soul, and with all your might. These words which I command you today shall be on your heart. Teach them repeatedly to your children, speaking of them when you sit at home and when you travel on the way, when you lie down and when you rise. Bind them as a sign on your hand, and they shall be an emblem between your eyes. Write them on the doorposts of your house and gates. *Deut. 6*

---

the people of Israel pour out their thanks for the gift of Torah and its "commandments, decrees and laws of justice." Here, law becomes love and love becomes law. God unites us to Him by teaching us how to act in accordance with His will – which becomes in turn "our life and the length of our days."

שְׁמַע יִשְׂרָאֵל *Listen, Israel: Shema* means not only "to hear" but also "to listen, understand, internalize, respond and obey." It is translated here as "Listen"

אַהֲבַת עוֹלָם בֵּית יִשְׂרָאֵל עַמְּךָ אָהָבְתָּ
תּוֹרָה וּמִצְוֹת, חֻקִּים וּמִשְׁפָּטִים, אוֹתָנוּ לִמַּדְתָּ
עַל כֵּן יהוה אֱלֹהֵינוּ בְּשָׁכְבֵנוּ וּבְקוּמֵנוּ נָשִׂיחַ בְּחֻקֶּיךָ
וְנִשְׂמַח בְּדִבְרֵי תוֹרָתֶךָ וּבְמִצְוֹתֶיךָ לְעוֹלָם וָעֶד
‹ כִּי הֵם חַיֵּינוּ וְאֹרֶךְ יָמֵינוּ, וּבָהֶם נֶהְגֶּה יוֹמָם וָלָיְלָה.
וְאַהֲבָתְךָ אַל תָּסִיר מִמֶּנּוּ לְעוֹלָמִים.
בָּרוּךְ אַתָּה יהוה, אוֹהֵב עַמּוֹ יִשְׂרָאֵל.

The שמע must be said with intense concentration.
When not with a מנין, say:

אֵל מֶלֶךְ נֶאֱמָן

The following verse should be said aloud, while covering the eyes with the right hand:

דברים ו **שְׁמַע יִשְׂרָאֵל, יהוה אֱלֹהֵינוּ, יהוה | אֶחָד:**

Quietly בָּרוּךְ שֵׁם כְּבוֹד מַלְכוּתוֹ לְעוֹלָם וָעֶד.

דברים ו וְאָהַבְתָּ אֵת יהוה אֱלֹהֶיךָ, בְּכָל־לְבָבְךָ וּבְכָל־נַפְשְׁךָ וּבְכָל־
מְאֹדֶךָ: וְהָיוּ הַדְּבָרִים הָאֵלֶּה, אֲשֶׁר אָנֹכִי מְצַוְּךָ הַיּוֹם, עַל־לְבָבֶךָ:
וְשִׁנַּנְתָּם לְבָנֶיךָ וְדִבַּרְתָּ בָּם, בְּשִׁבְתְּךָ בְּבֵיתֶךָ וּבְלֶכְתְּךָ בַדֶּרֶךְ,
וּבְשָׁכְבְּךָ וּבְקוּמֶךָ: וּקְשַׁרְתָּם לְאוֹת עַל־יָדֶךָ וְהָיוּ לְטֹטָפֹת בֵּין
עֵינֶיךָ: וּכְתַבְתָּם עַל־מְזֻזוֹת בֵּיתֶךָ וּבִשְׁעָרֶיךָ:

---

teaching us how to act with justice and compassion). The blessings surrounding the *Shema* are constructed on this pattern. This, the first, speaks of creation – heaven and earth, light and darkness, day and night. The next speaks of revelation, God's gift of the Torah to the children of Israel. The third, immediately after the *Shema,* speaks of redemption ("who redeemed Israel"). The siddur is our tutorial in belief, teaching us to see the world through the eyes of faith.

אַהֲבַת עוֹלָם *With everlasting love:* Nothing more eloquently refutes the idea that Judaism is a dry, legalistic religion than this magnificent poem in which

וְהָיָה If you indeed heed My commandments with which I charge *Deut. 11*
you today, to love the LORD your God and worship Him with all your heart and with all your soul, I will give rain in your land in its season, the early and late rain; and you shall gather in your grain, wine and oil. I will give grass in your field for your cattle, and you shall eat and be satisfied. Be careful lest your heart be tempted and you go astray and worship other gods, bowing down to them. Then the LORD's anger will flare against you and He will close the heavens so that there will be no rain. The land will not yield its crops, and you will perish swiftly from the good land that the LORD is giving you. Therefore, set these, My words, on your heart and soul. Bind them as a sign on your hand, and they shall be an emblem between your eyes. Teach them to your children, speaking of them when you sit at home and when you travel on the way, when you lie down and when you rise. Write them on the doorposts of your house and gates, so that you and your children may live long in the land that the LORD swore to your ancestors to give them, for as long as the heavens are above the earth.

וַיֹּאמֶר The LORD spoke to Moses, saying: Speak to the Israelites *Num. 15*
and tell them to make tassels on the corners of their garments for all generations. They shall attach to the tassel at each corner a thread of blue. This shall be your tassel, and you shall see it and remember all of the LORD's commandments and keep them, not straying after your heart and after your eyes, following your own sinful desires. Thus you will be reminded to keep all My

---

Secular terms for understanding are permeated with visual images. We speak of insight, foresight, vision, observation, perspective; when we understand, we say "I see." Judaism, with its belief in an invisible, transcendent God, is a culture of the ear, not the eye. The patriarchs and prophets did not see God; they heard Him. To emphasize the non-visual nature of Jewish belief, it is our custom to cover our eyes as we say these words.

דברים יא וְהָיָה אִם־שָׁמֹעַ תִּשְׁמְעוּ אֶל־מִצְוֺתַי אֲשֶׁר אָנֹכִי מְצַוֶּה אֶתְכֶם
הַיּוֹם, לְאַהֲבָה אֶת־יהוה אֱלֹהֵיכֶם וּלְעָבְדוֹ, בְּכָל־לְבַבְכֶם וּבְכָל־
נַפְשְׁכֶם: וְנָתַתִּי מְטַר־אַרְצְכֶם בְּעִתּוֹ, יוֹרֶה וּמַלְקוֹשׁ, וְאָסַפְתָּ דְגָנֶךָ
וְתִירֹשְׁךָ וְיִצְהָרֶךָ: וְנָתַתִּי עֵשֶׂב בְּשָׂדְךָ לִבְהֶמְתֶּךָ, וְאָכַלְתָּ וְשָׂבָעְתָּ:
הִשָּׁמְרוּ לָכֶם פֶּן־יִפְתֶּה לְבַבְכֶם, וְסַרְתֶּם וַעֲבַדְתֶּם אֱלֹהִים אֲחֵרִים
וְהִשְׁתַּחֲוִיתֶם לָהֶם: וְחָרָה אַף־יהוה בָּכֶם, וְעָצַר אֶת־הַשָּׁמַיִם
וְלֹא־יִהְיֶה מָטָר, וְהָאֲדָמָה לֹא תִתֵּן אֶת־יְבוּלָהּ, וַאֲבַדְתֶּם מְהֵרָה
מֵעַל הָאָרֶץ הַטֹּבָה אֲשֶׁר יהוה נֹתֵן לָכֶם: וְשַׂמְתֶּם אֶת־דְּבָרַי
אֵלֶּה עַל־לְבַבְכֶם וְעַל־נַפְשְׁכֶם, וּקְשַׁרְתֶּם אֹתָם לְאוֹת עַל־יֶדְכֶם,
וְהָיוּ לְטוֹטָפֹת בֵּין עֵינֵיכֶם: וְלִמַּדְתֶּם אֹתָם אֶת־בְּנֵיכֶם לְדַבֵּר בָּם,
בְּשִׁבְתְּךָ בְּבֵיתֶךָ, וּבְלֶכְתְּךָ בַדֶּרֶךְ וּבְשָׁכְבְּךָ וּבְקוּמֶךָ: וּכְתַבְתָּם
עַל־מְזוּזוֹת בֵּיתֶךָ וּבִשְׁעָרֶיךָ: לְמַעַן יִרְבּוּ יְמֵיכֶם וִימֵי בְנֵיכֶם עַל
הָאֲדָמָה אֲשֶׁר נִשְׁבַּע יהוה לַאֲבֹתֵיכֶם לָתֵת לָהֶם, כִּימֵי הַשָּׁמַיִם
עַל־הָאָרֶץ:

במדבר טו וַיֹּאמֶר יהוה אֶל־מֹשֶׁה לֵּאמֹר: דַּבֵּר אֶל־בְּנֵי יִשְׂרָאֵל וְאָמַרְתָּ
אֲלֵהֶם, וְעָשׂוּ לָהֶם צִיצִת עַל־כַּנְפֵי בִגְדֵיהֶם לְדֹרֹתָם, וְנָתְנוּ עַל־
צִיצִת הַכָּנָף פְּתִיל תְּכֵלֶת: וְהָיָה לָכֶם לְצִיצִת, וּרְאִיתֶם אֹתוֹ,
וּזְכַרְתֶּם אֶת־כָּל־מִצְוֺת יהוה וַעֲשִׂיתֶם אֹתָם, וְלֹא תָתֻרוּ אַחֲרֵי
לְבַבְכֶם וְאַחֲרֵי עֵינֵיכֶם, אֲשֶׁר־אַתֶּם זֹנִים אַחֲרֵיהֶם: לְמַעַן תִּזְכְּרוּ

---

because listening is active, while hearing is passive. This, the most famous line of Jewish prayer, is a call to action on the part of the mind, emotion and will. It asks us to reflect on, strive to understand, and to affirm the unity of God. God speaks in a "still, small voice" (1 Kings 19:12), and to serve Him is to listen with the totality of our being.

commandments, and be holy to your God. I am the Lord your God, who brought you out of the land of Egypt to be your God. I am the Lord your God.

True –

The Leader repeats:

▸ The Lord your God is true –

וֶאֱמוּנָה – and faithful is all this,
and firmly established for us
that He is the Lord our God,
and there is none beside Him,
and that we, Israel, are His people.
He is our King, who redeems us from the hand of kings
and delivers us from the grasp of all tyrants.
He is our God,
who on our behalf repays our foes
and brings just retribution on our mortal enemies;
who performs great deeds beyond understanding
and wonders beyond number;
who kept us alive, not letting our foot slip;
who led us on the high places of our enemies,
raising our pride above all our foes;
who did miracles for us
and brought vengeance against Pharaoh;
who performed signs and wonders
in the land of Ham's children;
who smote in His wrath all the firstborn of Egypt,
and brought out His people Israel from their midst
into everlasting freedom;
who led His children through the divided Reed Sea,
plunging their pursuers and enemies into the depths.

וַעֲשִׂיתֶם אֶת־כָּל־מִצְוֹתָי, וִהְיִיתֶם קְדֹשִׁים לֵאלֹהֵיכֶם: אֲנִי יְהוָה
אֱלֹהֵיכֶם, אֲשֶׁר הוֹצֵאתִי אֶתְכֶם מֵאֶרֶץ מִצְרַיִם, לִהְיוֹת לָכֶם
לֵאלֹהִים, אֲנִי יְהוָה אֱלֹהֵיכֶם:

אֱמֶת

The שליח ציבור *repeats:*

‹ יהוה אֱלֹהֵיכֶם אֱמֶת

וֶאֱמוּנָה כָּל זֹאת וְקַיָּם עָלֵינוּ
כִּי הוּא יהוה אֱלֹהֵינוּ וְאֵין זוּלָתוֹ
וַאֲנַחְנוּ יִשְׂרָאֵל עַמּוֹ.
הַפּוֹדֵנוּ מִיַּד מְלָכִים
מַלְכֵּנוּ הַגּוֹאֲלֵנוּ מִכַּף כָּל הֶעָרִיצִים.
הָאֵל הַנִּפְרָע לָנוּ מִצָּרֵינוּ
וְהַמְשַׁלֵּם גְּמוּל לְכָל אוֹיְבֵי נַפְשֵׁנוּ.
הָעוֹשֶׂה גְדוֹלוֹת עַד אֵין חֵקֶר, וְנִפְלָאוֹת עַד אֵין מִסְפָּר
הַשָּׂם נַפְשֵׁנוּ בַּחַיִּים, וְלֹא נָתַן לַמּוֹט רַגְלֵנוּ
הַמַּדְרִיכֵנוּ עַל בָּמוֹת אוֹיְבֵינוּ
וַיָּרֶם קַרְנֵנוּ עַל כָּל שׂוֹנְאֵינוּ.
הָעוֹשֶׂה לָּנוּ נִסִּים וּנְקָמָה בְּפַרְעֹה
אוֹתוֹת וּמוֹפְתִים בְּאַדְמַת בְּנֵי חָם.
הַמַּכֶּה בְעֶבְרָתוֹ כָּל בְּכוֹרֵי מִצְרָיִם
וַיּוֹצֵא אֶת עַמּוֹ יִשְׂרָאֵל מִתּוֹכָם לְחֵרוּת עוֹלָם.
הַמַּעֲבִיר בָּנָיו בֵּין גִּזְרֵי יַם סוּף
אֶת רוֹדְפֵיהֶם וְאֶת שׂוֹנְאֵיהֶם בִּתְהוֹמוֹת טִבַּע

When His children saw His might,
they gave praise and thanks to His name,
▸ and willingly accepted His Sovereignty.
Moses and the children of Israel
then sang a song to You with great joy, and they all exclaimed:

"Who is like You, LORD, among the mighty? *Ex. 15*
Who is like You, majestic in holiness,
awesome in praises, doing wonders?"

▸ Your children beheld Your majesty
as You parted the sea before Moses.
"This is my God!" they responded, and then said:

"The LORD shall reign for ever and ever." *Ex. 15*

▸ And it is said,
"For the LORD has redeemed Jacob *Jer. 31*
and rescued him from a power stronger than his own."
Blessed are You, LORD, who redeemed Israel.

הַשְׁכִּיבֵנוּ Help us lie down, O LORD our God, in peace,
and rise up, O our King, to life.
Spread over us Your canopy of peace.
Direct us with Your good counsel,
and save us for the sake of Your name.
Shield us and remove from us every enemy,
plague, sword, famine and sorrow.
Remove the adversary from before and behind us.
Shelter us in the shadow of Your wings,
for You, God, are our Guardian and Deliverer;
You, God, are a gracious and compassionate King.
▸ Guard our going out and our coming in,
for life and peace, from now and for ever.
Spread over us Your canopy of peace.
Blessed are You, LORD, who spreads a canopy of peace over us,
over all His people Israel, and over Jerusalem.

וְרָאוּ בָנָיו גְּבוּרָתוֹ, שִׁבְּחוּ וְהוֹדוּ לִשְׁמוֹ

◂ וּמַלְכוּתוֹ בְּרָצוֹן קִבְּלוּ עֲלֵיהֶם.

מֹשֶׁה וּבְנֵי יִשְׂרָאֵל, לְךָ עָנוּ שִׁירָה בְּשִׂמְחָה רַבָּה

וְאָמְרוּ כֻלָּם

מִי־כָמֹכָה בָּאֵלִם יהוה שמות טו

מִי כָּמֹכָה נֶאְדָּר בַּקֹּדֶשׁ

נוֹרָא תְהִלֹּת עֹשֵׂה פֶלֶא:

◂ מַלְכוּתְךָ רָאוּ בָנֶיךָ, בּוֹקֵעַ יָם לִפְנֵי מֹשֶׁה

זֶה אֵלִי עָנוּ, וְאָמְרוּ

יהוה יִמְלֹךְ לְעֹלָם וָעֶד: שמות טו

◂ וְנֶאֱמַר

כִּי־פָדָה יהוה אֶת־יַעֲקֹב, וּגְאָלוֹ מִיַּד חָזָק מִמֶּנּוּ: ירמיהו לא

בָּרוּךְ אַתָּה יהוה, גָּאַל יִשְׂרָאֵל.

הַשְׁכִּיבֵנוּ יהוה אֱלֹהֵינוּ לְשָׁלוֹם, וְהַעֲמִידֵנוּ מַלְכֵּנוּ לְחַיִּים

וּפְרֹשׂ עָלֵינוּ סֻכַּת שְׁלוֹמֶךָ, וְתַקְּנֵנוּ בְּעֵצָה טוֹבָה מִלְּפָנֶיךָ

וְהוֹשִׁיעֵנוּ לְמַעַן שְׁמֶךָ.

וְהָגֵן בַּעֲדֵנוּ, וְהָסֵר מֵעָלֵינוּ אוֹיֵב, דֶּבֶר וְחֶרֶב וְרָעָב וְיָגוֹן

וְהָסֵר שָׂטָן מִלְּפָנֵינוּ וּמֵאַחֲרֵינוּ, וּבְצֵל כְּנָפֶיךָ תַּסְתִּירֵנוּ

כִּי אֵל שׁוֹמְרֵנוּ וּמַצִּילֵנוּ אָתָּה

כִּי אֵל מֶלֶךְ חַנּוּן וְרַחוּם אָתָּה.

◂ וּשְׁמֹר צֵאתֵנוּ וּבוֹאֵנוּ לְחַיִּים וּלְשָׁלוֹם מֵעַתָּה וְעַד עוֹלָם.

וּפְרֹשׂ עָלֵינוּ סֻכַּת שְׁלוֹמֶךָ.

בָּרוּךְ אַתָּה יהוה

הַפּוֹרֵשׂ סֻכַּת שָׁלוֹם עָלֵינוּ וְעַל כָּל עַמּוֹ יִשְׂרָאֵל וְעַל יְרוּשָׁלָיִם.

The congregation stands and, together with the Leader, says:

וְשָׁמְרוּ The children of Israel must keep the Sabbath, *Ex. 31*
observing the Sabbath in every generation
as an everlasting covenant.
It is a sign between Me and the children of Israel for ever,
for in six days God made the heavens and the earth,
but on the seventh day He ceased work
and refreshed Himself.

HALF KADDISH

Leader: יִתְגַּדַּל Magnified and sanctified may His great name be,
in the world He created by His will.
May He establish His kingdom
in your lifetime and in your days,
and in the lifetime of all the house of Israel,
swiftly and soon –
and say: Amen.

All: May His great name be blessed
for ever and all time.

Leader: Blessed and praised,
glorified and exalted,
raised and honored,
uplifted and lauded
be the name of the Holy One,
blessed be He,
beyond any blessing,
song, praise and consolation
uttered in the world –
and say: Amen.

The קהל *stands and, together with the* שליח ציבור*, says:*

וְשָׁמְרוּ בְנֵי־יִשְׂרָאֵל אֶת־הַשַּׁבָּת שמות לא
לַעֲשׂוֹת אֶת־הַשַּׁבָּת לְדֹרֹתָם בְּרִית עוֹלָם:
בֵּינִי וּבֵין בְּנֵי יִשְׂרָאֵל, אוֹת הִוא לְעֹלָם
כִּי־שֵׁשֶׁת יָמִים עָשָׂה יהוה אֶת־הַשָּׁמַיִם וְאֶת־הָאָרֶץ
וּבַיּוֹם הַשְּׁבִיעִי שָׁבַת וַיִּנָּפַשׁ:

חצי קדיש

ש״ץ: יִתְגַּדַּל וְיִתְקַדַּשׁ שְׁמֵהּ רַבָּא (קהל: אָמֵן)
בְּעָלְמָא דִּי בְרָא כִרְעוּתֵהּ
וְיַמְלִיךְ מַלְכוּתֵהּ
בְּחַיֵּיכוֹן וּבְיוֹמֵיכוֹן וּבְחַיֵּי דְכָל בֵּית יִשְׂרָאֵל
בַּעֲגָלָא וּבִזְמַן קָרִיב
וְאִמְרוּ אָמֵן. (קהל: אָמֵן)

קהל וש״ץ: יְהֵא שְׁמֵהּ רַבָּא מְבָרַךְ לְעָלַם וּלְעָלְמֵי עָלְמַיָּא.

ש״ץ: יִתְבָּרַךְ וְיִשְׁתַּבַּח וְיִתְפָּאַר וְיִתְרוֹמַם וְיִתְנַשֵּׂא
וְיִתְהַדָּר וְיִתְעַלֶּה וְיִתְהַלָּל
שְׁמֵהּ דְּקֻדְשָׁא בְּרִיךְ הוּא (קהל: בְּרִיךְ הוּא)
לְעֵלָּא מִן כָּל בִּרְכָתָא
/בשבת שובה: לְעֵלָּא לְעֵלָּא מִכָּל בִּרְכָתָא/
וְשִׁירָתָא, תֻּשְׁבְּחָתָא וְנֶחֱמָתָא, דַּאֲמִירָן בְּעָלְמָא
וְאִמְרוּ אָמֵן. (קהל: אָמֵן)

THE AMIDA

The following prayer, until "in former years" on page 142, is said silently, standing with feet together. Take three steps forward and at the points indicated by ▾, bend the knees at the first word, bow at the second, and stand straight before saying God's name.

O Lord, open my lips, Ps. 51
so that my mouth may declare Your praise.

PATRIARCHS

▾בָּרוּךְ▾ Blessed are You, Lord our God and God of our fathers,
God of Abraham, God of Isaac and God of Jacob;
the great, mighty and awesome God, God Most High,
who bestows acts of loving-kindness and creates all,
who remembers the loving-kindness of the fathers
and will bring a Redeemer to their children's children
for the sake of His name, in love.

On Shabbat Shuva: Remember us for life, O King who desires life,
and write us in the book of life –
for Your sake, O God of life.

King, Helper, Savior, Shield:
▾Blessed are You, Lord, Shield of Abraham.

---

evening, we think of the birth of time; in the morning, of historical time, the remembered past and the living present; and in the afternoon, of the culmination of time, and the World to Come of which Shabbat is the foretaste. Shabbat becomes a journey through the three phases of faith: God's creation of the universe, His self-revelation to humanity, and His redemptive acts – collectively summoning us to build a world at peace with itself because it is at peace with God.

Another interpretation sees in the three stages of Shabbat the three parts of a wedding: first betrothal, *kiddushin*; then the marriage itself, symbolized by joy; then *yiḥud*, the coming together of the bride and groom (Abudarham). This idea, reflected in the language of the Amida, accords with the mystical understanding of Shabbat as a bride, and the day itself as a marriage of heaven and earth.

עמידה

The following prayer, until קַדְמֹנִיּוֹת on page 143, is said silently, standing with feet together. Take three steps forward and at the points indicated by ˅*, bend the knees at the first word, bow at the second, and stand straight before saying God's name.*

תהלים נא אֲדֹנָי, שְׂפָתַי תִּפְתָּח, וּפִי יַגִּיד תְּהִלָּתֶךָ:

אבות

˅בָּרוּךְ אַתָּה יהוה, אֱלֹהֵינוּ וֵאלֹהֵי אֲבוֹתֵינוּ
אֱלֹהֵי אַבְרָהָם, אֱלֹהֵי יִצְחָק, וֵאלֹהֵי יַעֲקֹב
הָאֵל הַגָּדוֹל הַגִּבּוֹר וְהַנּוֹרָא, אֵל עֶלְיוֹן
גּוֹמֵל חֲסָדִים טוֹבִים, וְקֹנֵה הַכֹּל
וְזוֹכֵר חַסְדֵי אָבוֹת
וּמֵבִיא גוֹאֵל לִבְנֵי בְנֵיהֶם לְמַעַן שְׁמוֹ בְּאַהֲבָה.

בשבת שובה: זָכְרֵנוּ לְחַיִּים, מֶלֶךְ חָפֵץ בַּחַיִּים
וְכָתְבֵנוּ בְּסֵפֶר הַחַיִּים, לְמַעַנְךָ אֱלֹהִים חַיִּים.

מֶלֶךְ עוֹזֵר וּמוֹשִׁיעַ וּמָגֵן.
˅בָּרוּךְ אַתָּה יהוה, מָגֵן אַבְרָהָם.

THE FRIDAY NIGHT AMIDA

On Shabbat and Yom Tov, the Amida, the "standing prayer," consists not of nineteen but seven blessings (in Musaf of Rosh HaShana, nine). The first and last three are, with minor variations, the same throughout the year. The seventh (middle) blessing is dedicated to the special "sanctity of the day." Uniquely on Shabbat, this blessing is different for each of the three services; evening, morning and afternoon (the Musaf prayer is in a category of its own). The quality of time on Shabbat is different from other days: like a symphony, it has several movements.

On Friday evening, we speak of the Shabbat of creation; in the morning, of the Shabbat of revelation, as it was commanded on Mount Sinai; and in the afternoon, we look forward to the Shabbat of redemption. Thus in the

DIVINE MIGHT

אַתָּה גִּבּוֹר You are eternally mighty, LORD.
You give life to the dead and have great power to save.

The phrase "He makes the wind blow and the rain fall" is added from Simḥat Torah until Pesaḥ. In Israel, the phrase "He causes the dew to fall" is added from Pesaḥ until Shemini Atzeret.

In fall & winter: He makes the wind blow and the rain fall.
In Israel, in spring & summer: He causes the dew to fall.

He sustains the living with loving-kindness,
and with great compassion revives the dead.
He supports the fallen, heals the sick, sets captives free,
and keeps His faith with those who sleep in the dust.
Who is like You, Master of might, and who can compare to You,
O King who brings death and gives life, and makes salvation grow?

On Shabbat Shuva: Who is like You, compassionate Father,
who remembers His creatures in compassion, for life?

Faithful are You to revive the dead.
Blessed are You, LORD, who revives the dead.

HOLINESS

אַתָּה קָדוֹשׁ You are holy and Your name is holy,
and holy ones praise You daily, Selah!
Blessed are You, LORD,
the holy God. / *On Shabbat Shuva:* the holy King./
(If forgotten, repeat the Amida.)

HOLINESS OF THE DAY

אַתָּה קִדַּשְׁתָּ You sanctified the seventh day
for Your name's sake,
as the culmination of the creation of heaven and earth.
Of all days, You blessed it; of all seasons You sanctified it –
and so it is written in Your Torah:

---

ning of time: the seventh day of creation when God rested and the universe was young. It also uses the word "sanctified," the key word of the betrothal declaration under the bridal canopy.

גבורות

אַתָּה גִּבּוֹר לְעוֹלָם, אֲדֹנָי
מְחַיֵּה מֵתִים אַתָּה, רַב לְהוֹשִׁיעַ

The phrase מַשִּׁיב הָרְוּחַ *is added from* שמחת תורה *until* פסח.
In ארץ ישראל *the phrase* מוֹרִיד הַטָּל *is added from* פסח *until* שמיני עצרת.

בחורף: מַשִּׁיב הָרְוּחַ וּמוֹרִיד הַגֶּשֶׁם / בארץ ישראל בקיץ: מוֹרִיד הַטָּל

מְכַלְכֵּל חַיִּים בְּחֶסֶד, מְחַיֵּה מֵתִים בְּרַחֲמִים רַבִּים
סוֹמֵךְ נוֹפְלִים, וְרוֹפֵא חוֹלִים, וּמַתִּיר אֲסוּרִים
וּמְקַיֵּם אֱמוּנָתוֹ לִישֵׁנֵי עָפָר.
מִי כָמְוֹךָ, בַּעַל גְּבוּרוֹת, וּמִי דּוֹמֶה לָּךְ
מֶלֶךְ, מֵמִית וּמְחַיֶּה וּמַצְמִיחַ יְשׁוּעָה.

בשבת שובה: מִי כָמְוֹךָ אַב הָרַחֲמִים, זוֹכֵר יְצוּרָיו לְחַיִּים בְּרַחֲמִים.

וְנֶאֱמָן אַתָּה לְהַחֲיוֹת מֵתִים.
בָּרוּךְ אַתָּה יהוה, מְחַיֵּה הַמֵּתִים.

קדושת השם

אַתָּה קָדוֹשׁ וְשִׁמְךָ קָדוֹשׁ, וּקְדוֹשִׁים בְּכָל יוֹם יְהַלְלְוּךָ סֶּלָה.
בָּרוּךְ אַתָּה יהוה, הָאֵל הַקָּדוֹשׁ. / בשבת שובה: הַמֶּלֶךְ הַקָּדוֹשׁ./
(*If forgotten, repeat the* עמידה.)

קדושת היום

אַתָּה קִדַּשְׁתָּ אֶת יוֹם הַשְּׁבִיעִי לִשְׁמֶךָ
תַּכְלִית מַעֲשֵׂה שָׁמַיִם וָאָרֶץ
וּבֵרַכְתּוֹ מִכָּל הַיָּמִים, וְקִדַּשְׁתּוֹ מִכָּל הַזְּמַנִּים
וְכֵן כָּתוּב בְּתוֹרָתֶךָ

אַתָּה קִדַּשְׁתָּ *You sanctified:* As signaled above, the Friday evening blessing speaks of creation: "You sanctified the seventh day for Your name's sake, as the culmination of the creation of heaven and earth." It refers to the begin-

וַיְכֻלּוּ Then the heavens and the earth were completed, Gen. 2
and all their array.
With the seventh day, God completed the work He had done.
He ceased on the seventh day from all the work He had done.
God blessed the seventh day and declared it holy,
because on it He ceased from all His work
He had created to do.

אֱלֹהֵינוּ Our God and God of our ancestors,
may You find favor in our rest.
Make us holy through Your commandments
and grant us our share in Your Torah.
Satisfy us with Your goodness, grant us joy in Your salvation,
and purify our hearts to serve You in truth.
In love and favor, O Lord our God,
grant us as our heritage Your holy Shabbat,
so that Israel, who sanctify Your name, may find rest on it.
Blessed are You, Lord, who sanctifies the Sabbath.

TEMPLE SERVICE

רְצֵה Find favor, Lord our God,
in Your people Israel and their prayer.
Restore the service to Your most holy House,
and accept in love and favor
the fire-offerings of Israel and their prayer.
May the service of Your people Israel
always find favor with You.

וַיְקַדֵּשׁ אֹתוֹ *And declared it holy:* This is the first time the word "holy" appears in the Torah, indicating that time, not just space, is holy. The Sages noted the similarities between Shabbat and the Sanctuary (*mishkan*) constructed by the Israelites in the wilderness. The 39 categories of work performed in the building of the Sanctuary are the same as those forbidden on Shabbat. Shabbat is thus a "sanctuary in time," and Israel, the "eternal people," is the nation called on to sanctify time.

בראשית ב

וַיְכֻלּוּ הַשָּׁמַיִם וְהָאָרֶץ וְכָל־צְבָאָם:
וַיְכַל אֱלֹהִים בַּיּוֹם הַשְּׁבִיעִי מְלַאכְתּוֹ אֲשֶׁר עָשָׂה
וַיִּשְׁבֹּת בַּיּוֹם הַשְּׁבִיעִי מִכָּל־מְלַאכְתּוֹ אֲשֶׁר עָשָׂה:
וַיְבָרֶךְ אֱלֹהִים אֶת־יוֹם הַשְּׁבִיעִי, וַיְקַדֵּשׁ אֹתוֹ
כִּי בוֹ שָׁבַת מִכָּל־מְלַאכְתּוֹ, אֲשֶׁר־בָּרָא אֱלֹהִים לַעֲשׂוֹת:

אֱלֹהֵינוּ וֵאלֹהֵי אֲבוֹתֵינוּ, רְצֵה בִמְנוּחָתֵנוּ.
קַדְּשֵׁנוּ בְּמִצְוֹתֶיךָ, וְתֵן חֶלְקֵנוּ בְּתוֹרָתֶךָ
שַׂבְּעֵנוּ מִטּוּבֶךָ, וְשַׂמְּחֵנוּ בִּישׁוּעָתֶךָ
וְטַהֵר לִבֵּנוּ לְעָבְדְּךָ בֶּאֱמֶת.
וְהַנְחִילֵנוּ, יהוה אֱלֹהֵינוּ, בְּאַהֲבָה וּבְרָצוֹן שַׁבַּת קָדְשֶׁךָ
וְיָנוּחוּ בָהּ יִשְׂרָאֵל מְקַדְּשֵׁי שְׁמֶךָ.
בָּרוּךְ אַתָּה יהוה, מְקַדֵּשׁ הַשַּׁבָּת.

עבודה

רְצֵה יהוה אֱלֹהֵינוּ בְּעַמְּךָ יִשְׂרָאֵל וּבִתְפִלָּתָם
וְהָשֵׁב אֶת הָעֲבוֹדָה לִדְבִיר בֵּיתֶךָ
וְאִשֵּׁי יִשְׂרָאֵל וּתְפִלָּתָם בְּאַהֲבָה תְקַבֵּל בְּרָצוֹן
וּתְהִי לְרָצוֹן תָּמִיד עֲבוֹדַת יִשְׂרָאֵל עַמֶּךָ.

וַיְכֻלּוּ הַשָּׁמַיִם וְהָאָרֶץ *Then the heavens and the earth were completed:* These three verses conclude the biblical account of creation. They contain 35 (5 × 7) words. The entire creation narrative (Gen. 1:1–2:3) is constructed in multiples of seven. The word "good" appears seven times, the word "God" thirty-five times, and the word "earth" twenty-one times. The opening verse contains seven words, the second fourteen, and the complete text 469 (7 × 67) words. From the very outset, seven dominates, as if to signal from the beginning that the seventh day was the culmination and purpose of creation: "last in deed, first in thought."

On Rosh Ḥodesh and Ḥol HaMo'ed:

אֱלֹהֵינוּ Our God and God of our ancestors, may there rise, come, reach, appear, be favored, heard, regarded and remembered before You, our recollection and remembrance, as well as the remembrance of our ancestors, and of the Messiah son of David Your servant, and of Jerusalem Your holy city, and of all Your people the house of Israel – for deliverance and well-being, grace, loving-kindness and compassion, life and peace, on this day of:

On Rosh Ḥodesh: Rosh Ḥodesh.
On Pesaḥ: the Festival of Matzot.
On Sukkot: the Festival of Sukkot.

On it remember us, LORD our God, for good; recollect us for blessing, and deliver us for life. In accord with Your promise of salvation and compassion, spare us and be gracious to us; have compassion on us and deliver us, for our eyes are turned to You because You, God, are a gracious and compassionate King.

וְתֶחֱזֶינָה And may our eyes witness Your return to Zion in compassion. Blessed are You, LORD, who restores His Presence to Zion.

THANKSGIVING

Bow at the first nine words.

מוֹדִים' We give thanks to You,
for You are the LORD our God and God of our ancestors
for ever and all time.
You are the Rock of our lives,
Shield of our salvation from generation to generation.
We will thank You and declare Your praise for our lives,
which are entrusted into Your hand;
for our souls, which are placed in Your charge;
for Your miracles which are with us every day;
and for Your wonders and favors
at all times, evening, morning and midday.
You are good – for Your compassion never fails.
You are compassionate – for Your loving-kindnesses never cease.
We have always placed our hope in You.

On חול המועד *and* ראש חודש:

אֱלֹהֵינוּ וֵאלֹהֵי אֲבוֹתֵינוּ, יַעֲלֶה וְיָבוֹא וְיַגִּיעַ, וְיֵרָאֶה וְיֵרָצֶה וְיִשָּׁמַע, וְיִפָּקֵד וְיִזָּכֵר זִכְרוֹנֵנוּ וּפִקְדוֹנֵנוּ וְזִכְרוֹן אֲבוֹתֵינוּ, וְזִכְרוֹן מָשִׁיחַ בֶּן דָּוִד עַבְדֶּךָ, וְזִכְרוֹן יְרוּשָׁלַיִם עִיר קָדְשֶׁךָ, וְזִכְרוֹן כָּל עַמְּךָ בֵּית יִשְׂרָאֵל, לְפָנֶיךָ, לִפְלֵיטָה לְטוֹבָה, לְחֵן וּלְחֶסֶד וּלְרַחֲמִים, לְחַיִּים וּלְשָׁלוֹם בְּיוֹם

בראש חודש: **רֹאשׁ הַחֹדֶשׁ** / בפסח: **חַג הַמַּצּוֹת** / בסוכות: **חַג הַסֻּכּוֹת**

הַזֶּה. זָכְרֵנוּ יהוה אֱלֹהֵינוּ בּוֹ לְטוֹבָה, וּפָקְדֵנוּ בוֹ לִבְרָכָה, וְהוֹשִׁיעֵנוּ בוֹ לְחַיִּים. וּבִדְבַר יְשׁוּעָה וְרַחֲמִים, חוּס וְחָנֵּנוּ וְרַחֵם עָלֵינוּ וְהוֹשִׁיעֵנוּ, כִּי אֵלֶיךָ עֵינֵינוּ, כִּי אֵל מֶלֶךְ חַנּוּן וְרַחוּם אָתָּה.

וְתֶחֱזֶינָה עֵינֵינוּ בְּשׁוּבְךָ לְצִיּוֹן בְּרַחֲמִים.
בָּרוּךְ אַתָּה יהוה, הַמַּחֲזִיר שְׁכִינָתוֹ לְצִיּוֹן.

הודאה

Bow at the first five words.

מוֹדִים אֲנַחְנוּ לָךְ
שָׁאַתָּה הוּא יהוה אֱלֹהֵינוּ וֵאלֹהֵי אֲבוֹתֵינוּ לְעוֹלָם וָעֶד.
צוּר חַיֵּינוּ, מָגֵן יִשְׁעֵנוּ, אַתָּה הוּא לְדוֹר וָדוֹר.
נוֹדֶה לְּךָ וּנְסַפֵּר תְּהִלָּתֶךָ
עַל חַיֵּינוּ הַמְּסוּרִים בְּיָדֶךָ
וְעַל נִשְׁמוֹתֵינוּ הַפְּקוּדוֹת לָךְ
וְעַל נִסֶּיךָ שֶׁבְּכָל יוֹם עִמָּנוּ
וְעַל נִפְלְאוֹתֶיךָ וְטוֹבוֹתֶיךָ שֶׁבְּכָל עֵת, עֶרֶב וָבֹקֶר וְצָהֳרָיִם.
הַטּוֹב, כִּי לֹא כָלוּ רַחֲמֶיךָ
וְהַמְרַחֵם, כִּי לֹא תַמּוּ חֲסָדֶיךָ
מֵעוֹלָם קִוִּינוּ לָךְ.

On Ḥanukka:

עַל הַנִּסִּים [We thank You also] for the miracles, the redemption, the mighty deeds, and the victories in battle which You performed for our ancestors in those days, at this time.

בִּימֵי מַתִּתְיָהוּ In the days of Mattityahu, son of Yoḥanan, the High Priest, the Hasmonean, and his sons, the wicked Greek kingdom rose up against Your people Israel to make them forget Your Torah and to force them to transgress the statutes of Your will. It was then that You in Your great compassion stood by them in the time of their distress. You championed their cause, judged their claim, and avenged their wrong. You delivered the strong into the hands of the weak, the many into the hands of the few, the impure into the hands of the pure, the wicked into the hands of the righteous, and the arrogant into the hands of those who were engaged in the study of Your Torah. You made for Yourself great and holy renown in Your world, and for Your people Israel You performed a great salvation and redemption as of this very day. Your children then entered the holiest part of Your House, cleansed Your Temple, purified Your Sanctuary, kindled lights in Your holy courts, and designated these eight days of Ḥanukka for giving thanks and praise to Your great name.

Continue with "For all these things."

On Shushan Purim in Jerusalem:

עַל הַנִּסִּים [We thank You also] for the miracles, the redemption, the mighty deeds, and the victories in battle which You performed for our ancestors in those days, at this time.

בִּימֵי מָרְדְּכַי In the days of Mordekhai and Esther, in Shushan the capital, the wicked Haman rose up against them and sought to destroy, slay and exterminate *Esther 3* all the Jews, young and old, children and women, on one day, the thirteenth day of the twelfth month, which is the month of Adar, and to plunder their possessions. Then You in Your great compassion thwarted his counsel, frustrated his plans, and caused his scheme to recoil on his own head, so that they hanged him and his sons on the gallows.

Continue with "For all these things."

וְעַל כֻּלָּם For all these things may Your name be blessed and exalted, our King, continually, for ever and all time.

On Shabbat Shuva: And write, for a good life,
all the children of Your covenant.

Let all that lives thank You, Selah! and praise Your name in truth,
God, our Savior and Help, Selah!
▾Blessed are You, LORD, whose name is "the Good"
and to whom thanks are due.

בחנוכה:

עַל הַנִּסִּים וְעַל הַפֻּרְקָן וְעַל הַגְּבוּרוֹת וְעַל הַתְּשׁוּעוֹת וְעַל הַמִּלְחָמוֹת שֶׁעָשִׂיתָ לַאֲבוֹתֵינוּ בַּיָּמִים הָהֵם בַּזְּמַן הַזֶּה.

בִּימֵי מַתִּתְיָהוּ בֶּן יוֹחָנָן כֹּהֵן גָּדוֹל חַשְׁמוֹנַאי וּבָנָיו, כְּשֶׁעָמְדָה מַלְכוּת יָוָן הָרְשָׁעָה עַל עַמְּךָ יִשְׂרָאֵל לְהַשְׁכִּיחָם תּוֹרָתֶךָ וּלְהַעֲבִירָם מֵחֻקֵּי רְצוֹנֶךָ, וְאַתָּה בְּרַחֲמֶיךָ הָרַבִּים עָמַדְתָּ לָהֶם בְּעֵת צָרָתָם, רַבְתָּ אֶת רִיבָם, דַּנְתָּ אֶת דִּינָם, נָקַמְתָּ אֶת נִקְמָתָם, מָסַרְתָּ גִבּוֹרִים בְּיַד חַלָּשִׁים, וְרַבִּים בְּיַד מְעַטִּים, וּטְמֵאִים בְּיַד טְהוֹרִים, וּרְשָׁעִים בְּיַד צַדִּיקִים, וְזֵדִים בְּיַד עוֹסְקֵי תוֹרָתֶךָ, וּלְךָ עָשִׂיתָ שֵׁם גָּדוֹל וְקָדוֹשׁ בְּעוֹלָמֶךָ, וּלְעַמְּךָ יִשְׂרָאֵל עָשִׂיתָ תְּשׁוּעָה גְדוֹלָה וּפֻרְקָן כְּהַיּוֹם הַזֶּה. וְאַחַר כֵּן בָּאוּ בָנֶיךָ לִדְבִיר בֵּיתֶךָ, וּפִנּוּ אֶת הֵיכָלֶךָ, וְטִהֲרוּ אֶת מִקְדָּשֶׁךָ, וְהִדְלִיקוּ נֵרוֹת בְּחַצְרוֹת קָדְשֶׁךָ, וְקָבְעוּ שְׁמוֹנַת יְמֵי חֲנֻכָּה אֵלּוּ, לְהוֹדוֹת וּלְהַלֵּל לְשִׁמְךָ הַגָּדוֹל.

Continue with וְעַל כֻּלָּם.

בשושן פורים בירושלים:

עַל הַנִּסִּים וְעַל הַפֻּרְקָן וְעַל הַגְּבוּרוֹת וְעַל הַתְּשׁוּעוֹת וְעַל הַמִּלְחָמוֹת שֶׁעָשִׂיתָ לַאֲבוֹתֵינוּ בַּיָּמִים הָהֵם בַּזְּמַן הַזֶּה.

בִּימֵי מָרְדְּכַי וְאֶסְתֵּר בְּשׁוּשַׁן הַבִּירָה, כְּשֶׁעָמַד עֲלֵיהֶם הָמָן הָרָשָׁע, בִּקֵּשׁ
לְהַשְׁמִיד לַהֲרֹג וּלְאַבֵּד אֶת־כָּל־הַיְּהוּדִים מִנַּעַר וְעַד־זָקֵן טַף וְנָשִׁים בְּיוֹם אסתר ג
אֶחָד, בִּשְׁלוֹשָׁה עָשָׂר לְחֹדֶשׁ שְׁנֵים־עָשָׂר, הוּא־חֹדֶשׁ אֲדָר, וּשְׁלָלָם לָבוֹז: וְאַתָּה בְּרַחֲמֶיךָ הָרַבִּים הֵפַרְתָּ אֶת עֲצָתוֹ, וְקִלְקַלְתָּ אֶת מַחֲשַׁבְתּוֹ, וַהֲשֵׁבוֹתָ לּוֹ גְּמוּלוֹ בְּרֹאשׁוֹ, וְתָלוּ אוֹתוֹ וְאֶת בָּנָיו עַל הָעֵץ.

Continue with וְעַל כֻּלָּם.

וְעַל כֻּלָּם יִתְבָּרַךְ וְיִתְרוֹמַם שִׁמְךָ מַלְכֵּנוּ תָּמִיד לְעוֹלָם וָעֶד.

בשבת שובה: וּכְתֹב לְחַיִּים טוֹבִים כָּל בְּנֵי בְרִיתֶךָ.

וְכֹל הַחַיִּים יוֹדוּךָ סֶּלָה, וִיהַלְלוּ אֶת שִׁמְךָ בֶּאֱמֶת הָאֵל יְשׁוּעָתֵנוּ וְעֶזְרָתֵנוּ סֶלָה.

בָּרוּךְ אַתָּה יהוה, הַטּוֹב שִׁמְךָ וּלְךָ נָאֶה לְהוֹדוֹת.

PEACE

שָׁלוֹם רָב Grant great peace to Your people Israel for ever,
for You are the sovereign LORD of all peace;
and may it be good in Your eyes
to bless Your people Israel
at every time, at every hour, with Your peace.

On Shabbat Shuva: In the book of life, blessing, peace and prosperity,
may we and all Your people the house of Israel
be remembered and written before You
for a good life, and for peace.*

Blessed are You, LORD, who blesses His people Israel with peace.

**On Shabbat Shuva in the Diaspora, many end the blessing:*
Blessed are You, LORD, who makes peace.

Some say the following verse:
May the words of my mouth and the meditation of my heart *Ps. 19*
find favor before You, LORD, my Rock and Redeemer.

אֱלֹהַי My God, *Berakhot 17a*
guard my tongue from evil and my lips from deceitful speech.
To those who curse me, let my soul be silent;
may my soul be to all like the dust.
Open my heart to Your Torah
and let my soul pursue Your commandments.
As for all who plan evil against me,
swiftly thwart their counsel and frustrate their plans.
Act for the sake of Your name; act for the sake of Your right hand;
act for the sake of Your holiness; act for the sake of Your Torah.
That Your beloved ones may be delivered, *Ps. 60*
save with Your right hand and answer me.
May the words of my mouth *Ps. 19*
and the meditation of my heart find favor before You,
LORD, my Rock and Redeemer.

Bow, take three steps back, then bow, first left, then right, then center, while saying:
May He who makes peace in His high places,
make peace for us and all Israel – and say: Amen.

ברכת שלום

שָׁלוֹם רָב עַל יִשְׂרָאֵל עַמְּךָ תָּשִׂים לְעוֹלָם
כִּי אַתָּה הוּא מֶלֶךְ אָדוֹן לְכָל הַשָּׁלוֹם.
וְטוֹב בְּעֵינֶיךָ לְבָרֵךְ אֶת עַמְּךָ יִשְׂרָאֵל
בְּכָל עֵת וּבְכָל שָׁעָה בִּשְׁלוֹמֶךָ.

בשבת שובה: בְּסֵפֶר חַיִּים, בְּרָכָה וְשָׁלוֹם, וּפַרְנָסָה טוֹבָה
נִזָּכֵר וְנִכָּתֵב לְפָנֶיךָ, אֲנַחְנוּ וְכָל עַמְּךָ בֵּית יִשְׂרָאֵל
לְחַיִּים טוֹבִים וּלְשָׁלוֹם.*

בָּרוּךְ אַתָּה יהוה, הַמְבָרֵךְ אֶת עַמּוֹ יִשְׂרָאֵל בַּשָּׁלוֹם.

**On* שבת שובה *in* חוץ לארץ*, many end the blessing:*

בָּרוּךְ אַתָּה יהוה, עוֹשֶׂה הַשָּׁלוֹם.

Some say the following verse:

יִהְיוּ לְרָצוֹן אִמְרֵי־פִי וְהֶגְיוֹן לִבִּי לְפָנֶיךָ, יהוה צוּרִי וְגֹאֲלִי: תהלים יט

אֱלֹהַי ברכות יז.

נְצֹר לְשׁוֹנִי מֵרָע וּשְׂפָתַי מִדַּבֵּר מִרְמָה
וְלִמְקַלְלַי נַפְשִׁי תִדֹּם, וְנַפְשִׁי כֶּעָפָר לַכֹּל תִּהְיֶה.
פְּתַח לִבִּי בְּתוֹרָתֶךָ, וּבְמִצְוֹתֶיךָ תִּרְדֹּף נַפְשִׁי.
וְכָל הַחוֹשְׁבִים עָלַי רָעָה
מְהֵרָה הָפֵר עֲצָתָם וְקַלְקֵל מַחֲשַׁבְתָּם.
עֲשֵׂה לְמַעַן שְׁמֶךָ, עֲשֵׂה לְמַעַן יְמִינֶךָ
עֲשֵׂה לְמַעַן קְדֻשָּׁתֶךָ, עֲשֵׂה לְמַעַן תּוֹרָתֶךָ.
לְמַעַן יֵחָלְצוּן יְדִידֶיךָ, הוֹשִׁיעָה יְמִינְךָ וַעֲנֵנִי: תהלים ס
יִהְיוּ לְרָצוֹן אִמְרֵי־פִי וְהֶגְיוֹן לִבִּי לְפָנֶיךָ, יהוה צוּרִי וְגֹאֲלִי: תהלים יט

Bow, take three steps back, then bow, first left, then right, then center, while saying:

עֹשֶׂה שָׁלוֹם/ בשבת שובה: הַשָּׁלוֹם/ בִּמְרוֹמָיו
הוּא יַעֲשֶׂה שָׁלוֹם עָלֵינוּ וְעַל כָּל יִשְׂרָאֵל, וְאִמְרוּ אָמֵן.

יְהִי רָצוֹן May it be Your will, LORD our God and God of our ancestors,
that the Temple be rebuilt speedily in our days, and grant us a share in Your Torah.
And there we will serve You with reverence,
as in the days of old and as in former years.
Then the offering of Judah and Jerusalem *Mal. 3*
will be pleasing to the LORD as in the days of old and as in former years.

All stand and say:

וַיְכֻלּוּ Then the heavens and the earth were completed, *Gen. 2*
and all their array.
With the seventh day, God completed the work He had done.
He ceased on the seventh day from all the work He had done. God
blessed the seventh day and declared it holy,
because on it He ceased from all His work He had created to do.

The following until "who sanctifies the Sabbath" on page 146, is omitted when praying with an occasional minyan or alone.
The Leader continues:

בָּרוּךְ Blessed are You, LORD our God and God of our fathers,
God of Abraham, God of Isaac and God of Jacob,
the great, mighty and awesome God,
God Most High, Creator of heaven and earth.

The congregation then the Leader:

מָגֵן אָבוֹת By His word, He was the Shield of our ancestors.
By His promise, He will revive the dead.
There is none like the holy God/*On Shabbat Shuva:* the holy King/
who gives rest to His people on His holy Sabbath day,
for He found them worthy of His favor to give them rest.
Before Him we will come in worship with reverence and awe,
giving thanks to His name daily, continually, with due blessings.
He is God to whom thanks are due, the LORD of peace

---

tion ascribes it to the fact that in Babylon – where synagogues were, for the most part, outside town – going home at night was fraught with danger. This prayer was added for the benefit of latecomers, so that the congregation could leave together.

יְהִי רָצוֹן מִלְּפָנֶיךָ יהוה אֱלֹהֵינוּ וֵאלֹהֵי אֲבוֹתֵינוּ
שֶׁיִּבָּנֶה בֵּית הַמִּקְדָּשׁ בִּמְהֵרָה בְיָמֵינוּ, וְתֵן חֶלְקֵנוּ בְּתוֹרָתֶךָ
וְשָׁם נַעֲבָדְךָ בְּיִרְאָה כִּימֵי עוֹלָם וּכְשָׁנִים קַדְמֹנִיּוֹת.
וְעָרְבָה לַיהוה מִנְחַת יְהוּדָה וִירוּשָׁלָםִ כִּימֵי עוֹלָם וּכְשָׁנִים קַדְמֹנִיּוֹת: מלאכי ג

All stand and say:

וַיְכֻלּוּ הַשָּׁמַיִם וְהָאָרֶץ וְכָל־צְבָאָם: בראשית ב
וַיְכַל אֱלֹהִים בַּיּוֹם הַשְּׁבִיעִי מְלַאכְתּוֹ אֲשֶׁר עָשָׂה
וַיִּשְׁבֹּת בַּיּוֹם הַשְּׁבִיעִי מִכָּל־מְלַאכְתּוֹ אֲשֶׁר עָשָׂה:
וַיְבָרֶךְ אֱלֹהִים אֶת־יוֹם הַשְּׁבִיעִי, וַיְקַדֵּשׁ אֹתוֹ
כִּי בוֹ שָׁבַת מִכָּל־מְלַאכְתּוֹ, אֲשֶׁר־בָּרָא אֱלֹהִים, לַעֲשׂוֹת:

The following until מְקַדֵּשׁ הַשַּׁבָּת *on page 147,*
is omitted when praying with an occasional מנין *or alone.*

The שליח ציבור *continues:*

בָּרוּךְ אַתָּה יהוה, אֱלֹהֵינוּ וֵאלֹהֵי אֲבוֹתֵינוּ
אֱלֹהֵי אַבְרָהָם, אֱלֹהֵי יִצְחָק, וֵאלֹהֵי יַעֲקֹב
הָאֵל הַגָּדוֹל הַגִּבּוֹר וְהַנּוֹרָא, אֵל עֶלְיוֹן, קֹנֵה שָׁמַיִם וָאָרֶץ.

The קהל *then the* שליח ציבור:

מָגֵן אָבוֹת בִּדְבָרוֹ, מְחַיֵּה מֵתִים בְּמַאֲמָרוֹ
הָאֵל / בשבת שובה: הַמֶּלֶךְ / הַקָּדוֹשׁ שֶׁאֵין כָּמוֹהוּ
הַמֵּנִיחַ לְעַמּוֹ בְּיוֹם שַׁבַּת קָדְשׁוֹ
כִּי בָם רָצָה לְהָנִיחַ לָהֶם
לְפָנָיו נַעֲבֹד בְּיִרְאָה וָפַחַד
וְנוֹדֶה לִשְׁמוֹ בְּכָל יוֹם תָּמִיד, מֵעֵין הַבְּרָכוֹת
אֵל הַהוֹדָאוֹת, אֲדוֹן הַשָּׁלוֹם

מָגֵן אָבוֹת בִּדְבָרוֹ *By His word, He was the Shield of our ancestors:* A summary of the seven blessings of the Amida, which is unique to Friday evening. Tradi-

who sanctifies the Sabbath and blesses the seventh day,
and in holiness gives rest to a people filled with delight,
in remembrance of the work of creation.

The Leader continues:
אֱלֹהֵינוּ Our God and God of our ancestors,
may You find favor in our rest.
Make us holy through Your commandments
and grant us our share in Your Torah.
Satisfy us with Your goodness, grant us joy in Your salvation,
and purify our hearts to serve You in truth.
In love and favor, LORD our God,
grant us as our heritage Your holy Sabbath,
so that Israel who sanctify Your name may find rest on it.
Blessed are You, LORD, who sanctifies the Sabbath.

FULL KADDISH

Leader: יִתְגַּדַּל Magnified and sanctified
may His great name be,
in the world He created by His will.
May He establish His kingdom
in your lifetime and in your days,
and in the lifetime of all the house of Israel,
swiftly and soon –
and say: Amen.

All: May His great name be blessed for ever and all time.

Leader: Blessed and praised,
glorified and exalted,
raised and honored,
uplifted and lauded be
the name of the Holy One,
blessed be He, beyond any blessing,

מְקַדֵּשׁ הַשַּׁבָּת וּמְבָרֵךְ שְׁבִיעִי
וּמֵנִיחַ בִּקְדֻשָּׁה לְעַם מְדֻשְּׁנֵי עֹנֶג
זֵכֶר לְמַעֲשֵׂה בְרֵאשִׁית.

The שליח ציבור *continues:*

אֱלֹהֵינוּ וֵאלֹהֵי אֲבוֹתֵינוּ, רְצֵה בִמְנוּחָתֵנוּ.
קַדְּשֵׁנוּ בְּמִצְוֹתֶיךָ וְתֵן חֶלְקֵנוּ בְּתוֹרָתֶךָ
שַׂבְּעֵנוּ מִטּוּבֶךָ וְשַׂמְּחֵנוּ בִּישׁוּעָתֶךָ
וְטַהֵר לִבֵּנוּ לְעָבְדְּךָ בֶּאֱמֶת.
וְהַנְחִילֵנוּ יהוה אֱלֹהֵינוּ בְּאַהֲבָה וּבְרָצוֹן שַׁבַּת קָדְשֶׁךָ
וְיָנוּחוּ בָהּ יִשְׂרָאֵל מְקַדְּשֵׁי שְׁמֶךָ.
בָּרוּךְ אַתָּה יהוה, מְקַדֵּשׁ הַשַּׁבָּת.

קדיש שלם

ש״ץ: יִתְגַּדַּל וְיִתְקַדַּשׁ שְׁמֵהּ רַבָּא (קהל: אָמֵן)
בְּעָלְמָא דִּי בְרָא כִרְעוּתֵהּ
וְיַמְלִיךְ מַלְכוּתֵהּ
בְּחַיֵּיכוֹן וּבְיוֹמֵיכוֹן וּבְחַיֵּי דְכָל בֵּית יִשְׂרָאֵל
בַּעֲגָלָא וּבִזְמַן קָרִיב, וְאִמְרוּ אָמֵן. (קהל: אָמֵן)

קהל וש״ץ: יְהֵא שְׁמֵהּ רַבָּא מְבָרַךְ לְעָלַם וּלְעָלְמֵי עָלְמַיָּא.

ש״ץ: יִתְבָּרַךְ וְיִשְׁתַּבַּח וְיִתְפָּאַר
וְיִתְרוֹמַם וְיִתְנַשֵּׂא וְיִתְהַדָּר וְיִתְעַלֶּה וְיִתְהַלָּל
שְׁמֵהּ דְּקֻדְשָׁא בְּרִיךְ הוּא (קהל: בְּרִיךְ הוּא)
לְעֵלָּא מִן כָּל בִּרְכָתָא
/בשבת שובה: לְעֵלָּא לְעֵלָּא מִכָּל בִּרְכָתָא/

song, praise and consolation uttered in the world –
and say: Amen.

May the prayers and pleas of all Israel
be accepted by their Father in heaven –
and say: Amen.

May there be great peace from heaven,
and life for us and all Israel – and say: Amen.

Bow, take three steps back, as if taking leave of the Divine Presence, then bow, first left, then right, then center, while saying:

May He who makes peace in His high places,
make peace for us and all Israel – and say: Amen.

KIDDUSH IN THE SYNAGOGUE

The Leader raises a cup of wine and says:

Please pay attention, my masters.

בָּרוּךְ Blessed are You, Lord our God, King of the Universe,
who creates the fruit of the vine.

בָּרוּךְ Blessed are You, Lord our God, King of the Universe,
who has made us holy with His commandments, has favored us,
and in love and favor given us His holy Sabbath as a heritage,
a remembrance of the work of creation.
It is the first among the holy days of assembly,
a remembrance of the exodus from Egypt.
For You chose us and sanctified us from all the peoples,
and in love and favor gave us Your holy Sabbath as a heritage.
Blessed are You, Lord, who sanctifies the Sabbath.

The wine should be drunk by children under the age of Bar/Bat Mitzva or, if there are none, by the Leader.

From the second night of Pesaḥ until the night before Shavuot, the Omer is counted on page 158.

קידוש *Kiddush.* As Kiddush is usually said "where we eat the meal," in order to avoid a blessing "said in vain," the wine is not drunk by an adult but by a child. The custom of saying Kiddush in the synagogue goes back to an age when the synagogue was also a hostel for visitors, who ate their meals nearby.

וְשִׁירָתָא, תֻּשְׁבְּחָתָא וְנֶחֱמָתָא
דַּאֲמִירָן בְּעָלְמָא, וְאִמְרוּ אָמֵן. (קהל: אָמֵן)
תִּתְקַבַּל צְלוֹתְהוֹן וּבָעוּתְהוֹן דְּכָל יִשְׂרָאֵל
קֳדָם אֲבוּהוֹן דִּי בִשְׁמַיָּא, וְאִמְרוּ אָמֵן. (קהל: אָמֵן)
יְהֵא שְׁלָמָא רַבָּא מִן שְׁמַיָּא
וְחַיִּים, עָלֵינוּ וְעַל כָּל יִשְׂרָאֵל, וְאִמְרוּ אָמֵן. (קהל: אָמֵן)

Bow, take three steps back, as if taking leave of the Divine Presence, then bow, first left, then right, then center, while saying:

עֹשֶׂה שָׁלוֹם/ בשבת שובה: הַשָּׁלוֹם/ בִּמְרוֹמָיו
הוּא יַעֲשֶׂה שָׁלוֹם עָלֵינוּ וְעַל כָּל יִשְׂרָאֵל
וְאִמְרוּ אָמֵן. (קהל: אָמֵן)

קידוש בבית הכנסת

The שליח ציבור *raises a cup of wine and says:*

סַבְרִי מָרָנָן
בָּרוּךְ אַתָּה יהוה אֱלֹהֵינוּ מֶלֶךְ הָעוֹלָם בּוֹרֵא פְּרִי הַגָּפֶן.

בָּרוּךְ אַתָּה יהוה אֱלֹהֵינוּ מֶלֶךְ הָעוֹלָם
אֲשֶׁר קִדְּשָׁנוּ בְּמִצְוֹתָיו, וְרָצָה בָנוּ
וְשַׁבַּת קָדְשׁוֹ בְּאַהֲבָה וּבְרָצוֹן הִנְחִילָנוּ
זִכָּרוֹן לְמַעֲשֵׂה בְרֵאשִׁית
כִּי הוּא יוֹם תְּחִלָּה לְמִקְרָאֵי קֹדֶשׁ, זֵכֶר לִיצִיאַת מִצְרָיִם
כִּי בָנוּ בָחַרְתָּ וְאוֹתָנוּ קִדַּשְׁתָּ מִכָּל הָעַמִּים
וְשַׁבַּת קָדְשְׁךָ בְּאַהֲבָה וּבְרָצוֹן הִנְחַלְתָּנוּ.
בָּרוּךְ אַתָּה יהוה, מְקַדֵּשׁ הַשַּׁבָּת.

The wine should be drunk by children under the age of בר מצווה *or* בת מצווה *or, if there are none, by the* שליח ציבור.

From the second night of פסח *until the night before* שבועות, *the* עומר *is counted* *on page 159.*

Stand while saying Aleinu. Bow at ▾.

עָלֵינוּ It is our duty to praise the Master of all,
and ascribe greatness to the Author of creation,
who has not made us like the nations of the lands
nor placed us like the families of the earth;
who has not made our portion like theirs,
nor our destiny like all their multitudes.
(For they worship vanity and emptiness,
and pray to a god who cannot save.)
▾But we bow in worship
and thank the Supreme King of kings, the Holy One, blessed be He,
who extends the heavens and establishes the earth,
whose throne of glory is in the heavens above,
and whose power's Presence is in the highest of heights.
He is our God; there is no other.
Truly He is our King, there is none else,
as it is written in His Torah:
"You shall know and take to heart this day *Deut. 4*
that the LORD is God, in heaven above and on earth below.
There is no other."

Therefore, we place our hope in You, LORD our God,
that we may soon see the glory of Your power,
when You will remove abominations from the earth,
and idols will be utterly destroyed,
when the world will be perfected under the sovereignty of the Almighty,
when all humanity will call on Your name,
to turn all the earth's wicked toward You.
All the world's inhabitants will realize and know
that to You every knee must bow and every tongue swear loyalty.
Before You, LORD our God, they will kneel and bow down
and give honor to Your glorious name.
They will all accept the yoke of Your kingdom,
and You will reign over them soon and for ever.

Stand while saying עָלֵינוּ*. Bow at* ˅.

עָלֵינוּ לְשַׁבֵּחַ לַאֲדוֹן הַכֹּל, לָתֵת גְּדֻלָּה לְיוֹצֵר בְּרֵאשִׁית
שֶׁלֹּא עָשָׂנוּ כְּגוֹיֵי הָאֲרָצוֹת, וְלֹא שָׂמָנוּ כְּמִשְׁפְּחוֹת הָאֲדָמָה
שֶׁלֹּא שָׂם חֶלְקֵנוּ כָּהֶם וְגוֹרָלֵנוּ כְּכָל הֲמוֹנָם.
(שֶׁהֵם מִשְׁתַּחֲוִים לְהֶבֶל וָרִיק וּמִתְפַּלְּלִים אֶל אֵל לֹא יוֹשִׁיעַ.)
˅וַאֲנַחְנוּ כּוֹרְעִים וּמִשְׁתַּחֲוִים וּמוֹדִים
לִפְנֵי מֶלֶךְ מַלְכֵי הַמְּלָכִים, הַקָּדוֹשׁ בָּרוּךְ הוּא
שֶׁהוּא נוֹטֶה שָׁמַיִם וְיוֹסֵד אָרֶץ
וּמוֹשַׁב יְקָרוֹ בַּשָּׁמַיִם מִמַּעַל
וּשְׁכִינַת עֻזּוֹ בְּגָבְהֵי מְרוֹמִים.
הוּא אֱלֹהֵינוּ, אֵין עוֹד.
אֱמֶת מַלְכֵּנוּ, אֶפֶס זוּלָתוֹ
כַּכָּתוּב בְּתוֹרָתוֹ
וְיָדַעְתָּ הַיּוֹם וַהֲשֵׁבֹתָ אֶל־לְבָבֶךָ דברים ד
כִּי יהוה הוּא הָאֱלֹהִים בַּשָּׁמַיִם מִמַּעַל וְעַל־הָאָרֶץ מִתָּחַת, אֵין עוֹד:

עַל כֵּן נְקַוֶּה לְּךָ יהוה אֱלֹהֵינוּ, לִרְאוֹת מְהֵרָה בְּתִפְאֶרֶת עֻזֶּךָ
לְהַעֲבִיר גִּלּוּלִים מִן הָאָרֶץ, וְהָאֱלִילִים כָּרוֹת יִכָּרֵתוּן
לְתַקֵּן עוֹלָם בְּמַלְכוּת שַׁדַּי.
וְכָל בְּנֵי בָשָׂר יִקְרְאוּ בִשְׁמֶךָ לְהַפְנוֹת אֵלֶיךָ כָּל רִשְׁעֵי אָרֶץ.
יַכִּירוּ וְיֵדְעוּ כָּל יוֹשְׁבֵי תֵבֵל
כִּי לְךָ תִּכְרַע כָּל בֶּרֶךְ, תִּשָּׁבַע כָּל לָשׁוֹן.
לְפָנֶיךָ יהוה אֱלֹהֵינוּ יִכְרְעוּ וְיִפֹּלוּ, וְלִכְבוֹד שִׁמְךָ יְקָר יִתֵּנוּ
וִיקַבְּלוּ כֻלָּם אֶת עֹל מַלְכוּתֶךָ
וְתִמְלֹךְ עֲלֵיהֶם מְהֵרָה לְעוֹלָם וָעֶד.

For the kingdom is Yours,
and to all eternity You will reign in glory,
as it is written in Your Torah: "The LORD will reign for ever and ever." *Ex. 15*
▸ And it is said: "Then the LORD shall be King over all the earth; *Zech. 14*
on that day the LORD shall be One and His name One."

Some add:
Have no fear of sudden terror or of the ruin when it overtakes the wicked. *Prov. 3*
Devise your strategy, but it will be thwarted; *Is. 8*
propose your plan, but it will not stand, for God is with us.
When you grow old, I will still be the same. *Is. 46*
When your hair turns gray, I will still carry you.
I made you, I will bear you, I will carry you, and I will rescue you.

MOURNER'S KADDISH

The following prayer, said by mourners, requires the presence of a minyan.
A transliteration can be found on page 199.

Mourner: יִתְגַּדַּל Magnified and sanctified
may His great name be,
in the world He created by His will.
May He establish His kingdom
in your lifetime and in your days,
and in the lifetime of all the house of Israel,
swiftly and soon –
and say: Amen.

All: May His great name be blessed for ever and all time.

Mourner: Blessed and praised,
glorified and exalted,
raised and honored,
uplifted and lauded
be the name of the Holy One,
blessed be He, beyond any blessing,

כִּי הַמַּלְכוּת שֶׁלְּךָ הִיא וּלְעוֹלְמֵי עַד תִּמְלֹךְ בְּכָבוֹד
כַּכָּתוּב בְּתוֹרָתֶךָ, יהוה יִמְלֹךְ לְעֹלָם וָעֶד: שמות טו
◂ וְנֶאֱמַר, וְהָיָה יהוה לְמֶלֶךְ עַל־כָּל־הָאָרֶץ זכריה יד
בַּיּוֹם הַהוּא יִהְיֶה יהוה אֶחָד וּשְׁמוֹ אֶחָד:

Some add:

אַל־תִּירָא מִפַּחַד פִּתְאֹם וּמִשֹּׁאַת רְשָׁעִים כִּי תָבֹא: משלי ג
עֻצוּ עֵצָה וְתֻפָר, דַּבְּרוּ דָבָר וְלֹא יָקוּם, כִּי עִמָּנוּ אֵל: ישעיה ח
וְעַד־זִקְנָה אֲנִי הוּא, וְעַד־שֵׂיבָה אֲנִי אֶסְבֹּל ישעיה מו
אֲנִי עָשִׂיתִי וַאֲנִי אֶשָּׂא וַאֲנִי אֶסְבֹּל וַאֲמַלֵּט:

קדיש יתום

The following prayer, said by mourners, requires the presence of a מנין.
A transliteration can be found on page 199.

אבל: יִתְגַּדַּל וְיִתְקַדַּשׁ שְׁמֵהּ רַבָּא (קהל: אָמֵן)
בְּעָלְמָא דִּי בְרָא כִרְעוּתֵהּ, וְיַמְלִיךְ מַלְכוּתֵהּ
בְּחַיֵּיכוֹן וּבְיוֹמֵיכוֹן וּבְחַיֵּי דְכָל בֵּית יִשְׂרָאֵל
בַּעֲגָלָא וּבִזְמַן קָרִיב
וְאִמְרוּ אָמֵן. (קהל: אָמֵן)

קהל ואבל: יְהֵא שְׁמֵהּ רַבָּא מְבָרַךְ לְעָלַם וּלְעָלְמֵי עָלְמַיָּא.

אבל: יִתְבָּרַךְ וְיִשְׁתַּבַּח וְיִתְפָּאַר
וְיִתְרוֹמַם וְיִתְנַשֵּׂא וְיִתְהַדָּר וְיִתְעַלֶּה וְיִתְהַלָּל
שְׁמֵהּ דְּקֻדְשָׁא בְּרִיךְ הוּא (קהל: בְּרִיךְ הוּא)
לְעֵלָּא מִן כָּל בִּרְכָתָא
/בשבת שובה: לְעֵלָּא לְעֵלָּא מִכָּל בִּרְכָתָא/

song, praise and consolation
uttered in the world –
and say: Amen.

May there be great peace from heaven,
and life for us and all Israel –
and say: Amen.

Bow, take three steps back, as if taking leave of the Divine Presence, then bow, first left, then right, then center, while saying:

May He who makes peace in His high places,
make peace for us and all Israel –
and say: Amen.

From the second day of Rosh Ḥodesh Elul until and including Shemini Atzeret (in Israel until and including Hoshana Raba), the following psalm is said:

לְדָוִד A psalm of David. The LORD is my light and my salvation – whom then shall I fear? The LORD is the stronghold of my life – of whom shall I be afraid? When evil men close in on me to devour my flesh, it is they, my enemies and foes, who stumble and fall. Should an army besiege me, my heart would not fear. Should war break out against me, still I would be confident. One thing I ask of the LORD, only this do I seek: to live in the House of the LORD all the days of my life, to gaze on the beauty of the LORD and worship in His Temple. For He will keep me safe in His pavilion on the day of trouble. He will hide me under the cover of His tent. He will set me high upon a rock. Now my head is high above my enemies who surround me. I will sacrifice in His tent with shouts of joy. I will sing and chant praises to the LORD. LORD, hear my voice when I call. Be gracious to me and answer me. On Your behalf my heart says, "Seek My face." Your face, LORD, will I seek. Do not hide Your face from me. Do not turn Your servant away in anger. You have been my help. Do not reject or forsake me, God, my Savior. Were my father and my mother to forsake me, the LORD would take me in. Teach me Your way, LORD, and lead me on a level path, because of my oppressors. Do not abandon me to the will of my foes, for false witnesses have risen against me, breathing violence. ▸ Were it not for my faith that I shall see the LORD's goodness in the land of the living. Hope in the LORD. Be strong and of good courage, and hope in the LORD! *Ps. 27*

Mourner's Kaddish (on previous page)

וְשִׁירָתָא, תֻּשְׁבְּחָתָא וְנֶחֱמָתָא
דַּאֲמִירָן בְּעָלְמָא, וְאִמְרוּ אָמֵן. (קהל: אָמֵן)

יְהֵא שְׁלָמָא רַבָּא מִן שְׁמַיָּא
וְחַיִּים, עָלֵינוּ וְעַל כָּל יִשְׂרָאֵל
וְאִמְרוּ אָמֵן. (קהל: אָמֵן)

Bow, take three steps back, as if taking leave of the Divine Presence, then bow, first left, then right, then center, while saying:

עֹשֶׂה שָׁלוֹם/ בשבת שובה: הַשָּׁלוֹם/ בִּמְרוֹמָיו
הוּא יַעֲשֶׂה שָׁלוֹם עָלֵינוּ וְעַל כָּל יִשְׂרָאֵל
וְאִמְרוּ אָמֵן. (קהל: אָמֵן)

From the second day of ראש חודש אלול *until and including* שמיני עצרת *(in* ארץ ישראל *until and including* הושענא רבה*), the following psalm is said:*

תהלים כז
לְדָוִד, יהוה אוֹרִי וְיִשְׁעִי, מִמִּי אִירָא, יהוה מָעוֹז־חַיַּי, מִמִּי אֶפְחָד: בִּקְרֹב עָלַי מְרֵעִים לֶאֱכֹל אֶת־בְּשָׂרִי, צָרַי וְאֹיְבַי לִי, הֵמָּה כָשְׁלוּ וְנָפָלוּ: אִם־תַּחֲנֶה עָלַי מַחֲנֶה, לֹא־יִירָא לִבִּי, אִם־תָּקוּם עָלַי מִלְחָמָה, בְּזֹאת אֲנִי בוֹטֵחַ: אַחַת שָׁאַלְתִּי מֵאֵת־יהוה, אוֹתָהּ אֲבַקֵּשׁ, שִׁבְתִּי בְּבֵית־יהוה כָּל־יְמֵי חַיַּי, לַחֲזוֹת בְּנֹעַם־יהוה, וּלְבַקֵּר בְּהֵיכָלוֹ: כִּי יִצְפְּנֵנִי בְּסֻכֹּה בְּיוֹם רָעָה, יַסְתִּרֵנִי בְּסֵתֶר אָהֳלוֹ, בְּצוּר יְרוֹמְמֵנִי: וְעַתָּה יָרוּם רֹאשִׁי עַל אֹיְבַי סְבִיבוֹתַי, וְאֶזְבְּחָה בְאָהֳלוֹ זִבְחֵי תְרוּעָה, אָשִׁירָה וַאֲזַמְּרָה לַיהוה: שְׁמַע־יהוה קוֹלִי אֶקְרָא, וְחָנֵּנִי וַעֲנֵנִי: לְךָ אָמַר לִבִּי בַּקְּשׁוּ פָנָי, אֶת־פָּנֶיךָ יהוה אֲבַקֵּשׁ: אַל־תַּסְתֵּר פָּנֶיךָ מִמֶּנִּי, אַל תַּט־בְּאַף עַבְדֶּךָ, עֶזְרָתִי הָיִיתָ, אַל־תִּטְּשֵׁנִי וְאַל־תַּעַזְבֵנִי, אֱלֹהֵי יִשְׁעִי: כִּי־אָבִי וְאִמִּי עֲזָבוּנִי, וַיהוה יַאַסְפֵנִי: הוֹרֵנִי יהוה דַּרְכֶּךָ, וּנְחֵנִי בְּאֹרַח מִישׁוֹר, לְמַעַן שׁוֹרְרָי: אַל־תִּתְּנֵנִי בְּנֶפֶשׁ צָרָי, כִּי קָמוּ־בִי עֵדֵי־שֶׁקֶר, וִיפֵחַ חָמָס: ‹ לוּלֵא הֶאֱמַנְתִּי לִרְאוֹת בְּטוּב־יהוה בְּאֶרֶץ חַיִּים: קַוֵּה אֶל־יהוה, חֲזַק וְיַאֲמֵץ לִבֶּךָ, וְקַוֵּה אֶל־יהוה:

קדיש יתום (*on previous page*)

Most congregations sing Yigdal at this point.
In Israel, most congregations sing Adon Olam on the following page.

GREAT
is the living God and praised.
He exists, and His existence is beyond time.

He is One, and there is no unity like His.
Unfathomable, His oneness is infinite.

He has neither bodily form nor substance;
His holiness is beyond compare.

He preceded all that was created.
He was first: there was no beginning to His beginning.

Behold He is Master of the Universe; every creature
shows His greatness and majesty.

The rich flow of His prophecy He gave
to His treasured people in whom He gloried.

Never in Israel has there arisen another like Moses,
a prophet who beheld God's image.

God gave His people a Torah of truth
by the hand of His prophet, most faithful of His House.

God will not alter or change His law
for any other, for eternity.

He sees and knows our secret thoughts;
as soon as something is begun, He foresees its end.

He rewards people with loving-kindness according to their deeds;
He punishes the wicked according to his wickedness.

At the end of days He will send our Messiah,
to redeem those who await His final salvation.

God will revive the dead in His great loving-kindness.
Blessed for evermore is His glorious name!

Most congregations sing יגדל *at this point.*
In ארץ ישראל*, most congregations sing* אדון עולם *on the following page.*

יִגְדַּל

אֱלֹהִים חַי וְיִשְׁתַּבַּח, נִמְצָא וְאֵין עֵת אֶל מְצִיאוּתוֹ.
אֶחָד וְאֵין יָחִיד כְּיִחוּדוֹ, נֶעְלָם וְגַם אֵין סוֹף לְאַחְדוּתוֹ.
אֵין לוֹ דְּמוּת הַגּוּף וְאֵינוֹ גוּף, לֹא נַעֲרֹךְ אֵלָיו קְדֻשָּׁתוֹ.
קַדְמוֹן לְכָל דָּבָר אֲשֶׁר נִבְרָא, רִאשׁוֹן וְאֵין רֵאשִׁית לְרֵאשִׁיתוֹ.
הִנּוֹ אֲדוֹן עוֹלָם, וְכָל נוֹצָר יוֹרֶה גְדֻלָּתוֹ וּמַלְכוּתוֹ.
שֶֽׁפַע נְבוּאָתוֹ נְתָנוֹ אֶל־אַנְשֵׁי סְגֻלָּתוֹ וְתִפְאַרְתּוֹ.
לֹא קָם בְּיִשְׂרָאֵל כְּמֹשֶׁה עוֹד נָבִיא וּמַבִּיט אֶת תְּמוּנָתוֹ.
תּוֹרַת אֱמֶת נָתַן לְעַמּוֹ אֵל עַל יַד נְבִיאוֹ נֶאֱמַן בֵּיתוֹ.
לֹא יַחֲלִיף הָאֵל וְלֹא יָמִיר דָּתוֹ לְעוֹלָמִים לְזוּלָתוֹ.
צוֹפֶה וְיוֹדֵעַ סְתָרֵינוּ, מַבִּיט לְסוֹף דָּבָר בְּקַדְמָתוֹ.
גּוֹמֵל לְאִישׁ חֶסֶד כְּמִפְעָלוֹ, נוֹתֵן לְרָשָׁע רָע כְּרִשְׁעָתוֹ.
יִשְׁלַח לְקֵץ יָמִין מְשִׁיחֵנוּ לִפְדּוֹת מְחַכֵּי קֵץ יְשׁוּעָתוֹ.
מֵתִים יְחַיֶּה אֵל בְּרֹב חַסְדּוֹ, בָּרוּךְ עֲדֵי עַד שֵׁם תְּהִלָּתוֹ.

יִגְדַּל אֱלֹהִים חַי *Great is the living God:* A poetic setting of Maimonides' Thirteen Principles of Jewish Faith, written by Rabbi Daniel bar Judah (Rome, fourteenth century), each line representing one of the principles. Like Adon Olam (see next page), the presence of Yigdal in the siddur reminds us that it is not only a book of prayer but also the supreme book of Jewish faith. Judaism contains little systematic theology. We speak *to* God more than we speak *about* God. Yet Judaism *is* a faith whose distinctive beliefs find their home in the prayer book. We do not analyze faith in academic detachment. We sing it, affirming faith with joy.

Lord of the universe,
who reigned before the birth of any thing –

When by His will all things were made
then was His name proclaimed King.

And when all things shall cease to be
He alone will reign in awe.

He was, He is, and He shall be
glorious for evermore.

He is One, there is none else,
alone, unique, beyond compare;

Without beginning, without end,
His might, His rule are everywhere.

He is my God; my Redeemer lives.
He is the Rock on whom I rely –

My banner and my safe retreat,
my cup, my portion when I cry.

Into His hand my soul I place,
when I awake and when I sleep.

The Lord is with me, I shall not fear;
body and soul from harm will He keep.

אֲדוֹן עוֹלָם

אֲשֶׁר מָלַךְ בְּטֶרֶם כָּל־יְצִיר נִבְרָא.
לְעֵת נַעֲשָׂה בְחֶפְצוֹ כֹּל אֲזַי מֶלֶךְ שְׁמוֹ נִקְרָא.
וְאַחֲרֵי כִּכְלוֹת הַכֹּל לְבַדּוֹ יִמְלֹךְ נוֹרָא.
וְהוּא הָיָה וְהוּא הֹוֶה וְהוּא יִהְיֶה בְּתִפְאָרָה.
וְהוּא אֶחָד וְאֵין שֵׁנִי לְהַמְשִׁיל לוֹ לְהַחְבִּירָה.
בְּלִי רֵאשִׁית בְּלִי תַכְלִית וְלוֹ הָעֹז וְהַמִּשְׂרָה.
וְהוּא אֵלִי וְחַי גּוֹאֲלִי וְצוּר חֶבְלִי בְּעֵת צָרָה.
וְהוּא נִסִּי וּמָנוֹס לִי מְנָת כּוֹסִי בְּיוֹם אֶקְרָא.
בְּיָדוֹ אַפְקִיד רוּחִי בְּעֵת אִישַׁן וְאָעִירָה.
וְעִם רוּחִי גְּוִיָּתִי יהוה לִי וְלֹא אִירָא.

COUNTING OF THE OMER

The Omer is counted each night from the second night of Pesaḥ until the night before Shavuot.
Some say the following meditation before the blessing:

For the sake of the unification of the Holy One, blessed be He,
and His Divine Presence, in reverence and love,
to unify the name *Yod-Heh* with *Vav-Heh*
in perfect unity in the name of all Israel.

הִנְנִי I am prepared and ready to fulfill the positive commandment of Counting the Omer, as is written in the Torah, "You shall count seven complete weeks from the day following the [Pesaḥ] rest day, when you brought the Omer as a wave-offering. To the day after the seventh week you shall count fifty days. Then you shall present a meal-offering of new grain to the LORD." May the pleasantness of the LORD our God be upon us. Establish for us the work of our hands, O establish the work of our hands.

Lev. 23

Ps. 90

בָּרוּךְ Blessed are You, LORD our God, King of the Universe,
who has made us holy through His commandments,
and has commanded us about counting the Omer.

16 Nisan

1. Today is the first day of the Omer.

17 Nisan

2. Today is the second day of the Omer.

18 Nisan

3. Today is the third day of the Omer.

19 Nisan

4. Today is the fourth day of the Omer.

20 Nisan

5. Today is the fifth day of the Omer.

21 Nisan

6. Today is the sixth day of the Omer.

Egypt with the giving of the Torah at Mount Sinai, are a time of preparation and growth – of leaving a world of slavery and getting ready to enter a world of personal, social and spiritual responsibility. The Jewish mystics attached special significance to this period of the year as one in which the various facets of the soul were cleansed, one by one.

סדר ספירת העומר

The עומר *is counted each night from the second night of* פסח *until the night before* שבועות*.*

Some say the following meditation before the blessing:

לְשֵׁם יִחוּד קֻדְשָׁא בְּרִיךְ הוּא וּשְׁכִינְתֵּהּ בִּדְחִילוּ וּרְחִימוּ
לְיַחֵד שֵׁם י״ה בו״ה בְּיִחוּדָא שְׁלִים בְּשֵׁם כָּל יִשְׂרָאֵל.

הִנְנִי מוּכָן וּמְזֻמָּן לְקַיֵּם מִצְוַת עֲשֵׂה שֶׁל סְפִירַת הָעְמֶר. כְּמוֹ שֶׁכָּתוּב בַּתּוֹרָה,
ויקרא כג וּסְפַרְתֶּם לָכֶם מִמָּחֳרַת הַשַּׁבָּת, מִיּוֹם הֲבִיאֲכֶם אֶת־עְמֶר הַתְּנוּפָה, שֶׁבַע
שַׁבָּתוֹת תְּמִימֹת תִּהְיֶינָה: עַד מִמָּחֳרַת הַשַּׁבָּת הַשְּׁבִיעִת תִּסְפְּרוּ חֲמִשִּׁים
תהלים צ יוֹם, וְהִקְרַבְתֶּם מִנְחָה חֲדָשָׁה לַיהוה: וִיהִי נֹעַם אֲדֹנָי אֱלֹהֵינוּ עָלֵינוּ, וּמַעֲשֵׂה
יָדֵינוּ כּוֹנְנָה עָלֵינוּ, וּמַעֲשֵׂה יָדֵינוּ כּוֹנְנֵהוּ:

בָּרוּךְ אַתָּה יהוה אֱלֹהֵינוּ מֶלֶךְ הָעוֹלָם
אֲשֶׁר קִדְּשָׁנוּ בְּמִצְוֹתָיו, וְצִוָּנוּ עַל סְפִירַת הָעְמֶר.

טז בניסן
1. הַיּוֹם יוֹם אֶחָד בָּעְמֶר.
חסד שבחסד

יז בניסן
2. הַיּוֹם שְׁנֵי יָמִים בָּעְמֶר.
גבורה שבחסד

יח בניסן
3. הַיּוֹם שְׁלֹשָׁה יָמִים בָּעְמֶר.
תפארת שבחסד

יט בניסן
4. הַיּוֹם אַרְבָּעָה יָמִים בָּעְמֶר.
נצח שבחסד

כ בניסן
5. הַיּוֹם חֲמִשָּׁה יָמִים בָּעְמֶר.
הוד שבחסד

כא בניסן
6. הַיּוֹם שִׁשָּׁה יָמִים בָּעְמֶר.
יסוד שבחסד

COUNTING THE OMER

When the Temple stood, on the day after the first day of Pesaḥ an offering was made of an Omer (approximately nine pounds) of new barley grain. There then began a count of forty-nine days – seven complete weeks – and on the fiftieth day, the festival of Shavuot was celebrated. When the Temple was destroyed, the Sages ordained that we should continue to count the days as a memory of this practice. The forty-nine days, connecting the exodus from

22 Nisan

7. Today is the seventh day,
making one week
of the Omer.

23 Nisan

8. Today is the eighth day,
making one week and one day
of the Omer.

24 Nisan

9. Today is the ninth day,
making one week and two days
of the Omer.

25 Nisan

10. Today is the tenth day,
making one week and three
days of the Omer.

26 Nisan

11. Today is the eleventh day,
making one week and four days
of the Omer.

27 Nisan

12. Today is the twelfth day, making
one week and five days of the
Omer.

28 Nisan

13. Today is the thirteenth day,
making one week and six days
of the Omer.

29 Nisan

14. Today is the fourteenth day,
making two weeks
of the Omer.

30 Nisan, 1st day Rosh Ḥodesh

15. Today is the fifteenth day,
making two weeks and one day
of the Omer.

1 Iyar, 2nd day Rosh Ḥodesh

16. Today is the sixteenth day,
making two weeks and two
days of the Omer.

2 Iyar

17. Today is the seventeenth day,
making two weeks and three
days of the Omer.

3 Iyar

18. Today is the eighteenth day,
making two weeks and four
days of the Omer.

4 Iyar

19. Today is the nineteenth day,
making two weeks and five days
of the Omer.

5 Iyar, Yom HaAtzma'ut

20. Today is the twentieth day,
making two weeks and six days
of the Omer.

כב בניסן

7. הַיּוֹם שִׁבְעָה יָמִים
שֶׁהֵם שָׁבוּעַ אֶחָד בָּעֹמֶר.
מלכות שבחסד

כג בניסן

8. הַיּוֹם שְׁמוֹנָה יָמִים
שֶׁהֵם שָׁבוּעַ אֶחָד וְיוֹם אֶחָד
בָּעֹמֶר.
חסד שבגבורה

כד בניסן

9. הַיּוֹם תִּשְׁעָה יָמִים
שֶׁהֵם שָׁבוּעַ אֶחָד וּשְׁנֵי יָמִים
בָּעֹמֶר.
גבורה שבגבורה

כה בניסן

10. הַיּוֹם עֲשָׂרָה יָמִים
שֶׁהֵם שָׁבוּעַ אֶחָד וּשְׁלֹשָׁה
יָמִים בָּעֹמֶר.
תפארת שבגבורה

כו בניסן

11. הַיּוֹם אַחַד עָשָׂר יוֹם
שֶׁהֵם שָׁבוּעַ אֶחָד וְאַרְבָּעָה
יָמִים בָּעֹמֶר.
נצח שבגבורה

כז בניסן

12. הַיּוֹם שְׁנֵים עָשָׂר יוֹם
שֶׁהֵם שָׁבוּעַ אֶחָד וַחֲמִשָּׁה
יָמִים בָּעֹמֶר.
הוד שבגבורה

כח בניסן

13. הַיּוֹם שְׁלֹשָׁה עָשָׂר יוֹם
שֶׁהֵם שָׁבוּעַ אֶחָד וְשִׁשָּׁה יָמִים
בָּעֹמֶר.
יסוד שבגבורה

כט בניסן

14. הַיּוֹם אַרְבָּעָה עָשָׂר יוֹם
שֶׁהֵם שְׁנֵי שָׁבוּעוֹת
בָּעֹמֶר.
מלכות שבגבורה

ל בניסן, א׳ דראש חודש

15. הַיּוֹם חֲמִשָּׁה עָשָׂר יוֹם
שֶׁהֵם שְׁנֵי שָׁבוּעוֹת וְיוֹם אֶחָד
בָּעֹמֶר.
חסד שבתפארת

א באייר, ב׳ דראש חודש

16. הַיּוֹם שִׁשָּׁה עָשָׂר יוֹם
שֶׁהֵם שְׁנֵי שָׁבוּעוֹת וּשְׁנֵי יָמִים
בָּעֹמֶר.
גבורה שבתפארת

ב באייר

17. הַיּוֹם שִׁבְעָה עָשָׂר יוֹם
שֶׁהֵם שְׁנֵי שָׁבוּעוֹת וּשְׁלֹשָׁה
יָמִים בָּעֹמֶר.
תפארת שבתפארת

ג באייר

18. הַיּוֹם שְׁמוֹנָה עָשָׂר יוֹם
שֶׁהֵם שְׁנֵי שָׁבוּעוֹת וְאַרְבָּעָה
יָמִים בָּעֹמֶר.
נצח שבתפארת

ד באייר

19. הַיּוֹם תִּשְׁעָה עָשָׂר יוֹם
שֶׁהֵם שְׁנֵי שָׁבוּעוֹת וַחֲמִשָּׁה
יָמִים בָּעֹמֶר.
הוד שבתפארת

ה באייר, יום העצמאות

20. הַיּוֹם עֶשְׂרִים יוֹם
שֶׁהֵם שְׁנֵי שָׁבוּעוֹת וְשִׁשָּׁה
יָמִים בָּעֹמֶר.
יסוד שבתפארת

6 Iyar

21. Today is the twenty-first day, making three weeks of the Omer.

7 Iyar

22. Today is the twenty-second day, making three weeks and one day of the Omer.

8 Iyar

23. Today is the twenty-third day, making three weeks and two days of the Omer.

9 Iyar

24. Today is the twenty-fourth day, making three weeks and three days of the Omer.

10 Iyar

25. Today is the twenty-fifth day, making three weeks and four days of the Omer.

11 Iyar

26. Today is the twenty-sixth day, making three weeks and five days of the Omer.

12 Iyar

27. Today is the twenty-seventh day, making three weeks and six days of the Omer.

13 Iyar

28. Today is the twenty-eighth day, making four weeks of the Omer.

14 Iyar, Pesaḥ Sheni

29. Today is the twenty-ninth day, making four weeks and one day of the Omer.

15 Iyar

30. Today is the thirtieth day, making four weeks and two days of the Omer.

16 Iyar

31. Today is the thirty-first day, making four weeks and three days of the Omer.

17 Iyar

32. Today is the thirty-second day, making four weeks and four days of the Omer.

18 Iyar, Lag BaOmer

33. Today is the thirty-third day, making four weeks and five days of the Omer.

19 Iyar

34. Today is the thirty-fourth day, making four weeks and six days of the Omer.

ו באייר

21. הַיּוֹם אֶחָד וְעֶשְׂרִים יוֹם
שֶׁהֵם שְׁלֹשָׁה שָׁבוּעוֹת בָּעֹמֶר.
מלכות שבתפארת

ז באייר

22. הַיּוֹם שְׁנַיִם וְעֶשְׂרִים יוֹם
שֶׁהֵם שְׁלֹשָׁה שָׁבוּעוֹת
וְיוֹם אֶחָד בָּעֹמֶר. חסד שבנצח

ח באייר

23. הַיּוֹם שְׁלֹשָׁה וְעֶשְׂרִים יוֹם
שֶׁהֵם שְׁלֹשָׁה שָׁבוּעוֹת
וּשְׁנֵי יָמִים בָּעֹמֶר. גבורה שבנצח

ט באייר

24. הַיּוֹם אַרְבָּעָה וְעֶשְׂרִים יוֹם
שֶׁהֵם שְׁלֹשָׁה שָׁבוּעוֹת וּשְׁלֹשָׁה
יָמִים בָּעֹמֶר. תפארת שבנצח

י באייר

25. הַיּוֹם חֲמִשָּׁה וְעֶשְׂרִים יוֹם
שֶׁהֵם שְׁלֹשָׁה שָׁבוּעוֹת
וְאַרְבָּעָה יָמִים בָּעֹמֶר. נצח שבנצח

יא באייר

26. הַיּוֹם שִׁשָּׁה וְעֶשְׂרִים יוֹם
שֶׁהֵם שְׁלֹשָׁה שָׁבוּעוֹת
וַחֲמִשָּׁה יָמִים בָּעֹמֶר. הוד שבנצח

יב באייר

27. הַיּוֹם שִׁבְעָה וְעֶשְׂרִים יוֹם
שֶׁהֵם שְׁלֹשָׁה שָׁבוּעוֹת
וְשִׁשָּׁה יָמִים בָּעֹמֶר. יסוד שבנצח

יג באייר

28. הַיּוֹם שְׁמוֹנָה וְעֶשְׂרִים יוֹם
שֶׁהֵם אַרְבָּעָה שָׁבוּעוֹת
בָּעֹמֶר. מלכות שבנצח

יד באייר, פסח שני

29. הַיּוֹם תִּשְׁעָה וְעֶשְׂרִים יוֹם
שֶׁהֵם אַרְבָּעָה שָׁבוּעוֹת
וְיוֹם אֶחָד בָּעֹמֶר. חסד שבהוד

טו באייר

30. הַיּוֹם שְׁלֹשִׁים יוֹם
שֶׁהֵם אַרְבָּעָה שָׁבוּעוֹת
וּשְׁנֵי יָמִים בָּעֹמֶר. גבורה שבהוד

טז באייר

31. הַיּוֹם אֶחָד וּשְׁלֹשִׁים יוֹם
שֶׁהֵם אַרְבָּעָה שָׁבוּעוֹת
וּשְׁלֹשָׁה יָמִים בָּעֹמֶר.
תפארת שבהוד

יז באייר

32. הַיּוֹם שְׁנַיִם וּשְׁלֹשִׁים יוֹם
שֶׁהֵם אַרְבָּעָה שָׁבוּעוֹת
וְאַרְבָּעָה יָמִים בָּעֹמֶר. נצח שבהוד

יח באייר, לג בעומר

33. הַיּוֹם שְׁלֹשָׁה וּשְׁלֹשִׁים יוֹם
שֶׁהֵם אַרְבָּעָה שָׁבוּעוֹת וַחֲמִשָּׁה
יָמִים בָּעֹמֶר. הוד שבהוד

יט באייר

34. הַיּוֹם אַרְבָּעָה וּשְׁלֹשִׁים יוֹם
שֶׁהֵם אַרְבָּעָה שָׁבוּעוֹת
וְשִׁשָּׁה יָמִים בָּעֹמֶר. יסוד שבהוד

20 Iyar

35. Today is the thirty-fifth day, making five weeks of the Omer.

21 Iyar

36. Today is the thirty-sixth day, making five weeks and one day of the Omer.

22 Iyar

37. Today is the thirty-seventh day, making five weeks and two days of the Omer.

23 Iyar

38. Today is the thirty-eighth day, making five weeks and three days of the Omer.

24 Iyar

39. Today is the thirty-ninth day, making five weeks and four days of the Omer.

25 Iyar

40. Today is the fortieth day, making five weeks and five days of the Omer.

26 Iyar

41. Today is the forty-first day, making five weeks and six days of the Omer.

27 Iyar

42. Today is the forty-second day, making six weeks of the Omer.

28 Iyar, Yom Yerushalayim

43. Today is the forty-third day, making six weeks and one day of the Omer.

29 Iyar

44. Today is the forty-fourth day, making six weeks and two days of the Omer.

1 Sivan, Rosh Ḥodesh

45. Today is the forty-fifth day, making six weeks and three days of the Omer.

2 Sivan

46. Today is the forty-sixth day, making six weeks and four days of the Omer.

3 Sivan

47. Today is the forty-seventh day, making six weeks and five days of the Omer.

4 Sivan

48. Today is the forty-eighth day, making six weeks and six days of the Omer.

כ באייר

35. הַיּוֹם חֲמִשָּׁה וּשְׁלֹשִׁים יוֹם שֶׁהֵם חֲמִשָּׁה שָׁבוּעוֹת בָּעֹֽמֶר. מלכות שבהוד

כא באייר

36. הַיּוֹם שִׁשָּׁה וּשְׁלֹשִׁים יוֹם שֶׁהֵם חֲמִשָּׁה שָׁבוּעוֹת וְיוֹם אֶחָד בָּעֹֽמֶר. חסד שביסוד

כב באייר

37. הַיּוֹם שִׁבְעָה וּשְׁלֹשִׁים יוֹם שֶׁהֵם חֲמִשָּׁה שָׁבוּעוֹת וּשְׁנֵי יָמִים בָּעֹֽמֶר. גבורה שביסוד

כג באייר

38. הַיּוֹם שְׁמוֹנָה וּשְׁלֹשִׁים יוֹם שֶׁהֵם חֲמִשָּׁה שָׁבוּעוֹת וּשְׁלֹשָׁה יָמִים בָּעֹֽמֶר. תפארת שביסוד

כד באייר

39. הַיּוֹם תִּשְׁעָה וּשְׁלֹשִׁים יוֹם שֶׁהֵם חֲמִשָּׁה שָׁבוּעוֹת וְאַרְבָּעָה יָמִים בָּעֹֽמֶר. נצח שביסוד

כה באייר

40. הַיּוֹם אַרְבָּעִים יוֹם שֶׁהֵם חֲמִשָּׁה שָׁבוּעוֹת וַחֲמִשָּׁה יָמִים בָּעֹֽמֶר. הוד שביסוד

כו באייר

41. הַיּוֹם אֶחָד וְאַרְבָּעִים יוֹם שֶׁהֵם חֲמִשָּׁה שָׁבוּעוֹת וְשִׁשָּׁה יָמִים בָּעֹֽמֶר. יסוד שביסוד

כז באייר

42. הַיּוֹם שְׁנַיִם וְאַרְבָּעִים יוֹם שֶׁהֵם שִׁשָּׁה שָׁבוּעוֹת בָּעֹֽמֶר. מלכות שביסוד

כח באייר, יום ירושלים

43. הַיּוֹם שְׁלֹשָׁה וְאַרְבָּעִים יוֹם שֶׁהֵם שִׁשָּׁה שָׁבוּעוֹת וְיוֹם אֶחָד בָּעֹֽמֶר. חסד שבמלכות

כט באייר

44. הַיּוֹם אַרְבָּעָה וְאַרְבָּעִים יוֹם שֶׁהֵם שִׁשָּׁה שָׁבוּעוֹת וּשְׁנֵי יָמִים בָּעֹֽמֶר. גבורה שבמלכות

א בסיון, ראש חודש

45. הַיּוֹם חֲמִשָּׁה וְאַרְבָּעִים יוֹם שֶׁהֵם שִׁשָּׁה שָׁבוּעוֹת וּשְׁלֹשָׁה יָמִים בָּעֹֽמֶר. תפארת שבמלכות

ב בסיון

46. הַיּוֹם שִׁשָּׁה וְאַרְבָּעִים יוֹם שֶׁהֵם שִׁשָּׁה שָׁבוּעוֹת וְאַרְבָּעָה יָמִים בָּעֹֽמֶר. נצח שבמלכות

ג בסיון

47. הַיּוֹם שִׁבְעָה וְאַרְבָּעִים יוֹם שֶׁהֵם שִׁשָּׁה שָׁבוּעוֹת וַחֲמִשָּׁה יָמִים בָּעֹֽמֶר. הוד שבמלכות

ד בסיון

48. הַיּוֹם שְׁמוֹנָה וְאַרְבָּעִים יוֹם שֶׁהֵם שִׁשָּׁה שָׁבוּעוֹת וְשִׁשָּׁה יָמִים בָּעֹֽמֶר. יסוד שבמלכות

5 Sivan, Erev Shavuot

49. Today is the forty-ninth day,
making seven weeks of the Omer.

הָרַחֲמָן May the Compassionate One restore the Temple service to its place speedily in our days. Amen, Selah.

Some add:

לַמְנַצֵּחַ For the conductor of music. With stringed instruments. A psalm, a song. *Ps. 67*
May God be gracious to us and bless us. May He make His face shine on us, Selah. Then will Your way be known on earth, Your salvation among all the nations. Let the peoples praise You, God; let all peoples praise You. Let nations rejoice and sing for joy, for You judge the peoples with equity, and guide the nations of the earth, Selah. Let the peoples praise You, God; let all peoples praise You. The earth has yielded its harvest. May God, our God, bless us. God will bless us, and all the ends of the earth will fear Him.

אָנָּא Please, by the power of Your great right hand, set the captive nation free. Accept Your people's prayer. Strengthen us, purify us, You who are revered. Please, mighty One, guard like the pupil of the eye those who seek Your unity. Bless them, cleanse them, have compassion on them, grant them Your righteousness always. Mighty One, holy One, in Your great goodness guide Your congregation. Only One, exalted One, turn to Your people, who proclaim Your holiness. Accept our plea and heed our cry, You who know all secret thoughts. Blessed be the name of His glorious kingdom for ever and all time.

רִבּוֹנוֹ שֶׁל עוֹלָם Master of the Universe, You commanded us through Your servant Moses to count the Omer, to cleanse our carapaces and impurities, as You have written in Your Torah: "You shall count seven complete weeks from the day *Lev. 23*
following the [Pesaḥ] rest day, when you brought the Omer as a wave-offering. To the day after the seventh week, you shall count fifty days." This is so that the souls of Your people Israel may be purified from their uncleanliness. May it also be Your will, Lord our God and God of our ancestors, that in the merit of the Omer count that I have counted today, there may be rectified any defect on my part in the counting of (*insert the appropriate sefira for this day*). May I be cleansed and sanctified with Your holiness on high, and through this may there flow a rich stream through all worlds, to rectify our lives, spirits and souls from any dross and defect, purifying and sanctifying us with Your sublime holiness. Amen, Selah.

The service continues with Aleinu on page 148.

ה בסיון, ערב שבועות

49. הַיּוֹם תִּשְׁעָה וְאַרְבָּעִים יוֹם
שֶׁהֵם שִׁבְעָה שָׁבוּעוֹת בָּעֹמֶר. מלכות שבמלכות

הָרַחֲמָן הוּא יַחֲזִיר לָנוּ עֲבוֹדַת בֵּית הַמִּקְדָּשׁ לִמְקוֹמָהּ בִּמְהֵרָה בְיָמֵינוּ, אָמֵן סֶלָה.

Some add:

תהלים סז
לַמְנַצֵּחַ בִּנְגִינֹת, מִזְמוֹר שִׁיר: אֱלֹהִים יְחָנֵּנוּ וִיבָרְכֵנוּ, יָאֵר פָּנָיו אִתָּנוּ סֶלָה: לָדַעַת בָּאָרֶץ דַּרְכֶּךָ, בְּכָל־גּוֹיִם יְשׁוּעָתֶךָ: יוֹדוּךָ עַמִּים אֱלֹהִים, יוֹדוּךָ עַמִּים כֻּלָּם: יִשְׂמְחוּ וִירַנְּנוּ לְאֻמִּים, כִּי־תִשְׁפֹּט עַמִּים מִישֹׁר, וּלְאֻמִּים בָּאָרֶץ תַּנְחֵם סֶלָה: יוֹדוּךָ עַמִּים אֱלֹהִים, יוֹדוּךָ עַמִּים כֻּלָּם: אֶרֶץ נָתְנָה יְבוּלָהּ, יְבָרְכֵנוּ אֱלֹהִים אֱלֹהֵינוּ: יְבָרְכֵנוּ אֱלֹהִים, וְיִירְאוּ אוֹתוֹ כָּל־אַפְסֵי־אָרֶץ:

אָנָּא, בְּכֹחַ גְּדֻלַּת יְמִינְךָ, תַּתִּיר צְרוּרָה. קַבֵּל רִנַּת עַמְּךָ, שַׂגְּבֵנוּ, טַהֲרֵנוּ, נוֹרָא. נָא גִבּוֹר, דּוֹרְשֵׁי יִחוּדְךָ כְּבָבַת שָׁמְרֵם. בָּרְכֵם, טַהֲרֵם, רַחֲמֵם, צִדְקָתְךָ תָּמִיד גָּמְלֵם. חֲסִין קָדוֹשׁ, בְּרֹב טוּבְךָ נַהֵל עֲדָתֶךָ. יָחִיד גֵּאֶה, לְעַמְּךָ פְּנֵה, זוֹכְרֵי קְדֻשָּׁתֶךָ. שַׁוְעָתֵנוּ קַבֵּל וּשְׁמַע צַעֲקָתֵנוּ, יוֹדֵעַ תַּעֲלוּמוֹת. בָּרוּךְ שֵׁם כְּבוֹד מַלְכוּתוֹ לְעוֹלָם וָעֶד.

רִבּוֹנוֹ שֶׁל עוֹלָם, אַתָּה צִוִּיתָנוּ עַל יְדֵי מֹשֶׁה עַבְדְּךָ לִסְפֹּר סְפִירַת הָעֹמֶר, כְּדֵי לְטַהֲרֵנוּ
ויקרא כג
מִקְּלִפּוֹתֵינוּ וּמִטֻּמְאוֹתֵינוּ. כְּמוֹ שֶׁכָּתַבְתָּ בְּתוֹרָתֶךָ: וּסְפַרְתֶּם לָכֶם מִמָּחֳרַת הַשַּׁבָּת, מִיּוֹם הֲבִיאֲכֶם אֶת־עֹמֶר הַתְּנוּפָה, שֶׁבַע שַׁבָּתוֹת תְּמִימֹת תִּהְיֶינָה: עַד מִמָּחֳרַת הַשַּׁבָּת הַשְּׁבִיעִת תִּסְפְּרוּ חֲמִשִּׁים יוֹם: כְּדֵי שֶׁיִּטָּהֲרוּ נַפְשׁוֹת עַמְּךָ יִשְׂרָאֵל מִזֻּהֲמָתָם. וּבְכֵן יְהִי רָצוֹן מִלְּפָנֶיךָ יהוה אֱלֹהֵינוּ וֵאלֹהֵי אֲבוֹתֵינוּ, שֶׁבִּזְכוּת סְפִירַת הָעֹמֶר שֶׁסָּפַרְתִּי הַיּוֹם, יְתֻקַּן מַה שֶּׁפָּגַמְתִּי בִּסְפִירָה (*insert appropriate* ספירה *for each day*) וְאֶטָּהֵר וְאֶתְקַדֵּשׁ בִּקְדֻשָּׁה שֶׁל מַעְלָה, וְעַל יְדֵי זֶה יֻשְׁפַּע שֶׁפַע רַב בְּכָל הָעוֹלָמוֹת, לְתַקֵּן אֶת נַפְשׁוֹתֵינוּ וְרוּחוֹתֵינוּ וְנִשְׁמוֹתֵינוּ מִכָּל סִיג וּפְגָם, וּלְטַהֲרֵנוּ וּלְקַדְּשֵׁנוּ בִּקְדֻשָּׁתְךָ הָעֶלְיוֹנָה, אָמֵן סֶלָה.

The service continues with עָלֵינוּ *on page 149.*

לַמְנַצֵּחַ *Psalm 67:* Selected to be said at this time because the Psalm (excluding the first verse, which is a superscription and not part of the Psalm itself) contains forty-nine words, corresponding to the days of the counting of the Omer.

רִבּוֹנוֹ שֶׁל עוֹלָם *Master of the Universe:* a prayer emphasizing the idea that the counting of the Omer is a time of spiritual purification.

Se'udat Leil Shabbat

BLESSING THE CHILDREN

On Shabbat evening, many have the custom to bless their children.

To sons, say:

יְשִׂמְךָ May God
make you like Ephraim
and Manasseh.

To daughters, say:

יְשִׂימֵךְ May God
make you like Sarah, Rebecca,
Rachel and Leah. *Gen. 48*

יְבָרֶכְךָ May the Lord bless you and protect you. *Num. 6*
May the Lord make His face shine on you and be gracious to you.
May the Lord turn His face toward you and grant you peace.

Many people sing each of the four verses of the following song three times:

שָׁלוֹם עֲלֵיכֶם Welcome,
ministering angels, angels of the Most High,
from the Supreme King of kings,
the Holy One, blessed be He.

Enter in peace,
angels of peace, angels of the Most High,
from the Supreme King of kings,
the Holy One, blessed be He.

Bless me with peace,
angels of peace, angels of the Most High,
from the Supreme King of kings,
the Holy One, blessed be He.

Go in peace,
angels of peace, angels of the Most High,
from the Supreme King of kings,
the Holy One, blessed be He.

כִּי מַלְאָכָיו He will command His angels about you, *Ps. 91*
to guard you in all your ways.
May the Lord guard your going out and your return, *Ps. 121*
from now and for all time.

סעודת ליל שבת

ברכת הבנים

On ליל שבת, many have the custom to bless their children.

To sons, say:

בראשית מח
יְשִׂמְךָ אֱלֹהִים
כְּאֶפְרַיִם וְכִמְנַשֶּׁה:

To daughters, say:

יְשִׂימֵךְ אֱלֹהִים
כְּשָׂרָה רִבְקָה רָחֵל וְלֵאָה.

במדבר ו
יְבָרֶכְךָ יהוה וְיִשְׁמְרֶךָ:
יָאֵר יהוה פָּנָיו אֵלֶיךָ וִיחֻנֶּךָּ:
יִשָּׂא יהוה פָּנָיו אֵלֶיךָ וְיָשֵׂם לְךָ שָׁלוֹם:

Many people sing each of the four verses of the following song three times:

שָׁלוֹם עֲלֵיכֶם, מַלְאֲכֵי הַשָּׁרֵת, מַלְאֲכֵי עֶלְיוֹן
מִמֶּלֶךְ מַלְכֵי הַמְּלָכִים, הַקָּדוֹשׁ בָּרוּךְ הוּא.

בּוֹאֲכֶם לְשָׁלוֹם, מַלְאֲכֵי הַשָּׁלוֹם, מַלְאֲכֵי עֶלְיוֹן
מִמֶּלֶךְ מַלְכֵי הַמְּלָכִים, הַקָּדוֹשׁ בָּרוּךְ הוּא.

בָּרְכוּנִי לְשָׁלוֹם, מַלְאֲכֵי הַשָּׁלוֹם, מַלְאֲכֵי עֶלְיוֹן
מִמֶּלֶךְ מַלְכֵי הַמְּלָכִים, הַקָּדוֹשׁ בָּרוּךְ הוּא.

צֵאתְכֶם לְשָׁלוֹם, מַלְאֲכֵי הַשָּׁלוֹם, מַלְאֲכֵי עֶלְיוֹן
מִמֶּלֶךְ מַלְכֵי הַמְּלָכִים, הַקָּדוֹשׁ בָּרוּךְ הוּא.

תהלים צא
כִּי מַלְאָכָיו יְצַוֶּה־לָּךְ, לִשְׁמָרְךָ בְּכָל־דְּרָכֶיךָ:
תהלים קכא
יהוה יִשְׁמָר־צֵאתְךָ וּבוֹאֶךָ, מֵעַתָּה וְעַד־עוֹלָם:

Some say:

רִבּוֹן כָּל הָעוֹלָמִים Master of all worlds, LORD of all souls, LORD of peace, mighty, blessed and great King, King who speaks peace, King who is glorious, enduring and pure, King who gives life to worlds, King who is good and does good, King alone and unique, great King who robes Himself in compassion, King who reigns over all kings, who is exalted and supports those who fall, King who is Author of creation, who redeems and rescues, who is radiant and ruddy, King who is holy, high and exalted, King who hears prayer, King whose way is just: I thank You, LORD my God and God of my ancestors, for all the loving-kindness You have done and will do for me, and all the members of my household and all my fellow creatures. Blessed are Your angels, holy and pure, who do Your will. LORD of peace, King to whom peace belongs, bless me with peace, and grant me and the members of my household, and all Your people the house of Israel, a good and peaceful life. King exalted over all the heavenly array, who formed me and who formed creation, I entreat Your radiant presence, that You find me and all the members of my household worthy of grace and good favor in Your eyes and the eyes of all people and all who see us, that we may serve You. May we be worthy to receive Sabbaths amidst great joy, wealth and honor, and few sins. May You remove from me and all the members of my household and all Your people the house of Israel all sickness and disease, all poverty, hardship and destitution. Grant us a virtuous desire to serve You in truth, awe and love. May we find honor in Your eyes and the eyes of all who see us, for You are the King of honor: to You it belongs, to You it accords. Please, King who reigns over all kings, command Your angels, ministering angels who minister to the Most High, to act compassionately toward me when they enter my house on our holy day, for I have lit my lights, spread my couch and changed my clothes in honor of the Sabbath; I have come to Your House to lay my pleas before You that You remove my sighs; I have testified that in six days You created all things, and said it a second time, and will testify to it a third time over my cup, in joy, as You commanded me to remember it, delighting in the extra soul You have given me. On it [the Sabbath] I shall rest as You have commanded me, thereby to serve You. So too I will declare Your greatness in joyful song, for I have set the LORD before me, that You may have compassion upon me in my exile, redeeming me and awakening my heart to Your love. Then I will keep Your commands and statutes without sadness, praying correctly as is right and fitting. Angels of peace, come in peace and bless me with peace; declare blessed the table I have prepared, and go in peace, now and forever. Amen, Selah.

Some say:

רִבּוֹן כָּל הָעוֹלָמִים, אֲדוֹן כָּל הַנְּשָׁמוֹת, אֲדוֹן הַשָּׁלוֹם. מֶלֶךְ אַבִּיר, מֶלֶךְ בָּרוּךְ, מֶלֶךְ גָּדוֹל, מֶלֶךְ דּוֹבֵר שָׁלוֹם, מֶלֶךְ הָדוּר, מֶלֶךְ וָתִיק, מֶלֶךְ זַךְ, מֶלֶךְ חֵי הָעוֹלָמִים, מֶלֶךְ טוֹב וּמֵטִיב, מֶלֶךְ יָחִיד וּמְיֻחָד, מֶלֶךְ כַּבִּיר, מֶלֶךְ לוֹבֵשׁ רַחֲמִים, מֶלֶךְ מַלְכֵי הַמְּלָכִים, מֶלֶךְ נִשְׂגָּב, מֶלֶךְ סוֹמֵךְ נוֹפְלִים, מֶלֶךְ עֹשֶׂה מַעֲשֵׂה בְרֵאשִׁית, מֶלֶךְ פּוֹדֶה וּמַצִּיל, מֶלֶךְ צַח וְאָדֹם, מֶלֶךְ קָדוֹשׁ, מֶלֶךְ רָם וְנִשָּׂא, מֶלֶךְ שׁוֹמֵעַ תְּפִלָּה, מֶלֶךְ תָּמִים דַּרְכּוֹ. מוֹדֶה אֲנִי לְפָנֶיךָ, יהוה אֱלֹהַי וֵאלֹהֵי אֲבוֹתַי, עַל כָּל הַחֶסֶד אֲשֶׁר עָשִׂיתָ עִמָּדִי וַאֲשֶׁר אַתָּה עָתִיד לַעֲשׂוֹת עִמִּי וְעִם כָּל בְּנֵי בֵיתִי וְעִם כָּל בְּרִיּוֹתֶיךָ, בְּנֵי בְרִיתִי. וּבְרוּכִים הֵם מַלְאָכֶיךָ הַקְּדוֹשִׁים וְהַטְּהוֹרִים שֶׁעוֹשִׂים רְצוֹנֶךָ. אֲדוֹן הַשָּׁלוֹם, מֶלֶךְ שֶׁהַשָּׁלוֹם שֶׁלּוֹ, בָּרְכֵנִי בַשָּׁלוֹם, וְתִפְקֹד אוֹתִי וְאֶת כָּל בְּנֵי בֵיתִי וְכָל עַמְּךָ בֵּית יִשְׂרָאֵל לְחַיִּים טוֹבִים וּלְשָׁלוֹם. מֶלֶךְ עֶלְיוֹן עַל כָּל צְבָא מָרוֹם, יוֹצְרֵנוּ, יוֹצֵר בְּרֵאשִׁית, אֲחַלֶּה פָנֶיךָ הַמְּאִירִים, שֶׁתְּזַכֶּה אוֹתִי וְאֶת כָּל בְּנֵי בֵיתִי לִמְצֹא חֵן וְשֵׂכֶל טוֹב בְּעֵינֶיךָ וּבְעֵינֵי כָּל בְּנֵי אָדָם וּבְעֵינֵי כָּל רוֹאֵינוּ לַעֲבוֹדָתֶךָ. וְזַכֵּנוּ לְקַבֵּל שַׁבָּתוֹת מִתּוֹךְ רֹב שִׂמְחָה וּמִתּוֹךְ עֹשֶׁר וְכָבוֹד וּמִתּוֹךְ מִעוּט עֲוֹנוֹת. וְהָסֵר מִמֶּנִּי וּמִכָּל בְּנֵי בֵיתִי וּמִכָּל עַמְּךָ בֵּית יִשְׂרָאֵל כָּל מִינֵי חֹלִי וְכָל מִינֵי מַדְוֶה וְכָל מִינֵי דַלּוּת וַעֲנִיּוּת וְאֶבְיוֹנוּת. וְתֵן בָּנוּ יֵצֶר טוֹב לְעָבְדְךָ בֶּאֱמֶת וּבְיִרְאָה וּבְאַהֲבָה. וְנִהְיֶה מְכֻבָּדִים בְּעֵינֶיךָ וּבְעֵינֵי כָּל רוֹאֵינוּ, כִּי אַתָּה הוּא מֶלֶךְ הַכָּבוֹד, כִּי לְךָ נָאֶה, כִּי לְךָ יָאֶה. אָנָּא, מֶלֶךְ מַלְכֵי הַמְּלָכִים, צַוֵּה לְמַלְאָכֶיךָ, מַלְאֲכֵי הַשָּׁרֵת, מְשָׁרְתֵי עֶלְיוֹן, שֶׁיִּפְקְדוּנִי בְּרַחֲמִים וִיבָרְכוּנִי בְּבוֹאָם לְבֵיתִי בְּיוֹם קָדְשֵׁנוּ, כִּי הִדְלַקְתִּי נֵרוֹתַי וְהִצַּעְתִּי מִטָּתִי וְהֶחֱלַפְתִּי שִׂמְלוֹתַי לִכְבוֹד יוֹם הַשַּׁבָּת וּבָאתִי לְבֵיתְךָ לְהַפִּיל תְּחִנָּתִי לְפָנֶיךָ, שֶׁתַּעֲבִיר אַנְחָתִי, וָאָעִיד אֲשֶׁר בָּרָאתָ בְשִׁשָּׁה יָמִים כָּל הַיְצוּר, וָאֶשְׁנֶה וַאֲשַׁלֵּשׁ עוֹד לְהָעִיד עַל כּוֹסִי בְּתוֹךְ שִׂמְחָתִי, כַּאֲשֶׁר צִוִּיתַנִי לְזָכְרוֹ וּלְהִתְעַנֵּג בְּיֶתֶר נִשְׁמָתִי אֲשֶׁר נָתַתָּ בִּי. בּוֹ אֶשְׁבֹּת כַּאֲשֶׁר צִוִּיתַנִי לְשָׁרְתֶךָ, וְכֵן אַגִּיד גְּדֻלָּתְךָ בְּרִנָּה, וְשִׁוִּיתִי יהוה לִקְרָאתִי שֶׁתְּרַחֲמֵנִי עוֹד בְּגָלוּתִי לְגָאֳלֵנִי לְעוֹרֵר לִבִּי לְאַהֲבָתֶךָ. וְאָז אֶשְׁמֹר פִּקּוּדֶיךָ וְחֻקֶּיךָ בְּלִי עֶצֶב, וְאֶתְפַּלֵּל כַּדָּת כָּרָאוּי וְכַנָּכוֹן. מַלְאֲכֵי הַשָּׁלוֹם, בּוֹאֲכֶם לְשָׁלוֹם, בָּרְכוּנִי לְשָׁלוֹם, וְאִמְרוּ בָּרוּךְ לְשֻׁלְחָנִי הֶעָרוּךְ, וְצֵאתְכֶם לְשָׁלוֹם מֵעַתָּה וְעַד עוֹלָם, אָמֵן סֶלָה.

אֵשֶׁת־חַיִל A woman of strength, who can find? Her worth is far beyond pearls. *Prov. 31*

Her husband's heart trusts in her, and he has no lack of gain.

She brings him good, not harm, all the days of her life.

She seeks wool and linen, and works with willing hands.

She is like a ship laden with merchandise, bringing her food from afar.

She rises while it is still night, providing food for her household, portions for her maids.

She considers a field and buys it; from her earnings she plants a vineyard.

She girds herself with strength, and braces her arms for her tasks.

She sees that her business goes well; her lamp does not go out at night.

She holds the distaff in her hand, and grasps the spindle with her palms.

She reaches out her palm to the poor, and extends her hand to the needy.

She has no fear for her family when it snows, for all her household is clothed in crimson wool.

She makes elegant coverings; her clothing is fine linen and purple wool.

Her husband is well known in the gates,
where he sits with the elders of the land.

She makes linen garments and sells them, and supplies merchants with sashes.

She is clothed with strength and dignity; she can laugh at the days to come.

She opens her mouth with wisdom,
and the law of kindness is on her tongue.

She watches over the ways of her household,
and never eats the bread of idleness.

Her children rise and call her happy; her husband also praises her:

"Many women have excelled, but you surpass them all."

Charm is deceptive and beauty vain:
it is the God-fearing woman who deserves praise.

Give her the reward she has earned;
let her deeds bring her praise in the gates.

אֵשֶׁת־חַיִל מִי יִמְצָא, וְרָחֹק מִפְּנִינִים מִכְרָהּ: משלי לא
בָּטַח בָּהּ לֵב בַּעְלָהּ, וְשָׁלָל לֹא יֶחְסָר:
גְּמָלַתְהוּ טוֹב וְלֹא־רָע, כֹּל יְמֵי חַיֶּיהָ:
דָּרְשָׁה צֶמֶר וּפִשְׁתִּים, וַתַּעַשׂ בְּחֵפֶץ כַּפֶּיהָ:
הָיְתָה כָּאֳנִיּוֹת סוֹחֵר, מִמֶּרְחָק תָּבִיא לַחְמָהּ:
וַתָּקָם בְּעוֹד לַיְלָה, וַתִּתֵּן טֶרֶף לְבֵיתָהּ, וְחֹק לְנַעֲרֹתֶיהָ:
זָמְמָה שָׂדֶה וַתִּקָּחֵהוּ, מִפְּרִי כַפֶּיהָ נָטְעָ כָּרֶם:
חָגְרָה בְעוֹז מָתְנֶיהָ, וַתְּאַמֵּץ זְרוֹעֹתֶיהָ:
טָעֲמָה כִּי־טוֹב סַחְרָהּ, לֹא־יִכְבֶּה בַלַּיְל נֵרָהּ:
יָדֶיהָ שִׁלְּחָה בַכִּישׁוֹר, וְכַפֶּיהָ תָּמְכוּ פָלֶךְ:
כַּפָּהּ פָּרְשָׂה לֶעָנִי, וְיָדֶיהָ שִׁלְּחָה לָאֶבְיוֹן:
לֹא־תִירָא לְבֵיתָהּ מִשָּׁלֶג, כִּי כָל־בֵּיתָהּ לָבֻשׁ שָׁנִים:
מַרְבַדִּים עָשְׂתָה־לָּהּ, שֵׁשׁ וְאַרְגָּמָן לְבוּשָׁהּ:
נוֹדָע בַּשְּׁעָרִים בַּעְלָהּ, בְּשִׁבְתּוֹ עִם־זִקְנֵי־אָרֶץ:
סָדִין עָשְׂתָה וַתִּמְכֹּר, וַחֲגוֹר נָתְנָה לַכְּנַעֲנִי:
עוֹז־וְהָדָר לְבוּשָׁהּ, וַתִּשְׂחַק לְיוֹם אַחֲרוֹן:
פִּיהָ פָּתְחָה בְחָכְמָה, וְתוֹרַת־חֶסֶד עַל־לְשׁוֹנָהּ:
צוֹפִיָּה הֲלִיכוֹת בֵּיתָהּ, וְלֶחֶם עַצְלוּת לֹא תֹאכֵל:
קָמוּ בָנֶיהָ וַיְאַשְּׁרוּהָ, בַּעְלָהּ וַיְהַלְלָהּ:
רַבּוֹת בָּנוֹת עָשׂוּ חָיִל, וְאַתְּ עָלִית עַל־כֻּלָּנָה:
שֶׁקֶר הַחֵן וְהֶבֶל הַיֹּפִי, אִשָּׁה יִרְאַת־יהוה הִיא תִתְהַלָּל:
תְּנוּ־לָהּ מִפְּרִי יָדֶיהָ, וִיהַלְלוּהָ בַשְּׁעָרִים מַעֲשֶׂיהָ:

Some say:

Prepare the feast of perfect faith, joy of the holy King.
Prepare the royal feast.

This is the feast [mystically known as] 'the Field of Holy Apples' –
and 'the Small Face' and 'the Holy Ancient One'
[mystical terms for aspects of the Divine] come to partake in the feast with it.

With songs of praise I will cut away [evil forces],
to enter the holy gates of 'the Field of Apples.'
We now invite Her [the Divine Presence] with a newly prepared table
and a fine candelabrum spreading light upon our heads.
Between right and left is the bride, decked with jewelry, adorned and robed.
Her husband embraces her, and in the joy of their togetherness
[evil forces] are crushed.
Cries and suffering stop and cease; a new face comes upon spirits and souls.
She will have great and doubled joy; light will come, and bounteous blessing.
Come near, dear friends, and prepare delicacies of many kinds, and fish and fowl.
Renewing souls and spirits through the thirty-two [paths of wisdom]
and the three branches [of Scripture].
She [the Divine Presence] has seventy crowns, and above,
the King is crowned with all in the Holy of Holies.
Engraved and hidden with her are all worlds,
but the pestle of the Ancient of Days releases all that is hidden.
May it be His will that the Divine Presence rest on His people who,
for His name's sake, delight in sweet foods and honey.
To the south, I will arrange the candelabrum of hidden [wisdom],
to the north I will set the table with bread.
With wine in the cup, and myrtle clusters for bridegroom and bride,
the weak will be given strength.
Let us make them crowns of precious words, seventy crowns beyond the fifty.
May the Divine Presence be crowned with six loaves on each side, like
the two sets of six loaves [of showbread] and other articles [in the Temple].
[On the Sabbath] impure powers and afflicting angels cease and desist; and
those who are confined have respite.
To break bread the size of an olive or an egg, for there are two ways of
interpreting the *Yod* [of the divine name], restrictively or expansively.
It is like pure olive oil, pressed in a mill, flowing like rivers, whispering secrets.
Let us speak of mysteries, secrets unrevealed, hidden and concealed.
To crown the bride with mysteries above, at this,
the holy angels' wedding celebration.

Some say:

אַתְקִינוּ סְעוּדְתָא דִמְהֵימְנוּתָא שְׁלִימְתָא
חֶדְוָתָא דְמַלְכָּא קַדִּישָׁא.
אַתְקִינוּ סְעוּדְתָא דְמַלְכָּא.
דָּא הִיא סְעוּדְתָא דַחֲקַל תַּפּוּחִין קַדִּישִׁין
וּזְעֵיר אַנְפִּין וְעַתִּיקָא קַדִּישָׁא אָתַיִן לְסַעֲדָה בַּהֲדַהּ.

אֲזַמֵּר בִּשְׁבָחִין / לְמֶעַל גּוֹ פִתְחִין / דְּבַחֲקַל תַּפּוּחִין / דְּאִנּוּן קַדִּישִׁין.
נְזַמֵּן לַהּ הַשְׁתָּא / בְּפָתוֹרָא חַדְתָּא / וּבִמְנָרְתָא טָבְתָא / דְּנָהֲרָה עַל רֵישִׁין.
יְמִינָא וּשְׂמָאלָא / וּבֵינַיְהוּ כַלָּה / בְּקִשּׁוּטִין אָזְלָא / וּמָנִין וּלְבוּשִׁין.
יְחַבֵּק לַהּ בַּעְלָהּ / וּבִיסוֹדָא דִי לַהּ / דְּעָבֵד נְיָחָא לַהּ / יְהֵא כָתֵשׁ כְּתִישִׁין.
צְוָחִין אוֹף עָקְתִין / בְּטִילִין וּשְׁבִיתִין / בְּרַם אַנְפִּין חַדְתִּין / וְרוּחִין עִם נַפְשִׁין.
חֲדוּ סַגִּי יֵיתֵי / וְעַל חֲדָה תַרְתֵּי / נְהוֹרָא לַהּ יַמְטֵי / וּבִרְכָן דִּנְפִישִׁין.
קְרִיבוּ שׁוֹשְׁבִינִין / עֲבִידוּ תִקּוּנִין / לְאַפָּשָׁה זֵינִין / וְנוּנִין עִם רַחֲשִׁין.
לְמֶעְבַּד נִשְׁמָתִין / וְרוּחִין חַדְתִּין / בְּתַרְתֵּי וּתְלָתִין / וּבִתְלָתָא שִׁבְשִׁין.
וְעִטְרִין שַׁבְעִין לַהּ / וּמַלְכָּא דִלְעֵלָּא / דְּיִתְעַטַּר כֹּלָּא / בְּקַדִּישׁ קַדִּישִׁין.
רְשִׁימִין וּסְתִימִין / בְּגַוַּהּ כָּל עָלְמִין / בְּרַם עַתִּיק יוֹמִין / הֲלָא בָטֵשׁ בְּטִישִׁין.
יְהֵא רַעֲוָה קַמֵּהּ / דְּתִשְׁרֵי עַל עַמֵּהּ / דְּיִתְעַנַּג לִשְׁמֵהּ / בְּמִתְקִין וְדֻבְשִׁין.
אֲסַדֵּר לִדְרוֹמָא / מְנָרְתָא דִסְתִימָא / וְשֻׁלְחָן עִם נַהְמָא / בִּצְפּוּנָא אַדְשִׁין.
בְּחַמְרָא גוֹ כָסָא / וּמַדָּנֵי אָסָא / לְאָרוּס וַאֲרוּסָה / לְאַתְקָפָא חַלָּשִׁין.
נְעַבֵּד לוֹן כִּתְרִין / בְּמִלִּין יַקִּירִין / בְּשִׁבְעִין עִטּוּרִין / דְּעַל גַּבֵּי חַמְשִׁין.
שְׁכִינְתָא תִתְעַטַּר / בְּשִׁית נַהֲמֵי לִסְטַר / בְּוָוִין תִּתְקַטַּר / וְזֵינִין דִּכְנִישִׁין.
(שְׁבִיתִין וּשְׁבִיקִין / מְסָאֲבִין דְּדָחֲקִין / חֲבִילִין דִּמְעִיקִין / וְכָל זֵינֵי חַרְשִׁין.)
לְמִבְצַע עַל רִיפְתָא / כְּזֵיתָא וּכְבֵיעְתָא / תְּרֵין יוּדִין נָקְטָא / סְתִימִין וּפְרִישִׁין.
מְשַׁח זֵיתָא דָכְיָא / דְּטָחֲנִין רֵיחַיָּא / וְנָגְדִין נַחְלַיָּא / בְּגַוַּהּ בִּלְחִישִׁין.
הֲלָא נֵימָא רָזִין / וּמִלִּין דִּגְנִיזִין / דְּלֵיתֵיהוֹן מִתְחֲזִין / טְמִירִין וּכְבִישִׁין.
לְאַעְטָרָה כַלָּה / בְּרָזִין דִּלְעֵלָּא / בְּגוֹ הַאי הִלּוּלָא / דְּעִירִין קַדִּישִׁין.

Kiddush for Shabbat Evening

Quietly: And it was evening, and it was morning – Gen. 1

יוֹם הַשִּׁשִּׁי the sixth day.

Then the heavens and the earth were completed, and all their array. Gen. 2
With the seventh day, God completed the work He had done.
He ceased on the seventh day from all the work He had done.
God blessed the seventh day and declared it holy,
because on it He ceased from all His work He had created to do.

When saying Kiddush for others, add:
Please pay attention, my masters.

Blessed are You, Lord our God, King of the Universe,
who creates the fruit of the vine.

Blessed are You, Lord our God, King of the Universe,
who has made us holy through His commandments,
who has favored us,
and in love and favor gave us His holy Sabbath as a heritage,
a remembrance of the work of creation.
It is the first among the holy days of assembly,
a remembrance of the exodus from Egypt.
For You chose us and sanctified us from all the peoples,
and in love and favor gave us Your holy Sabbath as a heritage.
Blessed are You, Lord, who sanctifies the Sabbath.

On Shabbat Ḥol HaMo'ed Sukkot, if Kiddush is made in the sukka, add:
Blessed are You, Lord our God, King of the Universe,
who has made us holy through his commandments and has
commanded us to dwell in the sukka.

It is customary for all present to drink of the wine.

קידוש לליל שבת

Quietly וַיְהִי־עֶרֶב וַיְהִי־בֹקֶר בראשית א
יוֹם הַשִּׁשִּׁי:

וַיְכֻלּוּ הַשָּׁמַיִם וְהָאָרֶץ וְכָל־צְבָאָם: בראשית ב
וַיְכַל אֱלֹהִים בַּיּוֹם הַשְּׁבִיעִי מְלַאכְתּוֹ אֲשֶׁר עָשָׂה
וַיִּשְׁבֹּת בַּיּוֹם הַשְּׁבִיעִי מִכָּל־מְלַאכְתּוֹ אֲשֶׁר עָשָׂה:
וַיְבָרֶךְ אֱלֹהִים אֶת־יוֹם הַשְּׁבִיעִי, וַיְקַדֵּשׁ אֹתוֹ
כִּי בוֹ שָׁבַת מִכָּל־מְלַאכְתּוֹ, אֲשֶׁר־בָּרָא אֱלֹהִים, לַעֲשׂוֹת:

When saying קידוש *for others, add:*

סַבְרִי מָרָנָן

בָּרוּךְ אַתָּה יהוה אֱלֹהֵינוּ מֶלֶךְ הָעוֹלָם, בּוֹרֵא פְּרִי הַגָּפֶן.

בָּרוּךְ אַתָּה יהוה אֱלֹהֵינוּ מֶלֶךְ הָעוֹלָם
אֲשֶׁר קִדְּשָׁנוּ בְּמִצְוֹתָיו, וְרָצָה בָנוּ
וְשַׁבַּת קָדְשׁוֹ בְּאַהֲבָה וּבְרָצוֹן הִנְחִילָנוּ
זִכָּרוֹן לְמַעֲשֵׂה בְרֵאשִׁית
כִּי הוּא יוֹם תְּחִלָּה לְמִקְרָאֵי קֹדֶשׁ, זֵכֶר לִיצִיאַת מִצְרָיִם
כִּי בָנוּ בָחַרְתָּ וְאוֹתָנוּ קִדַּשְׁתָּ מִכָּל הָעַמִּים
וְשַׁבַּת קָדְשְׁךָ בְּאַהֲבָה וּבְרָצוֹן הִנְחַלְתָּנוּ.
בָּרוּךְ אַתָּה יהוה, מְקַדֵּשׁ הַשַּׁבָּת.

On שבת חול המועד סוכות*, if* קידוש *is made in the* סוכה*, add:*

בָּרוּךְ אַתָּה יהוה אֱלֹהֵינוּ מֶלֶךְ הָעוֹלָם
אֲשֶׁר קִדְּשָׁנוּ בְּמִצְוֹתָיו וְצִוָּנוּ לֵישֵׁב בַּסֻּכָּה.

It is customary for all present to drink of the wine.

THE MEAL AND ITS BLESSINGS

On washing hands before eating bread:

Blessed are You, Lord our God, King of the Universe,
who has made us holy through His commandments,
and has commanded us about washing hands.

Before eating bread:

Blessed are You, Lord our God, King of the Universe,
who brings forth bread from the earth.

BIRKAT HAMAZON / GRACE AFTER MEALS

שִׁיר הַמַּעֲלוֹת A song of ascents. *Ps. 126*
When the Lord brought back the exiles of Zion
we were like people who dream.
Then were our mouths filled with laughter,
and our tongues with songs of joy.
Then was it said among the nations,
"The Lord has done great things for them."
The Lord did do great things for us and we rejoiced.
Bring back our exiles, Lord, like streams in a dry land.
May those who sowed in tears, reap in joy.
May one who goes out weeping, carrying a bag of seed,
come back with songs of joy, carrying his sheaves.

Some say:

תְּהִלַּת My mouth shall speak the praise of God, *Ps. 145*
and all creatures shall bless His holy name for ever and all time.
We will bless God now and for ever. Halleluya! *Ps. 115*
Thank the Lord for He is good; His loving-kindness is for ever. *Ps. 136*
Who can tell of the Lord's mighty acts *Ps. 106*
and make all His praise be heard?

סדר סעודה וברכותיה

On washing hands before eating bread:

בָּרוּךְ אַתָּה יהוה אֱלֹהֵינוּ מֶלֶךְ הָעוֹלָם
אֲשֶׁר קִדְּשָׁנוּ בְּמִצְוֹתָיו וְצִוָּנוּ עַל נְטִילַת יָדָיִם.

Before eating bread:

בָּרוּךְ אַתָּה יהוה אֱלֹהֵינוּ מֶלֶךְ הָעוֹלָם
הַמּוֹצִיא לֶחֶם מִן הָאָרֶץ.

ברכת המזון

שִׁיר הַמַּעֲלוֹת, בְּשׁוּב יהוה אֶת־שִׁיבַת צִיּוֹן, הָיִינוּ כְּחֹלְמִים׃ תהלים קכו
אָז יִמָּלֵא שְׂחוֹק פִּינוּ וּלְשׁוֹנֵנוּ רִנָּה
אָז יֹאמְרוּ בַגּוֹיִם הִגְדִּיל יהוה לַעֲשׂוֹת עִם־אֵלֶּה׃
הִגְדִּיל יהוה לַעֲשׂוֹת עִמָּנוּ, הָיִינוּ שְׂמֵחִים׃
שׁוּבָה יהוה אֶת־שְׁבִיתֵנוּ, כַּאֲפִיקִים בַּנֶּגֶב׃
הַזֹּרְעִים בְּדִמְעָה בְּרִנָּה יִקְצֹרוּ׃
הָלוֹךְ יֵלֵךְ וּבָכֹה נֹשֵׂא מֶשֶׁךְ־הַזָּרַע
בֹּא־יָבֹא בְרִנָּה נֹשֵׂא אֲלֻמֹּתָיו׃

Some say:

תְּהִלַּת יהוה יְדַבֶּר פִּי, וִיבָרֵךְ כָּל־בָּשָׂר שֵׁם קָדְשׁוֹ לְעוֹלָם וָעֶד׃ תהלים קמה
וַאֲנַחְנוּ נְבָרֵךְ יָהּ מֵעַתָּה וְעַד־עוֹלָם, הַלְלוּיָהּ׃ תהלים קטו
הוֹדוּ לַיהוה כִּי־טוֹב, כִּי לְעוֹלָם חַסְדּוֹ׃ תהלים קלו
מִי יְמַלֵּל גְּבוּרוֹת יהוה, יַשְׁמִיעַ כָּל־תְּהִלָּתוֹ׃ תהלים קו

ZIMMUN / INVITATION

When three or more men say Birkat HaMazon together, the following zimmun is said. When three or more women say Birkat HaMazon, substitute "Friends" for "Gentlemen." The leader should ask permission from those with precedence to lead the Birkat HaMazon.

Leader Gentlemen, let us say grace.

Others May the name of the LORD be blessed from now and for ever. *Ps. 113*

Leader May the name of the LORD be blessed from now and for ever.
With your permission, (my father and teacher / my mother and teacher / the Kohanim present / our teacher the Rabbi / the master of this house / the mistress of this house)
my masters and teachers,
let us bless (*in a minyan:* our God,) the One
from whose food we have eaten.

Others Blessed be (*in a minyan:* our God,) the One
from whose food we have eaten, and by whose goodness we live.

**People present who have not taken part in the meal say:*
*Blessed be (*in a minyan:* our God,) the One
whose name is continually blessed for ever and all time.

Leader Blessed be (*in a minyan:* our God,) the One
from whose food we have eaten, and by whose goodness we live.
Blessed be He, and blessed be His name.

BLESSING OF NOURISHMENT

בָּרוּךְ Blessed are You, LORD our God, King of the Universe,
who in His goodness feeds the whole world
with grace, kindness and compassion.
He gives food to all living things,
for His kindness is for ever.
Because of His continual great goodness,
we have never lacked food,
nor may we ever lack it, for the sake of His great name.
For He is God who feeds and sustains all,
does good to all,
and prepares food for all creatures He has created.
Blessed are You, LORD, who feeds all.

סדר הזימון

When three or more men say ברכת המזון *together, the following* זימון *is said.*
When three or more women say ברכת המזון*, substitute* חֲבֵרוֹתַי *for* רַבּוֹתַי.
The leader should ask permission from those with precedence to lead the ברכת המזון.

Leader רַבּוֹתַי, נְבָרֵךְ.

Others יְהִי שֵׁם יהוה מְבֹרָךְ מֵעַתָּה וְעַד־עוֹלָם: תהלים קיג

Leader יְהִי שֵׁם יהוה מְבֹרָךְ מֵעַתָּה וְעַד־עוֹלָם:
בִּרְשׁוּת (אָבִי מוֹרִי / אִמִּי מוֹרָתִי / כֹּהֲנִים / מוֹרֵנוּ הָרַב /
בַּעַל הַבַּיִת הַזֶּה / בַּעֲלַת הַבַּיִת הַזֶּה)
מָרָנָן וְרַבָּנָן וְרַבּוֹתַי
נְבָרֵךְ (במנין: אֱלֹהֵינוּ) שֶׁאָכַלְנוּ מִשֶּׁלּוֹ.

Others בָּרוּךְ (במנין: אֱלֹהֵינוּ) שֶׁאָכַלְנוּ מִשֶּׁלּוֹ וּבְטוּבוֹ חָיִינוּ.

**People present who have not taken part in the meal say:*

*בָּרוּךְ (במנין: אֱלֹהֵינוּ) וּמְבֹרָךְ שְׁמוֹ תָּמִיד לְעוֹלָם וָעֶד.

Leader בָּרוּךְ (במנין: אֱלֹהֵינוּ) שֶׁאָכַלְנוּ מִשֶּׁלּוֹ וּבְטוּבוֹ חָיִינוּ.
בָּרוּךְ הוּא וּבָרוּךְ שְׁמוֹ.

ברכת הזן

בָּרוּךְ אַתָּה יהוה אֱלֹהֵינוּ מֶלֶךְ הָעוֹלָם
הַזָּן אֶת הָעוֹלָם כֻּלּוֹ בְּטוּבוֹ, בְּחֵן בְּחֶסֶד וּבְרַחֲמִים
הוּא נוֹתֵן לֶחֶם לְכָל בָּשָׂר, כִּי לְעוֹלָם חַסְדּוֹ.
וּבְטוּבוֹ הַגָּדוֹל, תָּמִיד לֹא חָסַר לָנוּ
וְאַל יֶחְסַר לָנוּ מָזוֹן לְעוֹלָם וָעֶד
בַּעֲבוּר שְׁמוֹ הַגָּדוֹל.
כִּי הוּא אֵל זָן וּמְפַרְנֵס לַכֹּל, וּמֵטִיב לַכֹּל
וּמֵכִין מָזוֹן לְכָל בְּרִיּוֹתָיו אֲשֶׁר בָּרָא.
בָּרוּךְ אַתָּה יהוה, הַזָּן אֶת הַכֹּל.

BLESSING OF LAND

נוֹדֶה We thank You, LORD our God,
for having granted as a heritage to our ancestors
a desirable, good and spacious land;
for bringing us out, LORD our God, from the land of Egypt,
freeing us from the house of slavery;
for Your covenant which You sealed in our flesh;
for Your Torah which You taught us;
for Your laws which You made known to us;
for the life, grace and kindness You have bestowed on us;
and for the food by which You continually feed and sustain us,
every day, every season, every hour.

On Ḥanukka:

עַל הַנִּסִּים [We thank You also] for the miracles, the redemption, the mighty deeds, the salvations, and the victories in battle which You performed for our ancestors in those days, at this time.

בִּימֵי מַתִּתְיָהוּ In the days of Mattityahu, son of Yoḥanan, the High Priest, the Hasmonean, and his sons, the wicked Greek kingdom rose up against Your people Israel to make them forget Your Torah and to force them to transgress the statutes of Your will. It was then that You in Your great compassion stood by them in the time of their distress. You championed their cause, judged their claim, and avenged their wrong. You delivered the strong into the hands of the weak, the many into the hands of the few, the impure into the hands of the pure, the wicked into the hands of the righteous, and the arrogant into the hands of those who were engaged in the study of Your Torah. You made for Yourself great and holy renown in Your world, and for Your people Israel You performed a great salvation and redemption as of this very day. Your children then entered the holiest part of Your House, cleansed Your Temple, purified Your Sanctuary, kindled lights in Your holy courts, and designated these eight days of Ḥanukka for giving thanks and praise to Your great name.

Continue with "For all this."

ברכת הארץ

נוֹדֶה לְּךָ, יהוה אֱלֹהֵינוּ
עַל שֶׁהִנְחַלְתָּ לַאֲבוֹתֵינוּ אֶרֶץ חֶמְדָּה טוֹבָה וּרְחָבָה
וְעַל שֶׁהוֹצֵאתָנוּ יהוה אֱלֹהֵינוּ מֵאֶרֶץ מִצְרַיִם
וּפְדִיתָנוּ מִבֵּית עֲבָדִים
וְעַל בְּרִיתְךָ שֶׁחָתַמְתָּ בִּבְשָׂרֵנוּ
וְעַל תּוֹרָתְךָ שֶׁלִּמַּדְתָּנוּ
וְעַל חֻקֶּיךָ שֶׁהוֹדַעְתָּנוּ
וְעַל חַיִּים חֵן וָחֶסֶד שֶׁחוֹנַנְתָּנוּ
וְעַל אֲכִילַת מָזוֹן
שָׁאַתָּה זָן וּמְפַרְנֵס אוֹתָנוּ תָּמִיד
בְּכָל יוֹם וּבְכָל עֵת וּבְכָל שָׁעָה.

בחנוכה:

עַל הַנִּסִּים וְעַל הַפֻּרְקָן וְעַל הַגְּבוּרוֹת וְעַל הַתְּשׁוּעוֹת וְעַל הַמִּלְחָמוֹת שֶׁעָשִׂיתָ לַאֲבוֹתֵינוּ בַּיָּמִים הָהֵם בַּזְּמַן הַזֶּה.

בִּימֵי מַתִּתְיָהוּ בֶּן יוֹחָנָן כֹּהֵן גָּדוֹל חַשְׁמוֹנַאי וּבָנָיו, כְּשֶׁעָמְדָה מַלְכוּת יָוָן הָרְשָׁעָה עַל עַמְּךָ יִשְׂרָאֵל לְהַשְׁכִּיחָם תּוֹרָתֶךָ וּלְהַעֲבִירָם מֵחֻקֵּי רְצוֹנֶךָ, וְאַתָּה בְּרַחֲמֶיךָ הָרַבִּים עָמַדְתָּ לָהֶם בְּעֵת צָרָתָם, רַבְתָּ אֶת רִיבָם, דַּנְתָּ אֶת דִּינָם, נָקַמְתָּ אֶת נִקְמָתָם, מָסַרְתָּ גִבּוֹרִים בְּיַד חַלָּשִׁים, וְרַבִּים בְּיַד מְעַטִּים, וּטְמֵאִים בְּיַד טְהוֹרִים, וּרְשָׁעִים בְּיַד צַדִּיקִים, וְזֵדִים בְּיַד עוֹסְקֵי תוֹרָתֶךָ, וּלְךָ עָשִׂיתָ שֵׁם גָּדוֹל וְקָדוֹשׁ בְּעוֹלָמֶךָ, וּלְעַמְּךָ יִשְׂרָאֵל עָשִׂיתָ תְּשׁוּעָה גְדוֹלָה וּפֻרְקָן כְּהַיּוֹם הַזֶּה. וְאַחַר כֵּן בָּאוּ בָנֶיךָ לִדְבִיר בֵּיתֶךָ, וּפִנּוּ אֶת הֵיכָלֶךָ, וְטִהֲרוּ אֶת מִקְדָּשֶׁךָ, וְהִדְלִיקוּ נֵרוֹת בְּחַצְרוֹת קָדְשֶׁךָ, וְקָבְעוּ שְׁמוֹנַת יְמֵי חֲנֻכָּה אֵלּוּ, לְהוֹדוֹת וּלְהַלֵּל לְשִׁמְךָ הַגָּדוֹל.

Continue with וְעַל הַכֹּל.

On Shushan Purim in Jerusalem:

עַל הַנִּסִּים [We thank You also] for the miracles, the redemption, the mighty deeds, the salvations, and the victories in battle which You performed for our ancestors in those days, at this time.

בִּימֵי מָרְדְּכַי In the days of Mordekhai and Esther, in Shushan the capital, the wicked Haman rose up against them and sought to destroy, slay and exterminate all the Jews, young and old, children and women, on one day, the thirteenth day of the twelfth month, which is the month of Adar, and to plunder their possessions. Then You in Your great compassion thwarted his counsel, frustrated his plans, and caused his scheme to recoil on his own head, so that they hanged him and his sons on the gallows. *Esther 3*

Continue with "For all this."

וְעַל הַכֹּל For all this, Lord our God, we thank and bless You.
May Your name be blessed continually
by the mouth of all that lives, for ever and all time –
for so it is written: "You will eat and be satisfied, then you shall bless the Lord your God for the good land He has given you." *Deut. 8*
Blessed are You, Lord, for the land and for the food.

BLESSING FOR JERUSALEM

רַחֵם נָא Have compassion, please, Lord our God,
on Israel Your people,
on Jerusalem Your city,
on Zion the dwelling place of Your glory,
on the royal house of David Your anointed,
and on the great and holy House that bears Your name.
Our God, our Father,
tend us, feed us, sustain us and support us,
relieve us and send us relief,
Lord our God, swiftly from all our troubles.
Please, Lord our God, do not make us dependent
on the gifts or loans of other people,
but only on Your full, open, holy and generous hand
so that we may suffer neither shame nor humiliation
for ever and all time.

בשושן פורים בירושלים:

עַל הַנִּסִּים וְעַל הַפֻּרְקָן וְעַל הַגְּבוּרוֹת וְעַל הַתְּשׁוּעוֹת וְעַל הַמִּלְחָמוֹת שֶׁעָשִׂיתָ לַאֲבוֹתֵינוּ בַּיָּמִים הָהֵם בַּזְּמַן הַזֶּה.

בִּימֵי מָרְדְּכַי וְאֶסְתֵּר בְּשׁוּשַׁן הַבִּירָה, כְּשֶׁעָמַד עֲלֵיהֶם הָמָן הָרָשָׁע, בִּקֵּשׁ לְהַשְׁמִיד לַהֲרֹג וּלְאַבֵּד אֶת־כָּל־הַיְּהוּדִים מִנַּעַר וְעַד־זָקֵן טַף וְנָשִׁים בְּיוֹם אֶחָד, בִּשְׁלוֹשָׁה עָשָׂר לְחֹדֶשׁ שְׁנֵים־עָשָׂר, הוּא־חֹדֶשׁ אֲדָר, וּשְׁלָלָם לָבוֹז: וְאַתָּה בְּרַחֲמֶיךָ הָרַבִּים הֵפַרְתָּ אֶת עֲצָתוֹ, וְקִלְקַלְתָּ אֶת מַחֲשַׁבְתּוֹ, וַהֲשֵׁבוֹתָ לּוֹ גְּמוּלוֹ בְּרֹאשׁוֹ, וְתָלוּ אוֹתוֹ וְאֶת בָּנָיו עַל הָעֵץ. אסתר ג

Continue with וְעַל הַכֹּל.

וְעַל הַכֹּל, יהוה אֱלֹהֵינוּ, אֲנַחְנוּ מוֹדִים לָךְ וּמְבָרְכִים אוֹתָךְ
יִתְבָּרַךְ שִׁמְךָ בְּפִי כָּל חַי תָּמִיד לְעוֹלָם וָעֶד
כַּכָּתוּב: וְאָכַלְתָּ וְשָׂבָעְתָּ, וּבֵרַכְתָּ אֶת־יהוה אֱלֹהֶיךָ דברים ח
עַל־הָאָרֶץ הַטֹּבָה אֲשֶׁר נָתַן־לָךְ:
בָּרוּךְ אַתָּה יהוה, עַל הָאָרֶץ וְעַל הַמָּזוֹן.

ברכת ירושלים

רַחֵם נָא, יהוה אֱלֹהֵינוּ
עַל יִשְׂרָאֵל עַמֶּךָ, וְעַל יְרוּשָׁלַיִם עִירֶךָ
וְעַל צִיּוֹן מִשְׁכַּן כְּבוֹדֶךָ, וְעַל מַלְכוּת בֵּית דָּוִד מְשִׁיחֶךָ
וְעַל הַבַּיִת הַגָּדוֹל וְהַקָּדוֹשׁ שֶׁנִּקְרָא שִׁמְךָ עָלָיו.
אֱלֹהֵינוּ, אָבִינוּ
רְעֵנוּ, זוּנֵנוּ, פַּרְנְסֵנוּ וְכַלְכְּלֵנוּ
וְהַרְוִיחֵנוּ, וְהַרְוַח לָנוּ יהוה אֱלֹהֵינוּ מְהֵרָה מִכָּל צָרוֹתֵינוּ.
וְנָא אַל תַּצְרִיכֵנוּ, יהוה אֱלֹהֵינוּ
לֹא לִידֵי מַתְּנַת בָּשָׂר וָדָם, וְלֹא לִידֵי הַלְוָאָתָם
כִּי אִם לְיָדְךָ הַמְּלֵאָה, הַפְּתוּחָה, הַקְּדוֹשָׁה וְהָרְחָבָה
שֶׁלֹּא נֵבוֹשׁ וְלֹא נִכָּלֵם לְעוֹלָם וָעֶד.

רְצֵה Favor and strengthen us, LORD our God,
through Your commandments,
especially through the commandment of the seventh day,
this great and holy Sabbath.
For it is, for You, a great and holy day.
On it we cease work and rest in love
in accord with Your will's commandment.
May it be Your will, LORD our God,
to grant us rest without distress, grief, or lament on our day of rest.
May You show us the consolation of Zion Your city,
and the rebuilding of Jerusalem Your holy city,
for You are the Master of salvation and consolation.

On Rosh Ḥodesh and Festivals, say:

אֱלֹהֵינוּ Our God and God of our ancestors,
may there rise, come, reach, appear, be favored, heard, regarded
and remembered before You, our recollection and remembrance,
as well as the remembrance of our ancestors,
and of the Messiah son of David Your servant,
and of Jerusalem Your holy city,
and of all Your people the house of Israel –
for deliverance and well-being, grace,
loving-kindness and compassion, life and peace,
on this day of:

On Rosh Ḥodesh:	Rosh Ḥodesh.
On Pesaḥ:	the Festival of Matzot.
On Shavuot:	the Festival of Shavuot.
On Sukkot:	the Festival of Sukkot.
On Shemini Atzeret & Simḥat Torah:	the Festival of Shemini Atzeret.

On it remember us, LORD our God, for good;
recollect us for blessing,
and deliver us for life.
In accord with Your promise of salvation and compassion,
spare us and be gracious to us;
have compassion on us and deliver us,
for our eyes are turned to You because You are God,
gracious and compassionate.

רְצֵה וְהַחֲלִיצֵנוּ, יהוה אֱלֹהֵינוּ, בְּמִצְוֹתֶיךָ
וּבְמִצְוַת יוֹם הַשְּׁבִיעִי הַשַּׁבָּת הַגָּדוֹל וְהַקָּדוֹשׁ הַזֶּה
כִּי יוֹם זֶה גָּדוֹל וְקָדוֹשׁ הוּא לְפָנֶיךָ
לִשְׁבָּת בּוֹ, וְלָנוּחַ בּוֹ בְּאַהֲבָה כְּמִצְוַת רְצוֹנֶךָ
וּבִרְצוֹנְךָ הָנִיחַ לָנוּ, יהוה אֱלֹהֵינוּ
שֶׁלֹּא תְהֵא צָרָה וְיָגוֹן וַאֲנָחָה בְּיוֹם מְנוּחָתֵנוּ
וְהַרְאֵנוּ, יהוה אֱלֹהֵינוּ, בְּנֶחָמַת צִיּוֹן עִירֶךָ
וּבְבִנְיַן יְרוּשָׁלַיִם עִיר קָדְשֶׁךָ
כִּי אַתָּה הוּא בַּעַל הַיְשׁוּעוֹת וּבַעַל הַנֶּחָמוֹת.

On ראש חודש *and* חגים*, say:*

אֱלֹהֵינוּ וֵאלֹהֵי אֲבוֹתֵינוּ
יַעֲלֶה וְיָבוֹא וְיַגִּיעַ, וְיֵרָאֶה וְיֵרָצֶה וְיִשָּׁמַע
וְיִפָּקֵד וְיִזָּכֵר זִכְרוֹנֵנוּ וּפִקְדוֹנֵנוּ, וְזִכְרוֹן אֲבוֹתֵינוּ
וְזִכְרוֹן מָשִׁיחַ בֶּן דָּוִד עַבְדֶּךָ
וְזִכְרוֹן יְרוּשָׁלַיִם עִיר קָדְשֶׁךָ
וְזִכְרוֹן כָּל עַמְּךָ בֵּית יִשְׂרָאֵל
לְפָנֶיךָ, לִפְלֵיטָה לְטוֹבָה, לְחֵן וּלְחֶסֶד וּלְרַחֲמִים
לְחַיִּים וּלְשָׁלוֹם בְּיוֹם

בראש חודש: רֹאשׁ הַחֹדֶשׁ הַזֶּה.

בפסח: חַג הַמַּצּוֹת הַזֶּה.

בשבועות: חַג הַשָּׁבוּעוֹת הַזֶּה.

בסוכות: חַג הַסֻּכּוֹת הַזֶּה.

בשמיני עצרת ושמחת תורה: הַשְּׁמִינִי חַג הָעֲצֶרֶת הַזֶּה.

זָכְרֵנוּ יהוה אֱלֹהֵינוּ בּוֹ לְטוֹבָה
וּפָקְדֵנוּ בוֹ לִבְרָכָה, וְהוֹשִׁיעֵנוּ בוֹ לְחַיִּים.
וּבִדְבַר יְשׁוּעָה וְרַחֲמִים, חוּס וְחָנֵּנוּ וְרַחֵם עָלֵינוּ, וְהוֹשִׁיעֵנוּ
כִּי אֵלֶיךָ עֵינֵינוּ, כִּי אֵל חַנּוּן וְרַחוּם אָתָּה.

וּבְנֵה And may Jerusalem the holy city be rebuilt soon, in our time.
Blessed are You, LORD, who in His compassion
will rebuild Jerusalem. Amen.

BLESSING OF GOD'S GOODNESS

בָּרוּךְ Blessed are You, LORD our God, King of the Universe –
God our Father, our King, our Sovereign,
our Creator, our Redeemer, our Maker,
our Holy One, the Holy One of Jacob.
He is our Shepherd, Israel's Shepherd,
the good King who does good to all.
Every day He has done, is doing, and will do good to us.
He has acted, is acting, and will always act kindly toward us for ever,
granting us grace, kindness and compassion, relief and rescue,
prosperity, blessing, redemption and comfort,
sustenance and support, compassion, life, peace and all good things,
and of all good things may He never let us lack.

ADDITIONAL REQUESTS

הָרַחֲמָן May the Compassionate One reign over us
for ever and all time.
May the Compassionate One be blessed
in heaven and on earth.
May the Compassionate One be praised
from generation to generation,
be glorified by us to all eternity,
and honored among us for ever and all time.
May the Compassionate One
grant us an honorable livelihood.
May the Compassionate One break the yoke from our neck
and lead us upright to our land.
May the Compassionate One send us many blessings to this house
and this table at which we have eaten.
May the Compassionate One send us Elijah the prophet –
may he be remembered for good –
to bring us good tidings of salvation and consolation.

וּבְנֵה יְרוּשָׁלַיִם עִיר הַקֹּדֶשׁ בִּמְהֵרָה בְיָמֵינוּ.
בָּרוּךְ אַתָּה יהוה, בּוֹנֵה בְרַחֲמָיו יְרוּשָׁלָיִם, אָמֵן.

ברכת הטוב והמטיב

בָּרוּךְ אַתָּה יהוה אֱלֹהֵינוּ מֶלֶךְ הָעוֹלָם
הָאֵל אָבִינוּ, מַלְכֵּנוּ, אַדִּירֵנוּ
בּוֹרְאֵנוּ, גּוֹאֲלֵנוּ, יוֹצְרֵנוּ, קְדוֹשֵׁנוּ, קְדוֹשׁ יַעֲקֹב
רוֹעֵנוּ, רוֹעֵה יִשְׂרָאֵל, הַמֶּלֶךְ הַטּוֹב וְהַמֵּטִיב לַכֹּל
שֶׁבְּכָל יוֹם וָיוֹם
הוּא הֵטִיב, הוּא מֵטִיב, הוּא יֵיטִיב לָנוּ
הוּא גְמָלָנוּ, הוּא גוֹמְלֵנוּ, הוּא יִגְמְלֵנוּ לָעַד
לְחֵן וּלְחֶסֶד וּלְרַחֲמִים, וּלְרֶוַח, הַצָּלָה וְהַצְלָחָה
בְּרָכָה וִישׁוּעָה, נֶחָמָה, פַּרְנָסָה וְכַלְכָּלָה
וְרַחֲמִים וְחַיִּים וְשָׁלוֹם וְכָל טוֹב, וּמִכָּל טוּב לְעוֹלָם אַל יְחַסְּרֵנוּ.

בקשות נוספות

הָרַחֲמָן הוּא יִמְלֹךְ עָלֵינוּ לְעוֹלָם וָעֶד.
הָרַחֲמָן הוּא יִתְבָּרַךְ בַּשָּׁמַיִם וּבָאָרֶץ.
הָרַחֲמָן הוּא יִשְׁתַּבַּח לְדוֹר דּוֹרִים, וְיִתְפָּאַר בָּנוּ לָעַד וּלְנֵצַח נְצָחִים
וְיִתְהַדַּר בָּנוּ לָעַד וּלְעוֹלְמֵי עוֹלָמִים.
הָרַחֲמָן הוּא יְפַרְנְסֵנוּ בְּכָבוֹד.
הָרַחֲמָן הוּא יִשְׁבֹּר עֻלֵּנוּ מֵעַל צַוָּארֵנוּ
וְהוּא יוֹלִיכֵנוּ קוֹמְמִיּוּת לְאַרְצֵנוּ.
הָרַחֲמָן הוּא יִשְׁלַח לָנוּ בְּרָכָה מְרֻבָּה בַּבַּיִת הַזֶּה
וְעַל שֻׁלְחָן זֶה שֶׁאָכַלְנוּ עָלָיו.
הָרַחֲמָן הוּא יִשְׁלַח לָנוּ אֶת אֵלִיָּהוּ הַנָּבִיא זָכוּר לַטּוֹב
וִיבַשֶּׂר לָנוּ בְּשׂוֹרוֹת טוֹבוֹת יְשׁוּעוֹת וְנֶחָמוֹת.

May the Compassionate One bless the State of Israel,
first flowering of our redemption.

May the Compassionate One bless
the members of Israel's Defense Forces,
who stand guard over our land.

A guest says:

יְהִי רָצוֹן May it be Your will that the master of this house shall not suffer shame in this world, nor humiliation in the World to Come. May all he owns prosper greatly, and may his and our possessions be successful and close to hand. Let not the Accuser hold sway over his deeds or ours, and may no thought of sin, iniquity or transgression enter him or us from now and for evermore.

הָרַחֲמָן May the Compassionate One bless –

When eating at one's own table, say (include the words in parentheses that apply):
me, (my wife/husband, / my father, my teacher / my mother,
my teacher/ my children,) and all that is mine,

A guest at someone else's table says (include the words in parentheses that apply):
the master of this house, him (and his wife,
the mistress of this house / and his children,) and all that is his,

Children at their parents' table say (include the words in parentheses that apply):
my father, my teacher, (master of this house,) and my mother,
my teacher, (mistress of this house,) them, their household,
their children, and all that is theirs.

For all other guests, add:
and all the diners here,

אוֹתָנוּ – together with us and all that is ours.
Just as our forefathers
Abraham, Isaac and Jacob were blessed
in all, from all, with all,
so may He bless all of us together with a complete blessing,
and let us say: Amen.

הָרַחֲמָן הוּא יְבָרֵךְ אֶת מְדִינַת יִשְׂרָאֵל, רֵאשִׁית צְמִיחַת גְּאֻלָּתֵנוּ.
הָרַחֲמָן הוּא יְבָרֵךְ אֶת חַיָּלֵי צְבָא הַהֲגָנָה לְיִשְׂרָאֵל
הָעוֹמְדִים עַל מִשְׁמַר אַרְצֵנוּ.

A guest says:

יְהִי רָצוֹן שֶׁלֹּא יֵבוֹשׁ בַּעַל הַבַּיִת בָּעוֹלָם הַזֶּה, וְלֹא יִכָּלֵם לָעוֹלָם הַבָּא, וְיִצְלַח מְאֹד בְּכָל נְכָסָיו, וְיִהְיוּ נְכָסָיו וּנְכָסֵינוּ מֻצְלָחִים וּקְרוֹבִים לָעִיר, וְאַל יִשְׁלֹט שָׂטָן לֹא בְּמַעֲשֵׂה יָדָיו וְלֹא בְּמַעֲשֵׂה יָדֵינוּ. וְאַל יִזְדַּקֵּק לֹא לְפָנָיו וְלֹא לְפָנֵינוּ שׁוּם דְּבַר הִרְהוּר חֵטְא, עֲבֵירָה וְעָוֹן, מֵעַתָּה וְעַד עוֹלָם.

הָרַחֲמָן הוּא יְבָרֵךְ

When eating at one's own table, say (include the words in parentheses that apply):

אוֹתִי (וְאֶת אִשְׁתִּי / וְאֶת בַּעְלִי / וְאֶת אָבִי מוֹרִי /
וְאֶת אִמִּי מוֹרָתִי / וְאֶת זַרְעִי) וְאֶת כָּל אֲשֶׁר לִי.

A guest at someone else's table says (include the words in parentheses that apply):

אֶת בַּעַל הַבַּיִת הַזֶּה, אוֹתוֹ (וְאֶת אִשְׁתּוֹ בַּעֲלַת הַבַּיִת הַזֶּה /
וְאֶת זַרְעוֹ) וְאֶת כָּל אֲשֶׁר לוֹ.

Children at their parents' table say (include the words in parentheses that apply):

אֶת אָבִי מוֹרִי (בַּעַל הַבַּיִת הַזֶּה), וְאֶת אִמִּי מוֹרָתִי (בַּעֲלַת הַבַּיִת הַזֶּה), אוֹתָם וְאֶת בֵּיתָם וְאֶת זַרְעָם וְאֶת כָּל אֲשֶׁר לָהֶם

For all other guests, add:

וְאֶת כָּל הַמְּסֻבִּין כָּאן

אוֹתָנוּ וְאֶת כָּל אֲשֶׁר לָנוּ
כְּמוֹ שֶׁנִּתְבָּרְכוּ אֲבוֹתֵינוּ
אַבְרָהָם יִצְחָק וְיַעֲקֹב, בַּכֹּל, מִכֹּל, כֹּל
כֵּן יְבָרֵךְ אוֹתָנוּ כֻּלָּנוּ יַחַד בִּבְרָכָה שְׁלֵמָה, וְנֹאמַר אָמֵן.

בַּמָּרוֹם On high, may grace be invoked for them and for us,
as a safeguard of peace.
May we receive a blessing from the LORD
and a just reward from the God of our salvation,
and may we find grace and good favor in the eyes of God and man.

On Shabbat: May the Compassionate One let us inherit the time,
that will be entirely Shabbat and rest for life everlasting.

On Rosh Ḥodesh: May the Compassionate One renew this month for us,
for good and blessing.

On Yom Tov: May the Compassionate One let us inherit the day,
that is all good.

On Sukkot: May the Compassionate One restore for us,
the fallen Tabernacle of David.

הָרַחֲמָן May the Compassionate One make us worthy
of the Messianic Age and life in the World to Come.
He is a tower of salvation to His king, *II Sam. 22*
showing kindness to His anointed,
to David and his descendants for ever.
He who makes peace in His high places,
may He make peace for us and all Israel,
and let us say: Amen.

יְראוּ Fear the LORD, you His holy ones; *Ps. 34*
those who fear Him lack nothing.
Young lions may grow weak and hungry,
but those who seek the LORD lack no good thing.
Thank the LORD for He is good; His loving-kindness is for ever. *Ps. 118*
You open Your hand, and satisfy every living thing with favor. *Ps. 145*
Blessed is the person who trusts in the LORD, *Jer. 17*
whose trust is in the LORD alone.
Once I was young, and now I am old, yet I have never watched *Ps. 37*
a righteous man forsaken or his children begging for bread.
The LORD will give His people strength. *Ps. 29*
The LORD will bless His people with peace.

If Birkat HaMazon was made on a cup of wine, then the blessing over wine is made and the majority of the cup is drunk, after which Al HaMiḥya, on the next page, is said.

בַּמָּרוֹם יְלַמְּדוּ עֲלֵיהֶם וְעָלֵינוּ זְכוּת שֶׁתְּהֵא לְמִשְׁמֶרֶת שָׁלוֹם
וְנִשָּׂא בְרָכָה מֵאֵת יהוה וּצְדָקָה מֵאֱלֹהֵי יִשְׁעֵנוּ
וְנִמְצָא חֵן וְשֵׂכֶל טוֹב בְּעֵינֵי אֱלֹהִים וְאָדָם.

בשבת: הָרַחֲמָן הוּא יַנְחִילֵנוּ
יוֹם שֶׁכֻּלּוֹ שַׁבָּת וּמְנוּחָה לְחַיֵּי הָעוֹלָמִים.

בראש חודש: הָרַחֲמָן הוּא יְחַדֵּשׁ עָלֵינוּ
אֶת הַחֹדֶשׁ הַזֶּה לְטוֹבָה וְלִבְרָכָה.

ביום טוב: הָרַחֲמָן הוּא יַנְחִילֵנוּ יוֹם שֶׁכֻּלּוֹ טוֹב.

בסוכות: הָרַחֲמָן הוּא יָקִים לָנוּ אֶת סֻכַּת דָּוִד הַנּוֹפֶלֶת.

הָרַחֲמָן הוּא יְזַכֵּנוּ לִימוֹת הַמָּשִׁיחַ וּלְחַיֵּי הָעוֹלָם הַבָּא
מִגְדּוֹל יְשׁוּעוֹת מַלְכּוֹ שמואל ב׳ כב
וְעֹשֶׂה־חֶסֶד לִמְשִׁיחוֹ, לְדָוִד וּלְזַרְעוֹ עַד־עוֹלָם:
עֹשֶׂה שָׁלוֹם בִּמְרוֹמָיו
הוּא יַעֲשֶׂה שָׁלוֹם עָלֵינוּ וְעַל כָּל יִשְׂרָאֵל
וְאִמְרוּ אָמֵן.

יְראוּ אֶת־יהוה קְדֹשָׁיו, כִּי־אֵין מַחְסוֹר לִירֵאָיו: תהלים לד
כְּפִירִים רָשׁוּ וְרָעֵבוּ, וְדֹרְשֵׁי יהוה לֹא־יַחְסְרוּ כָל־טוֹב:
הוֹדוּ לַיהוה כִּי־טוֹב, כִּי לְעוֹלָם חַסְדּוֹ: תהלים קיח
פּוֹתֵחַ אֶת־יָדֶךָ, וּמַשְׂבִּיעַ לְכָל־חַי רָצוֹן: תהלים קמה
בָּרוּךְ הַגֶּבֶר אֲשֶׁר יִבְטַח בַּיהוה, וְהָיָה יהוה מִבְטַחוֹ: ירמיה יז
נַעַר הָיִיתִי גַּם־זָקַנְתִּי, וְלֹא־רָאִיתִי צַדִּיק נֶעֱזָב וְזַרְעוֹ מְבַקֶּשׁ־לָחֶם: תהלים לז
יהוה עֹז לְעַמּוֹ יִתֵּן, יהוה יְבָרֵךְ אֶת־עַמּוֹ בַשָּׁלוֹם: תהלים כט

If ברכת המזון *was made on a cup of wine, then* בּוֹרֵא פְּרִי הַגָּפֶן *is said and the majority of the cup is drunk, after which* ברכה מעין שלוש*, on the next page, is said.*

BLESSING AFTER FOOD – AL HAMIḤYA

Grace after eating from the "seven species" of produce with which Israel is blessed: food made from the five grains (but not bread); wine or grape juice; grapes, figs, pomegranates, olives, or dates.

בָּרוּךְ Blessed are You, Lord our God, King of the Universe,

After grain products (but not bread or matza):	*After wine or grape juice:*	*After grapes, figs, olives, pomegranates or dates:*
for the nourishment and sustenance,	for the vine and the fruit of the vine,	for the tree and the fruit of the tree,

After grain products (but not bread or matza), and wine or grape juice:
for the nourishment and sustenance
and for the vine and the fruit of the vine,

and for the produce of the field; for the desirable, good and spacious land that You willingly gave as heritage to our ancestors, that they might eat of its fruit and be satisfied with its goodness. Have compassion, please, Lord our God, on Israel Your people, on Jerusalem, Your city, on Zion the home of Your glory, on Your altar and Your Temple. May You rebuild Jerusalem, the holy city swiftly in our time, and may You bring us back there, rejoicing in its rebuilding, eating from its fruit, satisfied by its goodness, and blessing You for it in holiness and purity. Be pleased to refresh us on this Sabbath Day.

On Rosh Ḥodesh: Remember us for good on this day of the New Moon.

On Pesaḥ: Grant us joy on this Festival of Matzot.

On Shavuot: Grant us joy on this Festival of Shavuot.

On Sukkot: Grant us joy on this Festival of Sukkot.

On Shemini Atzeret & Simḥat Torah: Grant us joy on this Festival of Shemini Atzeret.

For You, God, are good and do good to all and we thank You for the land

ברכה מעין שלוש

Grace after eating from the "seven species" of produce with which ארץ ישראל *is blessed: food made from the five grains (but not bread); wine or grape juice; grapes, figs, pomegranates, olives, or dates.*

בָּרוּךְ אַתָּה יהוה אֱלֹהֵינוּ מֶלֶךְ הָעוֹלָם, עַל

After grain products (but not bread or מצה*):*
הַמִּחְיָה וְעַל הַכַּלְכָּלָה

After wine or grape juice:
הַגֶּפֶן וְעַל פְּרִי הַגֶּפֶן

After grapes, figs, olives, pomegranates or dates:
הָעֵץ וְעַל פְּרִי הָעֵץ

After grain products (but not bread or מצה*), and wine or grape juice:*
הַמִּחְיָה וְעַל הַכַּלְכָּלָה וְעַל הַגֶּפֶן וְעַל פְּרִי הַגֶּפֶן

וְעַל תְּנוּבַת הַשָּׂדֶה וְעַל אֶרֶץ חֶמְדָּה טוֹבָה וּרְחָבָה, שֶׁרָצִיתָ וְהִנְחַלְתָּ לַאֲבוֹתֵינוּ לֶאֱכֹל מִפִּרְיָהּ וְלִשְׂבֹּעַ מִטּוּבָהּ. רַחֶם נָא יהוה אֱלֹהֵינוּ עַל יִשְׂרָאֵל עַמֶּךָ וְעַל יְרוּשָׁלַיִם עִירֶךָ וְעַל צִיּוֹן מִשְׁכַּן כְּבוֹדֶךָ וְעַל מִזְבְּחֶךָ וְעַל הֵיכָלֶךָ. וּבְנֵה יְרוּשָׁלַיִם עִיר הַקֹּדֶשׁ בִּמְהֵרָה בְיָמֵינוּ, וְהַעֲלֵנוּ לְתוֹכָהּ וְשַׂמְּחֵנוּ בְּבִנְיָנָהּ וְנֹאכַל מִפִּרְיָהּ וְנִשְׂבַּע מִטּוּבָהּ, וּנְבָרֶכְךָ עָלֶיהָ בִּקְדֻשָּׁה וּבְטָהֳרָה. וּרְצֵה וְהַחֲלִיצֵנוּ בְּיוֹם הַשַּׁבָּת הַזֶּה

בראש חודש: וְזָכְרֵנוּ לְטוֹבָה בְּיוֹם רֹאשׁ הַחֹדֶשׁ הַזֶּה

בפסח: וְשַׂמְּחֵנוּ בְּיוֹם חַג הַמַּצּוֹת הַזֶּה

בשבועות: וְשַׂמְּחֵנוּ בְּיוֹם חַג הַשָּׁבוּעוֹת הַזֶּה

בסוכות: וְשַׂמְּחֵנוּ בְּיוֹם חַג הַסֻּכּוֹת הַזֶּה

בשמיני עצרת ושמחת תורה: וְשַׂמְּחֵנוּ בְּיוֹם הַשְּׁמִינִי חַג הָעֲצֶרֶת הַזֶּה

כִּי אַתָּה יהוה טוֹב וּמֵטִיב לַכֹּל, וְנוֹדֶה לְּךָ עַל הָאָרֶץ

After grain products (but not bread or matza):	*After wine or grape juice:*	*After grapes, figs, olives, pomegranates or dates:*
and for the nourishment. Blessed are You, LORD, for the land and for the nourishment.	and for the fruit of the vine.* Blessed are You, LORD, for the land and for the fruit of the vine.*	and for the fruit.** Blessed are You, LORD, for the land and for the fruit.**

After grain products (but not bread or matza), and wine or grape juice:

and for the nourishment and for the fruit of the vine.*
Blessed are You, LORD, for the land and for the
nourishment and the fruit of the vine.*

** If the wine is from Israel, then substitute "her vine" for "the vine."*
*** If the fruit is from Israel, then substitute "her fruit" for "the fruit."*

BLESSING AFTER FOOD – BOREH NEFASHOT

After food or drink that does not require Birkat HaMazon or Al HaMiḥya – such as meat, fish, dairy products, vegetables, beverages, or fruit other than grapes, figs, pomegranates, olives or dates – say:

בָּרוּךְ Blessed are You, LORD our God,
King of the Universe,
who creates the many forms of life and their needs.
For all You have created
to sustain the life of all that lives,
blessed be He, Giver of life to the worlds.

After grain products (but not bread or מצה):

וְעַל הַמִּחְיָה.
בָּרוּךְ אַתָּה יהוה עַל
הָאָרֶץ וְעַל הַמִּחְיָה.

After wine or grape juice:

וְעַל פְּרִי הַגָּפֶן.*
בָּרוּךְ אַתָּה יהוה עַל
הָאָרֶץ וְעַל פְּרִי הַגָּפֶן.*

After grapes, figs, olives, pomegranates or dates:

וְעַל הַפֵּרוֹת.**
בָּרוּךְ אַתָּה יהוה עַל
הָאָרֶץ וְעַל הַפֵּרוֹת.**

After grain products (but not bread or מצה), and wine or grape juice:

וְעַל הַמִּחְיָה וְעַל פְּרִי הַגָּפֶן.*
בָּרוּךְ אַתָּה יהוה, עַל הָאָרֶץ וְעַל הַמִּחְיָה וְעַל פְּרִי הַגָּפֶן.*

**If the wine is from ארץ ישראל, then substitute גַּפְנָהּ for הַגָּפֶן.*
***If the fruit is from ארץ ישראל, then substitute פֵּרוֹתֶיהָ for הַפֵּרוֹת.*

בורא נפשות

After food or drink that does not require ברכת המזון or מעין שלוש – such as meat, fish, dairy products, vegetables, beverages, or fruit other than grapes, figs, pomegranates, olives or dates – say:

בָּרוּךְ אַתָּה יהוה אֱלֹהֵינוּ מֶלֶךְ הָעוֹלָם
בּוֹרֵא נְפָשׁוֹת רַבּוֹת וְחֶסְרוֹנָן
עַל כָּל מַה שֶּׁבָּרָאתָ
לְהַחֲיוֹת בָּהֶם נֶפֶשׁ כָּל חָי.
בָּרוּךְ חֵי הָעוֹלָמִים.

TRANSLITERATION OF RABBIS' KADDISH

Mourner: Yitgadal ve-yitkadash shemeh raba. (*Cong:* Amen)
Be-alema di vera khir'uteh, ve-yamlikh malkhuteh,
be-ḥayyeikhon, uv-yomeikhon,
uv-ḥayyei de-khol beit Yisrael, ba-agala uvi-zman kariv,
ve-imru Amen. (*Cong:* Amen)

All: Yeheh shemeh rabba mevarakh le'alam ul-alemei alemaya.

Mourner: Yitbarakh ve-yishtabaḥ ve-yitpa'ar ve-yitromam ve-yitnaseh
ve-yit-hadar ve-yit'aleh ve-yit-hallal
shemeh dekudsha, berikh hu. (*Cong:* Berikh hu)
Le-ela min kol birkhata
/*Between Rosh HaShana & Yom Kippur:* Le-ela le-ela mi-kol birkhata/
ve-shirata, tushbeḥata ve-neḥemata, da-amiran be-alema,
ve-imru, Amen. (*Cong:* Amen)

Al Yisrael, ve-al rabanan,
ve-al talmideihon, ve-al kol talmidei talmideihon,
ve-al kol man de-asekin be-oraita
di be-atra (*In Israel:* kadisha) ha-dein ve-di be-khol atar
va-atar, yeheh lehon ul-khon shelama raba,
ḥina ve-ḥisda, ve-raḥamei,
ve-ḥayyei arikhei, um-zonei re-viḥei,
u-furkana min kodam avuhon di vish-maya,
ve-imru Amen. (*Cong:* Amen)

Yeheh shelama raba min shemaya
ve-ḥayyim (tovim) aleinu ve-al kol Yisrael,
ve-imru Amen. (*Cong:* Amen)

Bow, take three steps back, as if taking leave of the Divine Presence, then bow, first left, then right, then center, while saying:

Oseh shalom/*Between Rosh HaShana & Yom Kippur:* ha-shalom/
bim-romav,
hu ya'aseh ve-raḥamav shalom aleinu, ve-al kol Yisrael,
ve-imru Amen. (*Cong:* Amen)

TRANSLITERATION OF MOURNER'S KADDISH

Mourner: Yitgadal ve-yitkadash shemeh raba. (*Cong:* Amen)
Be-alema di vera khir'uteh, ve-yamlikh malkhuteh,
be-ḥayyeikhon, uv-yomeikhon,
uv-ḥayyei de-khol beit Yisrael, ba-agala uvi-zman kariv,
ve-imru Amen. (*Cong:* Amen)

All: Yeheh shemeh rabba mevarakh le'alam ul-alemei alemaya.

Mourner: Yitbarakh ve-yishtabaḥ ve-yitpa'ar ve-yitromam ve-yitnaseh
ve-yit-hadar ve-yit'aleh ve-yit-hallal
shemeh dekudsha, berikh hu. (*Cong:* Berikh hu)
Le-ela min kol birkhata
/*Between Rosh HaShana & Yom Kippur:* Le-ela le-ela mi-kol birkhata/
ve-shirata, tushbeḥata ve-neḥemata, da-amiran be-alema,
ve-imru, Amen. (*Cong:* Amen)

Yeheh shelama raba min shemaya
ve-ḥayyim aleinu ve-al kol Yisrael,
ve-imru Amen. (*Cong:* Amen)

Bow, take three steps back, as if taking leave of the Divine Presence, then bow, first left, then right, then center, while saying:

Oseh shalom/*Between Rosh HaShana & Yom Kippur:* ha-shalom/
bim-romav,
hu ya'aseh shalom aleinu, ve-al kol Yisrael,
ve-imru Amen. (*Cong:* Amen)

LAWS AND GUIDES

EREV SHABBAT

1 Minḥa: as for weekdays. *Taḥanun* is omitted [שו״ע או״ח, רסז: א].

2 There is a set time period every afternoon during which the Minḥa Amida may be said. At the earliest, one may say the Amida one half of a halakhic "hour" from midday (a halakhic hour is 1⁄12 of the day measured from daybreak to nightfall). At the latest, the Amida must be said before nightfall. It is preferable to say the Amida at least 3½ halakhic "hours" after midday [שו״ע או״ח, רלג: א].

3 One should wash hands before saying Minḥa, even if they are not dirty; but if no water is available, one need not wash [שו״ע או״ח, רלג: ב]. No blessing is said on the hand-washing.

4 Candle lighting: At least two candles are lit [שו״ע או״ח, רסג: א]. There is a custom to light one candle for each member of the household. After lighting, one says the blessing **לְהַדְלִיק נֵר שֶׁל שַׁבָּת** [שו״ע ורמ״א או״ח, רסג: ה]. It is customary to cover one's eyes when saying the blessing [רמ״א, שם].

5 The custom is to light Shabbat candles 18 minutes prior to sunset. In any case, the candles must be lit before sunset, at which time all labor must cease [שו״ע ורמ״א או״ח, רסא: א]. After lighting the candles, one may not perform any labor, even if one lit prior to sunset, unless one's intention to perform necessary labor before sunset is articulated explicitly prior to lighting [רמ״א או״ח, רסג: י; משנ״ב, שם: מב].

6 The candles must be lit in a location where one will benefit from the light before the candles burn out [שו״ע, שם: ט].

7 If one is not eating at home on Friday night, one should still light candles at home [שו״ע, שם: ו]. If one is not sleeping at home on Friday night, one should light where one sleeps or make a nominal payment to one's host, so as to participate in the host's candle lighting. This is not required if a family member is at home and lights candles with one in mind [שו״ע, שם: ו].

LEIL SHABBAT

8 Kabbalat Shabbat: Many congregations sing *Yedid Nefesh* before Kabbalat Shabbat. Because Kabbalat Shabbat is not considered part of Ma'ariv, it is customary for the *Shaliaḥ Tzibbur* to stand at the *bima*, rather than at the front of the synagogue [אשי ישראל, לו: יד]. For the same reason, it is permissible for a male under the age of 13 to lead Kabbalat Shabbat.

9 When saying the last stanza of *Lekha Dodi*, the custom is to stand facing the door, which is usually the western side of the synagogue [משנ״ב או״ח, רסב: י].

10 By custom, mourners who are sitting *shiva* remain outside the synagogue for Kabbalat Shabbat, entering when the congregation finishes *Lekha Dodi*. As they enter, the congregation calls out in unison הַמָּקוֹם יְנַחֵם אֶתְכֶם בְּתוֹךְ שְׁאָר אֲבֵלֵי צִיּוֹן וִירוּשָׁלָיִם (page 63) [ערוה״ש יו״ד, ת: ה].

11 The congregation says the last two psalms of Kabbalat Shabbat, מִזְמוֹר שִׁיר לְיוֹם הַשַּׁבָּת (Ps. 92) and יהוה מָלָךְ (Ps. 93). This is followed by the Mourner's Kaddish and the second chapter of Mishna *Shabbat* (בַּמֶּה מַדְלִיקִין) [שו״ע או״ח, ער: א]. Some congregations outside Israel say בַּמֶּה מַדְלִיקִין after Full Kaddish at the end of Ma'ariv instead [משנ״ב, שם: ב].

12 Ma'ariv for Shabbat: וְהוּא רַחוּם is omitted [טור או״ח, רסז]. The *Shaliaḥ Tzibbur* moves to the front of the synagogue to say *Barekhu*. It is preferable for Ma'ariv to begin after nightfall. If it does not, the congregation needs to repeat the Shema after nightfall [משנ״ב או״ח, רסז: ג]. The conclusion of הַשְׁכִּיבֵנוּ is different from the weekday formula, and בָּרוּךְ יהוה לְעוֹלָם is omitted [שו״ע שם, ג]. If one erroneously concludes הַשְׁכִּיבֵנוּ with the weekday blessing, one should say the correct blessing, provided one remembers immediately. If not, one does not repeat the blessing [משנ״ב, שם: ט]. It is customary to say וְשָׁמְרוּ (page 129) before the Amida [משנ״ב, שם].

13 The Shabbat Ma'ariv Amida is said (page 131). On Rosh Ḥodesh, יַעֲלֶה וְיָבוֹא is added in the fifth blessing (page 137). On Ḥanukka (and Shushan Purim in Jerusalem), עַל הַנִּסִּים is added in the sixth blessing (page 139).

14 If one begins to say the Amida for weekdays on Shabbat and remembers in the middle of the Amida, one should complete the blessing already started, then begin the fourth blessing for the appropriate Shabbat Amida [שו״ע או״ח, רסח: ב]. If one remembers after completing the Amida, the correct Amida should be said from the beginning [שם: ד].

15 One who says the Amida for the wrong Shabbat service (e.g., saying the Amida for Shaḥarit during Minḥa), does not repeat the Amida. The exception is one who says the wrong Amida during Musaf, or the Musaf Amida during a different service, in which case the Amida must be repeated [שם: ו]. If, however, one remembers during the Amida, one goes back to the beginning of the fourth blessing of the correct Amida [משנ״ב, שם: טז].

16 After the Amida, the *Shaliaḥ Tzibbur* and congregation say וַיְכֻלּוּ (page 143) [שו״ע או״ח, רסח: ז]. The *Shaliaḥ Tzibbur* says the abbreviated repetition of the Amida, unless prayers are said in a location where (a) services are not held in a regular fashion, or (b) there is no Torah scroll [משנ״ב, שם: כד]. The *Shaliaḥ Tzibbur* says the Full Kaddish. Some congregations say בַּמֶּה מַדְלִיקִין (page 107) at this point. From Shabbat Hol HaMo'ed Pesaḥ until Shavuot, the Omer is counted (page 159). The congregation says Aleinu, followed by the Mourner's Kaddish. From the 1st of Elul through Shemini Atzeret, Psalm 27 (page 153) is said. It is customary to conclude with the singing of Yigdal or Adon Olam.

17 Some congregations have the custom to say Kiddush in the synagogue prior to Aleinu. However, since Kiddush should generally be said where the Shabbat meal is eaten, where possible, the Kiddush wine should be drunk by a child (or children) under the age of bar/bat mitzva. If this is not possible, the person making Kiddush may drink the wine [שו״ע או״ח, רסט: א].

18 Upon returning home, the custom is to say (or sing) a number of traditional songs and prayers. Some have the custom to bless their children. The Kiddush for Shabbat is an affirmative mitzva from the Torah. By custom, one person says Kiddush and the others listen attentively, fulfilling their obligation by proxy (based on the principle of שומע כעונה – "one who hears is as one who says"). Women are obligated in this mitzva, and a woman is permitted to say Kiddush for herself and others [שו״ע או״ח, רעא: ב]. It is customary to punctuate the meal with *Zemirot*. After the meal, one adds רְצֵה to the third blessing of *Birkat HaMazon*. On Rosh Ḥodesh, יַעֲלֶה וְיָבוֹא is added after רְצֵה [שו״ע או״ח, קפח: ה].

Laws of Mourner's Kaddish

19 The Mourner's Kaddish is generally said after specific chapters of Psalms at the beginning and end of a service. It is said by one who is either (a) in mourning for a relative, or (b) commemorating the *yahrzeit* of a relative. When no such person is present, the Mourner's Kaddish is generally omitted, except after Aleinu at the end of Shaḥarit [רמ"א או"ח, קלב: ב], when it is said by one whose parents have died or whose parents do not object to their child saying the Mourner's Kaddish [שם].

20 Historically, the Mourner's Kaddish was said by one individual. A set of rules developed for allocating among different mourners the various opportunities for saying it [ביאור הלכה, שם; קונטרס מאמר קדישין, י]. Today, most congregations allow group recitation of the Mourner's Kaddish. In such cases, they should say the words in unison [סידור יעב"ץ].

Photograph Credits:

Photographs by Yehoshua Halevi, www.yehoshuahalevi.com:
p. 42: Mt. Hermon
p. 44: Date Palms
p. 46: Old City of Jerusalem
p. 48: Man blowing Shofar, Judean Mountains
p. 50: Sunset at Caesarea Beach
p. 52: Eilat Mountains
p. 55: Pomegranate star
p. 56: Candles
p. 58: Kotel Ramparts
p. 60: Blessing of the Sun, Eitam Hill, Gush Etzion
p. 62: Ripe Pomegranates
p. 64: Rosh HaNiqra
p. 66: HaBonim Beach
p. 95: Full moon set over Gush Etzion
p. 101: Date Palm
p. 105: Grapes and Vines

Other Photographs:
p. 83 (left): Narcissus tazetta © Oren Rosenfeld
p. 83 (right): Scolymus maculatus © Prof. Avinoam Danin:
http://flora.org.il/plants/SCOMAC/
p. 85: Baby fig © Dena Landowne Bailey
p. 87: View from Patzel, Jordan Valley © Ella Koblenz
p. 89: Meron © Yonit Schiller
p. 91: Kinneret © Yonit Schiller
p. 93: Saffron crocus flowers © iStockphoto.com/viperagp
p. 97: Pancratium maritimum © iStockphoto.com/parisvas
p. 99: Pomegranate buds © Eliahu Misgav
p. 103: Parchment phylacteries in production © Eliahu Misgav

We extend our thanks to Joy Elias, Elana Knoller, and Gabrielle Lasher for their assistance in developing the concept and design of the siddur.

A deep debt of gratitude is owed as well to Abe Katz for his invaluable research provided through www.beureihatefila.com

קורן ירושלים